War in Colombia: Made in U.S.A.

Edited and Compiled by
Rebeca Toledo, Teresa Gutierrez,
Sara Flounders and Andy McInerney

International Action Center
New York

War in Colombia: Made in U.S.A.

© Copyright 2003

ISBN 0-9656916-9-1

International Action Center
39 West 14th Street, Rm. 206
New York, NY 10011

Phone: (212) 633-6646
Fax: (212) 633-2889
Website: www.iacenter.org
E-mail: iacenter@action-mail.org

Cover Design: Lal Roohk

Library of Congress Cataloging-in-Publication Data

War in Colombia : made in U.S.A.
    p. cm.
Includes bibliographical references and index.
ISBN 0-9656916-9-1 (alk. paper)
    1. Narcotics, Control of—Colombia. 2 United States—Foreign rela-
tions—Colombia. 3. Colombia—Foreign relations—United States. 4. United
States—Military relations—Colombia. 5. Colombia—Military relations—
United States. I. International Action Center (New York, N.Y.)

HV5840.C7W37 2003
327.730861—dc21   2002191308

TABLE OF CONTENTS

II. VOICES FROM COLOMBIA

III. U.S. INTERVENTION: THE REGIONAL PICTURE

VI. APPENDIX

PREFACE

There is a risk inherent in producing a book like this. By the time it gets widely distributed, it could become obsolete, as events in Colombia unfold rapidly.

But *War in Colombia: Made in U.S.A.* will never be outdated. And that is because this book provides the necessary analysis to understand the complex relations between Colombia and the United States, now and for years to come.

Furthermore, *War in Colombia: Made in U.S.A.* discusses Colombia's importance within the context of developments in the entire region.

Latin America and the Caribbean are the battlegrounds for tumultuous developments that will soon have profound importance. Mass movements throughout the continent have risen against the Free Trade Area of the Americas. Independence-minded leaders such as those in Venezuela and Brazil have been popularly elected, challenging the status quo set by Wall Street.

These are signs that this continent will be the scene of great advances for humanity, despite the best efforts of Washington.

What is Colombia's role in all of this? Why is Colombia the number one recipient of U.S. aid in Latin America? What does it indicate that while the trend today in Latin America is to fight for sovereignty, Colombia has the distinct dishonor of presiding over the United Nations Security Council at the very moment the U.S. government is about to launch a horrific war against the people of Iraq?

The answers to these questions will be found within these pages. They will help orient readers, now and long after the Colombian people win the peace for which they so desperately yearn.

Colombia has the highest murder rate in the world. It has one of the highest rates of displaced people. Four out of every five trade unionists murdered in the world today are in Colombia. Latin America's oldest guerrilla organization is in Colombia.

So when the Clinton administration proposed a $2 billion aid package for Colombia, it signaled that Colombia was a top priority in U.S.-Latin American relations.

Hence it is a top priority for the anti-war movement.

For too many decades, U.S. imperialism has intervened throughout Latin America. From blockading revolutionary Cuba to ousting Guatemalan President Jacobo Arbenz, to quelling the revolutionary movements in Central America, it has spread its bloody tentacles far and wide.

From the robbery of one-half of Mexico to splitting Colombia to build the Panama Canal, the U.S. government has done whatever it takes to rob the resources of Latin America and the Caribbean.

It is the U.S. that still maintains the oldest colony in this hemisphere: Puerto Rico. This history is why the perspective provided in the pages of this book will never be outdated.

Colombia is at a crossroads. At this writing, Colombian President Álvaro Uribe Vélez is imposing measures similar to President George W. Bush's "Homeland Security." The right to dissent is being criminalized; Uribe is relentlessly militarizing and privatizing the country.

Some Colombians even view Uribe's policies as fascistic.

Which road Colombia takes depends on the strength of not only the people's movement in Colombia, but also the solidarity movement in this country. *War in Colombia: Made in U.S.A.* is written with the goal of contributing to that movement.

Teresa Gutierrez
National Co-Director, International Action Center
New York, NY
January, 2003

ACKNOWLEDGEMENTS

War in Colombia: Made in U.S.A. represents a major contribution and valuable resource for all in the U.S. and worldwide who oppose U.S. intervention in Colombia.

This book was produced by the collective effort of many people who brought their skills, experience and dedication to this project. First, we thank all the writers and activists who contributed essays to this important work. We also appreciate all who worked on editorial, technical and promotional tasks to finish this edition and make it available to readers, activists and progressive forces worldwide.

Berta Joubert-Ceci, Alicia Jrapko, Alicia Rivera, Carl Glenn and Andy McInerney skillfully translated major articles written by leading figures from Colombia, as well as from popular movements in other Latin American and Caribbean nations.

Imani Henry was very helpful in doing needed publicity and varied tasks for this project. Gery Armsby did essential research. Alejandra Serrano assisted this endeavor in many ways. She and Nathalie Alsop assembled and wrote the excellent chronology that reviews the history of U.S. intervention in Colombia, political repression and popular resistance.

Lal Roohk designed the beautiful cover. Shelley Ettinger carefully copyedited the entire text. She and John Catalinotto made editorial corrections. A book like this requires a thorough index; this was thoughtfully constructed by Janet Mayes and Rebeca Toledo. Kathy Durkin contacted supporters about funding this effort and did promotional work.

We thank the volunteer staff at the International Action Center national office for their tireless efforts in promoting and distributing all of the International Action Center's publications. They have done much to help on this work, from sending out mailings to answering phone call inquiries, to processing orders and shipping the books out worldwide. They include Marie Jay, Carol Holland, Kadouri Al-Kaysi, William Mason and Henri Nereaux. Deirdre Sinnott and Sarah Sloan e-mailed information about the book to potential readers and activists.

Several chapters in this compilation have already appeared in print elsewhere. "An Empire in Search of a War," by Mumia Abu-Jamal, is copyrighted 2000 by Mumia Abu-Jamal.

"The Geopolitics of Plan Colombia," by James Petras, first appeared in the May 2001 issue of *Monthly Review*. It appears here with the permission of the editors.

"Workers United with Students and Campesinos," by Nathalie Alsop and Ramón Acevedo, first appeared on the New Colombia News Agency (ANNCOL) website in September 2002.

The chapter by Antonio Garcia, "The National Liberation Army Speaks," first appeared as a longer piece entitled, "An Interview with ELN Commander Antonio Garcia" on the official ELN website, www.webnet/eln/.

ACKNOWLEDGEMENTS TO DONORS

The publication of *War in Colombia: Made in U.S.A.* would not have been possible without the support of International Action Center friends and supporters who provided financial backing for this effort.

We extend our thanks to the People's Rights Fund for their assistance and to Phyllis Lucero for her generosity. We appreciate Stuart Anderson, Ed Gibney, Hal Jamison and Robert Precious for their sponsorship of this project.

Many friends came forward to contribute towards this book's publication. We are grateful for the assistance of those listed below and the many others who donated but could not at this time list their names.

DONORS: Arizona Rountree Acors, Archie Wayne Blumhorst, Wanita L. Blumhorst, Lee Booth, Phil Booth, Harlan Girard, James E. Gonzales II, Richard J. Haviland, E. Roy John, Robert K. Johnson, David Klein, Merle G. Krause, Stephen L. Kreznar, Irene Leiby, Ray Leszczak, Aaron Moss, Balquis Muhammad, Kenneth Reiner, Al Strasburger, Joe Yuskaitis

FRIENDS: Timothy Brennan, Arthur Carney, Lillian Carney, Madeline Casey, Angela Durso, Beatrice Einhorn, C. Steven Fate, George Fay, Michael Gambale, George Harrison, Wayne Kelpien, Kamel T. Khalaf, Rev. George J. Kuhn, Margaret Lopez-Ambrosoni, Linden P. Martineau, Dr. Austin Murphy, Edith Oxfeld, Sue Peters, Randolph C. Richter, Armando G. Rosa, Jeannette Safran, Ethel Sanjines, Barbara Ann Scott, Joe Sekin, Mike Shaw, Dick Tidwell, Lisa Vargas, Radmila Veselinovic, Brian Zabowski

Author Biographies

MUMIA ABU-JAMAL, former Black Panther. He is currently a political prisoner and death-row inmate in Pennsylvania and a renowned radio and print journalist.

RAMÓN ACEVEDO, co-founder of the Committee for a New Colombia. He is a student at San Francisco State University.

ARTURO ALAPE, renowned Colombian reporter, writer and journalist. His books include *The Bogotazo: Memories of the Forgotten* and a three-volume biography of Manuel Marulanda Vélez.

NATHALIE ALSOP, organizer with the International ANSWER coalition and the Committee for a New Colombia. She is a student at City College of San Francisco.

FR. ROY BOURGEOIS, Vietnam Veteran and Catholic priest of the Maryknoll order who has spent over four years in prison for protesting against the School of the Americas and U.S. policy in Latin America, also visit: www.soawne.org.

FIDEL CASTRO RUZ, commander in chief of the Cuban military, first secretary of the Communist Party of Cuba, president of the Council of State and the Council of Ministers and leader of the 1959 Cuban Revolution.

RAMSEY CLARK, the U.S. attorney general in the Lyndon Johnson administration. He is an international attorney and human-rights advocate and has opposed U.S. military intervention all around the world. Clark is the founder of the International Action Center and author of *Crime in America* and *The Fire This Time*. He traveled to Colombia in December 2000, where he visited San Vincente del Caguán, the center of the talks between the FARC-EP and the government.

NARCISO ISA CONDE, a veteran of the 1965 revolution in the Dominican Republic who currently leads the Fuerza de la Revolución (Force of the Revolution), a Dominican political party. He is the author of many articles and books on political struggles in the Dominican Republic, Latin America, and around the world, including *Rearming Utopia* (Editora Tropical, 2000).

JAVIER CORREA SUÁREZ, president of the National Union of Food Industry Workers (Sinaltrainal) in Colombia. He is a spokesman for the lawsuit filed against Coca-Cola in the U.S. and a leader for workers' rights in Colombia.

HEATHER COTTIN, activist in civil rights, anti-war and women's movements in the United States. Contributed to *NATO in the Balkans* and *Hidden Agenda*.

SARA FLOUNDERS, a co-director of the International Action Center. She co-edited the following four books: *Hidden Agenda*; *NATO in the Balkans*; *Metal of Dishonor* and *Challenge to Genocide: Let Iraq Live*.

GLORIA GAITÁN, daughter of Jorge Eliécer Gaitán, a popular leader of Colombia's Liberal Party in the 1940s, assassinated while running for president of Colombia in 1948 on a campaign of social justice and anti-imperialism.

ANTONIO GARCIA, guerrilla leader who has over-all military command of the National Liberation Army (ELN), Colombia's second largest guerrilla movement. An engineer by profession he joined the ELN when he was 19 years old.

CARL GLENN, an editor of the Spanish section of *Workers World* newspaper, *Mundo Obrero,* and an organizer of solidarity actions with Panama during and after the 1989 U.S. military intervention.

STAN GOFF, a former member of the 7th Special Forces Group. Author of *Hideous Dream: A Soldier's Memoir of the U.S. Invasion of Haiti* (Soft Skull Press, 2000).

ISMAEL GUADALUPE, leads the Committee for the Rescue and Development of Vieques, which has fought to force the U.S. Navy off the Puerto Rican island of Vieques. Originally a teacher in Vieques, he now travels around the world organizing against the U.S. military occupation of his homeland.

BISHOP THOMAS GUMBLETON, from Detroit, founding president of Pax Christi USA (1972-1991), author of *A Call to Holiness, A Call to Action* and a participant in several delegations to Colombia.

LUCIO GUTIÉRREZ, elected president of Ecuador in November 2002. He was a colonel in the Ecuadorian military when he helped lead a coalition of Indigenous, working class and low-ranking military officers that toppled the Ecuadorian government in January 2000. His presidential campaign became a lightning rod for mass disgust over the government's pro-International Monetary Fund policies.

TERESA GUTIERREZ, a co-director of the International Action Center, responsible for IAC committees in solidarity with the people of Colombia and Venezuela and for the Cuban 5 political prisoners in the U.S. Also produced the video, "Plan Colombia: We Say No."

IMANI HENRY, poet, performance artist and activist in the anti-war, Black liberation and transgender movements in the U.S.

DR. ARISTÓBULO ISTÚRIZ, minister of education in the Venezuelan government of President Hugo Chávez, a former teachers' union leader and vice-president of the Constituent Assembly.

BERTA JOUBERT-CECI, Puerto Rican community organizer from Philadelphia active in mobilizing support for the struggle to oust the U.S. Navy from Vieques, Puerto Rico.

GARRY M. LEECH, editor of the online journal *Colombia Report* (www.colombiareport.org) and author of the book *Killing Peace: Colombia's Conflict and the Failure of U.S. Intervention.*

MANUEL MARULANDA VÉLEZ, founding member and commander in chief of the Central General Staff of the Revolutionary Armed Forces of Colombia-People's Army (FARC-EP).

DIANNE MATHIOWETZ, Atlanta organizer and United Auto Workers member at General Motors, organizing solidarity with Colombian workers against Coca-Cola.

ANDY MCINERNEY, a journalist and lecturer specializing in social struggles in Latin America. His articles appear frequently in *Workers World* newspaper.

CYNTHIA MCKINNEY, served in the U.S. House of Representatives from 1992-2003. She was one of the few voices in Congress who questioned President George W. Bush's "war on terrorism" following the Sept. 11, 2001 events.

LINDA PANETTA, founder and director of School of the Americas Watch Northeast, a photojournalist who has been active on issues regarding Latin America for 20 years.

LUIS GUILLERMO PÉREZ CASAS, an attorney with the Lawyers Collective Corporation based in Bogotá, Colombia. The Corporation is a human rights organization founded in 1980.

JAMES PETRAS, Bartle Professor (Emeritus) of Sociology at the State University of New York at Binghamton and the author of some 30 books on Latin America and U.S. policy.

RAÚL REYES, commander of the Revolutionary Armed Forces of Colombia-People's Army (FARC-EP) and member of the FARC-EP's leading body.

REBECA TOLEDO, Latina, lesbian activist and member of the International Action Center delegation to the Tribunal Against the Violence of Coca-Cola in Bogotá, Colombia, in December 2002.

MIGUEL URBANO, former member of the European Parliament. He is a writer and a journalist living in Havana and for many years the editor-in-chief of the Portuguese daily *O Diario*.

PAUL WELLSTONE, served in the U.S. Senate from 1990 until his death in 2002. Outspoken critic of Plan Colombia and U.S. war plans in the region.

CHRONOLOGY OF COLOMBIA

1819 South America's Liberator, Simón Bolívar, declares the independence of Gran Colombia from Spanish rule.

1823 In the Monroe Doctrine, the United States declares that Latin America is within its sphere of influence. The former imperial powers in Latin America, like Spain and Britain, were barred from attempting to control the region. The United States thus declares itself the new colonial overlord of all Latin America.

1828-29 Regional differences prompt the collapse of Gran Colombia into what is now Colombia, Venezuela, and Ecuador.

1849 The two parties of Colombia's ruling elite, the Liberal and Conservative Parties, are formed. Differences break out into armed clashes, with over 50 insurrections and eight civil wars taking place between 1849 and 1899.

1899 Outbreak of the "Thousand Days War" between the Liberal and Conservative Parties. Up to 130,000 people killed before the end of the war in 1903.

1903 U.S. engineers Panama's secession from Colombia in order to gain control of the Panama Canal.

1948 The CIA-backed assassination of Jorge Eliécer Gaitán on April 9 sparks the "Bogotazo," a massive uprising throughout the capital city. Over 300,000 people are killed in the ensuing civil war known as "La Violencia," which lasts until 1958.

1952 The Military Assistance Agreement signed between Colombia and the United States. Colombia is the site of the first Latin American counterinsurgency training school.

1953 Washington financially and politically supports the military coup that brings General Rojas Pinilla to power.

1955 Washington gives Rojas Pinilla a $170 million dollar loan, following the strategy of the National Security Doctrine. Rojas Pinilla uses this money to increase the repression of armed resistance groups and peasant organizations.

1958 Rojas Pinilla's dictatorship collapses. The Liberal and Conservative Parties agree to a 16-year National Front, alternating the presidency and dividing all political posts equally between the parties.

1959 Victory of the Cuban Revolution.

1961 U.S. initiates Alliance for Progress, providing aid to Latin America to counter the growing influence of the 1959 Cuban Revolution.

1962 Pres. Kennedy sends an armed military mission to Colombia to reorganize the Colombian military. This mission created the State Security Corps, attacking anyone accused of being a communist along with peasants, workers and opposition political groups.

1964 The Colombian government unleashes "Operation Marquetalia," an air-and-land attack on peasant self-defense communities that had formed in response to inequity and repression. The operation was designed by the Pentagon within the framework of the Latin American Security Operation. The start of "Operation Marquetalia" is considered the official birth of the Revolutionary Armed Forces of Colombia (FARC).

1964 The National Liberation Army (ELN) is formed in Santander province by students inspired by the Cuban Revolution.

1974 The National Front formally ends, but Liberal and Conservative Parties still monopolize political power.

1981 Two hundred and twenty-three drug traffickers form the paramilitary group "Death to Kidnappers" (MAS) in Cali.

1984 The FARC enters into talks with the government of Pres. Belisario Betancourt. Both sides sign the Uribe Accords, providing the FARC a political opening. The FARC agrees to a bilateral cease-fire.

1985 The FARC backs the creation of the Patriotic Union (UP), a leftist political party.

1985 The M-19, a guerrilla group, responds to repression by seizing the Palace of Justice, Colombia's Supreme Court. The government responds by bombarding the building, killing 128 people including 41 M-19 militants and 11 Supreme Court justices.

1986 The CIA and Colombian military create and implement the Condor Plan, a military plan designed to exterminate all progressive, liberal and revolutionary sectors of society. During and after the 1986 elections, in which many UP members were elected to congressional seats, mayoral positions and other local and regional offices, UP members are consistently assassinated. In the next decade, over 4,000 UP members are murdered.

1987 Pres. Virgilio Barco launches an attack on the FARC leadership, breaking the cease-fire and ending the dialog period opened by the Uribe Accords.

1987 The FARC, the ELN and the Popular Liberation Army (EPL) form the Simón Bolívar Guerrilla Coordinating Committee (CGSB).

1989 U.S. sends $125 million to Bolivia, Colombia and Peru in "anti-drug" military aid.

1991 The Defense Intelligence Agency creates 41 military intelligence networks in Colombia, all of which incorporate paramilitaries and foster death squads. U.S. sends $550 million in police and military aid to Bolivia, Colombia and Peru.

1991-93 The CGSB conducts talks with the government of Pres. César Gaviria.

1993 The FARC adds "People's Army" to its name, becoming the FARC-EP.

1996 The FARC-EP launches nationwide offensive, dealing the government a string of crippling defeats and taking prisoner over 60 police and government troops. Millions of workers and peasants take to the streets against Pres. Ernesto Samper's economic policies.

1996 Tens of thousands of workers and peasants take to the streets separately to protest defoliation, ecomonic austerity measures and cutbacks in social services

1997 U.S. gives $88.5 million in military and police aid to Colombia.

1998 U.S. gives $112 million in military aid to Colombia. Colombian President Andrés Pastrana announces Plan Colombia, a huge international aid package to begin strengthening the Colombian military, which is losing the civil war.

1999 Pres. Pastrana agrees to clear troops out of a zone of five municipalities, centered in the town of San Vicente del Caguán, to open talks with the FARC-EP. Talks are to proceed "amid war." U.S. gives $308 million in military and police aid programs to Colombia.

2000 U.S. gives $1.3 billion in military and police aid programs to Colombia as part of Plan Colombia.

2001 FARC-EP conducts public audiences in the cleared zone, allowing tens of thousands of Colombians to take part in the dialog process. President Bush adds another $153.4 million to the military and police aid for Colombia under the Andean Regional Initiative.

2002 Pres. Pastrana invades dialog zone after a series of provocations and accusations against the FARC-EP. The FARC-EP charges that the Pastrana government is unwilling to address needed social changes.

2002 Álvaro Uribe Vélez, backed by the paramilitaries, becomes president of Colombia.

2002 Emergency Anti-terrorism package signed in August by the U.S. includes $35 million in additional military aid to Colombia.

I.

U.S.

INTERVENTION

IN

COLOMBIA

THE FUTURE OF LATIN AMERICA

RAMSEY CLARK

I. FREED OF FOREIGN EXPLOITATION AND DOMESTIC REPRESSION, COLOMBIA HAS UNLIMITED POTENTIAL

Colombia is a country of stunning riches and unlimited potential. Its physical location, size, diversity and natural wealth, its history, peoples, cultures and independence are important to every individual, society and nation.

Colombia is the only South American country fronting both the Caribbean Sea and the Pacific Ocean. It has hundreds of miles of coastline on each, with fine harbors and important cities nearing half a millennium in age. Its three chains of Andean mountains running parallel north-south courses exceed 18,000 feet in height and are the country's dominant physical feature. Roughly three-fifths of its lands lie east of the mountains in the vast basin of the Amazon rain forest and the broad llanos of the Orinoco. These parts of the country drain into the distant Atlantic Ocean through the Amazon and Orinoco river systems. It is here that most of the nearly one-half of Colombia that remains inaccessible and thinly populated is found.

Colombia's own great river, the Magdalena, traverses from near the Ecuadorian border in the south between the central and eastern ranges of the Andes to the Caribbean in the north near Barranquilla. Navigable for some 600 miles to the city of Neiva, southwest of Bogotá, the Magdalena has been called the lifeline of Colombia. Rio Cauca, a major tributary, flows between the central and western range of the Andes past Medellín, joining the Magdalena about 100 miles from the sea. It is navigable for two stretches of 200 miles each. The nature and importance of the uses of the flatboat, barge and steamboat on the Magdalena and Cauca from the 18th to the 20th century provide a history reminiscent of Mark Twain's *Life on the Mississippi*.

In area, Colombia exceeds Spain and France together, equaling California, Texas and New England, or eight New Yorks combined.

Among the nations of South America, Colombia is second only to Brazil in population, with more than 40 million people. Its capital, Santa Fe de Bogotá, with 7 million citizens, is the third largest city on the continent. Three-fourths of the population live in the Andean highlands and valleys, a region covering one-fourth of the nation, where the climate is temperate and healthy. Life expectancy at birth is over 70 years.

Colombians today are a vital mixture of peoples from America, Africa and Europe. The majority, approximately 60%, is of Native American-European mixture. There is close to 20% full-blooded European population, predominately Spanish, and a large African, American, Indigenous, European mixed-blood group composing about 18% of the society. A smaller all African and even smaller all Native American segment measure 4% and 1% of the population, respectively.

The nation's productivity is enormous. Colombia has 26 million head of cattle, 60% more in proportion to its population than the United States, a chicken for every pot and abundant fish. Annually, Colombia grows 180 pounds of plantains for every man, woman and child; 130 pounds of potatoes; 110 pounds of bananas and 90 pounds of rice and 50 pounds of corn. Colombia produces 830,000 tons of the best coffee in the world and 32 million tons of sugar cane a year, largely for export.

It can feed itself and help others less fortunate. Colombian adults average 2,800 calories a day, 84% vegetable and 16% animal, 119% of the U.N. FAO recommended minimum requirement.

Literacy is above 91%,—with female literacy slightly higher than male—compared to U.S. tests measuring functional literacy at 85%. Infant mortality is 26 deaths per thousand live births within the first year, less than half that of Brazil or Peru, but more than twice the rate for Cuba and the United States.

The nation's natural resources are vast. It extracts close to 200 million barrels of oil a year with new fields awaiting development and 24 million tons of coal, the largest coal deposits in South America. More than 700,000 troy ounces of gold are mined annually and more than 6 million carats of emeralds are mined, half the world production.

Colombian culture thrives, producing abstract painters like Leonardo Nierman. Fusion musicians like Shakira, Juanes, Carlos Vives and the young Andrés Cabas, who says his lyrics portray the "real Colombia," are heard throughout the hemisphere. The magical writer Gabriel García Márquez offers Colombia to all the world.

In the midst of this vast potential for social and economic justice, the human condition in Colombia is desperate. Per capita income is barely over $2,000 with more than half the population living on less than $500. The gap between the rich few and many poor is a human and national tragedy. A very small part of the population holds most of the wealth. The richest 1% control 45% of the wealth. Half the farmland is held by 37 interests. Malnutrition is widespread. Unemployment is close to 25%. Nearly 3 million Colombians are refugees fleeing violence and poverty. And year after recent year, the major cause of death has been "homicide with firearms."[1] The violence of the conquistadores still infects the culture. The badge of colonial servitude has never been lifted from the poor. But U.S. intervention and a modern regime of foreign exploitation and domestic repression by the oligarchy hold the masses in poverty and subjugation.

The reasons are to be found in part in the past.

II. THE CONQUISTADORES EMPLOYED GENOCIDAL VIOLENCE AND THE COLONIAL PERIOD CREATED INTOLERABLE CONDITIONS YET TO BE OVERCOME

The Indigenous of Colombia lived largely in the high plateau of the eastern chain of the Andes, where Bogotá is situated, and in the valleys between the eastern and central chains. Most living in this region were Chibcha-speaking tribes. They practiced intensive agriculture among a fairly dense population that lived in villages. They had organized religion, class divisions and matrilineal inheritance of political and religious offices. Among the more aggressive Chibcha, war was waged for political ends by large forces using darts, dart throwers, shields and wooden clubs. When met by the sword and armor of the Spanish, the Indigenous population was slaughtered.

The arrival of the Conquistadores meant death and destruction for the Indigenous of Colombia. In 1500 Alfonso de Ojeda came ashore on Colombian soil near the site of the present city of Cartagena. Several years later a Spanish colony was established further west in Colombia on the Isthmus of Panama. From there, Vasco Nuñez de Balboa, directed by some Indigenous people, crossed the isthmus to reach the Pacific Ocean at the Gulf of San Miguel in 1513. En route, Captain Balboa, accompanied by chained dogs led by his famous veteran Leoncico, will preside over a "ceremony ... the dogs will sink their teeth into the naked flesh of fifty Indigenous of Panama. They will disembowel and devour fifty who were guilty of the abominable sin of sodomy. ... The spectacle will take place in this mountain clearing. By torchlight the soldiers quarrel and jockey for the best places. ... In two days time Balboa will discover the Pacific Ocean."[2]

Reaching the vast "South Ocean" Balboa splashed into the waters in full armor and full faith that he had found the long-sought way to the Indies. Eduardo Galeano reports the event in his epic work: "His men carve an immense cross in the sand. The scribe Valderrabano registers the names of those who have just discovered the new ocean, and Father Andres intones the Te Deum Laudamus.'[3]

As word spread of how narrow the land barrier blocking voyages directly to the far east was and knowledge of the great distances and hazards of the southern passage spread from Magellan's voyage, the idea of a direct passage between the oceans obsessed the Conquistadores and infected those who came after.

In 1533, Cartagena was founded, decades before the French built a fort near

Saint Augustine in Florida, which would become the first permanent European habitation in North America. By 1538, Santa Fe de Bogotá was founded at 8,000 feet above sea level. It grew, though it could be reached from either coast only by an arduous journey of several weeks until the 20th century.

The impact of European conquest on Colombia was genocidal, as was true in most of the Americas. The death rate of the Indigenous population skyrocketed in the first decades. Their population continued its decline for a century and a half. In Colombia this led to the absorption of Indigenous people into the European population so that today the majority of Colombians are mestizo. One percent of the nation remains pure Indigenous, but even their culture is frozen, or largely imagined and adapted. Spanish profit from the genocide of the Indigenous of Colombia meant more gold for the coffers of murderous conquistadores and their foreign kings than was taken from any other colony in the Americas.

III. THE STRUGGLE FOR INDEPENDENCE FROM EUROPE FAILED TO LIBERATE COLOMBIA FROM FOREIGN DOMINATION OR ITS OWN OLIGARCHY

The struggle of the Amerindians for political independence from Spain continued for three centuries before Spanish Americans revolted against their motherland. The Indigenous struggle continues still through the Indian blood in the veins of the poor. The colonizers struggled for several decades to take Colombia for themselves before the final victory of forces led by Simón Bolívar over the Spanish army at Boyacá, north of Bogotá, in 1819.

Bolívar received critically needed assistance in arms, men and money from Haiti, whose President Petion could see African blood in Bolívar and sought the abolition of slavery as well as the end of colonial domination. Legal abolition of slavery came finally in 1851, two decades after Bolívar's death. Colonial domination has merged into a more pervasive and debilitating repression by oligarchy.

The government of New Granada that was established in the 1820s included Colombia, Venezuela and Peru. It was forged by a recognition of the weaknesses of the new nations separately and a commitment to strong international relations. The realization that federation of the new nations was essential to any hope for real independence was widespread. His understanding of it is the source of Bolívar's place in history, more than his military exploits romanticized by European Colombians.

IV. FEDERATION AS A MEANS OF UNITY AGAINST FOREIGN EXPLOITATION

Shortly after the independence of Mexico in 1820, the United States of Mexico were expanded briefly to include four former Spanish provinces in

Central America. The inclusion of the small Central American countries would make them less vulnerable to intervention and exploitation. It would also prevent the often tragic arbitrary division of lands and peoples by European powers drawing artificial lines without regard for the people who live there, or their segregation from needed resources and accesses. In the Mexican federation the large Mayan population in Chiapas and the larger Guatemalan Mayan population were within the same federal government. This Mexican federation ended by 1822.

The colonists along the Atlantic coast of North America who fought Great Britain for their independence knew they must hang together, or they would be hanged separately, that 13 clocks must strike as one. The history of the continent would have been different had they gone their separate ways.

The federation of New Granada was similar to the Central American federation established in 1824 which included the countries between Mexico and Colombia and including Guatemala, Honduras, El Salvador, Nicaragua and Costa Rica. Panama was part of Colombia until 1903. Both federations offered a better opportunity for full sovereign independence and economic development free from foreign domination and exploitation than the nations separately could hope to attain.

The United States was opposed to these federations because of the more formidable resistance to exploitation they presented and the greater concentration of power they possessed. It acted to undermine federations, except its own, as did European powers. These same considerations were part of the reasons the United States, Germany and others acted to balkanize the Federal Republic of Yugoslavia in the 1990s into easily exploited parts.

As Bolívar's health broke and ambitious nationalists within New Granada, supported by foreign interests, sought sole power for themselves, leaders in Ecuador and Venezuela moved for separation from New Granada by force. Near death and aware that his hopes for a large United States of South America were failing, Bolívar wrote, "We have ploughed the seas." He doubted that his struggle which gave birth to six new nations from Spanish colonies had benefited the peoples of the continent. New Granada survived until 1830, the year of Bolívar's death.

The Central American Federation lasted until 1839. The five small, weak nations that survived, joined by Panama after the United States took it from Colombia in 1903, have never been independent from foreign political and economic influences; domestic insurrections; war with neighbors or the threat and frequent fact of U.S. intervention. Within 15 years, Nicaragua experienced conquest by William Walker, the U.S. adventurer whose brief kingdom symbolizes the ways of imperial power. Walker decreed English, which only a few isolated communities spoke, to be the national language and restored slavery.

V. THE GROWTH OF U.S. DOMINATION AND EXPLOITATION OF THE WESTERN HEMISPHERE BEGAN BEFORE ITS OWN INDE-PENDENCE AND HAS CONTINUED TO THIS DAY

U.S. expansion was aggressively pursued before and from the earliest days after the 13 colonies drove Great Britain from their lands and established a federal republic. Major milestones included the Northwest Ordinance of 1778, resulting from pressure by land speculators, the Ohio Company of Associates and the Society of the Cincinnatus. The Louisiana Purchase in 1803 wrested an empire from European control stretching from the important port of New Orleans to the far northwest corner of what is now the state of Montana. Control of Florida, secured by force, was consolidated by treaty in 1819.

The U.S. population had grown by more than 33% each decade between 1790 and 1820, increasing from 3.9 million to 9.6 million people. Its land empire had doubled from 888,000 square miles to 1,798,000 square miles. Manifest destiny was ready to extend its grasp to non-contiguous territories.

Before the new and extremely fragile nations freed from Spain in the first two decades of the 1800s had a fair chance to establish themselves, they were confronted by the spectre of U.S. power and the Monroe Doctrine of December 2, 1823.

The Russian Imperial government formally claimed rights to Alaska and the northwest coast of North America in the early 1820s. His Imperial Majesty to the government of Great Britain claimed to be concerned that the Holy Alliance among Russia, Austria and Prussia, which had as its purpose the preservation of monarchy as the best form of government, might seek to protect the Spanish monarchy then threatened by Spanish revolutionaries by encouraging France to intervene. The British monarch claimed to fear an intervention by France supported by the Holy Alliance might lead to assistance to Spain to regain its colonies in the Americas. This could interfere with Great Britain's ability to exploit the vast resources of these lands. The defense of the monarchy was a lesser priority for all parties.

There was no evidence of any intention by Spain itself, much less by the Holy Alliance, that Spain would reclaim its colonies. The Holy Alliance was concerned with maintaining monarchy as the reigning form of government. It proclaimed, much as President Bush has asserted in his "war on terrorism," "the principle that legitimate kings should not be restrained by constitutions."[4]

Russia was powerful. In 1823, its population was twice that of Great Britain and more than four times that of the United States. Its army was over seven times larger than any other nation's force. Fear of Russian interference with its plans fostered a policy by Great Britain designed to enlist the United States as a junior partner to obtain domination of the Western Hemisphere. Never mind that it had sacked Washington only nine years earlier.

In August 1823, British Foreign Secretary George Canning summoned U.S. Minister Richard Rush to the Foreign Office to propose Great Britain and the United States "going hand in hand" to protect the Western Hemisphere from further European intervention.

Great Britain held Canada, claimed the Oregon territory in North America, British Honduras in Central America, British Guyana in South America and numerous islands in the Caribbean. With its powerful Navy and large Merchant Marine, it engaged in lucrative trade throughout the hemisphere and the sun never set on its empire.

A proposal of alliance from Great Britain could not be rejected out of hand by Washington. While U.S. merchant ship tonnage was nearing one-half that of Britannia, its navy had only one-sixteenth as many guns. War with Great Britain was dangerous and costly. It too could seek to reclaim its colonies.

Monroe obtained written comments on the British proposal from his two predecessors and neighbors, Jefferson and Madison. Jefferson argued strongly for acceptance. Madison favored it as well.

The Canning proposal raised important issues and concerns in domestic politics in the United States, including presidential ambitions in the 1824 elections only a year away. Because it implied an end to outright acquisition of colonial lands in the hemisphere by either Great Britain or the United States, it sought a new era of market domination and economic exploitation of the hemisphere, not political colonization.

Slave states in the United States were concerned about the imbalance of power created by the admission of new free states and sought territory for the expansion of slavery. Secretary of State John Quincy Adams asked John C. Calhoun of South Carolina whether he would forfeit claims to Cuba and Texas in order to support the Canning concept. Both Cuba and Texas were desired for the expansion of slavery. Both Adams and Calhoun were major presidential candidates. The Monroe Doctrine gave an advantage to Adams' presidential aspirations.

Monroe, guided by Adams who succeeded him in the presidency, seized the opportunity to steal the Canning proposal for economic exploitation of the hemisphere and the exclusion of new European colonies by announcing his unilateral doctrine and evading an alignment with the old enemy, Great Britain, in the enterprise.

President Monroe's message to Congress is worth remembering. It stated:

> The American continents, by the free and independent condition which they have assumed and maintain, are henceforth not to be considered as subjects for future colonization by any European powers.

We owe it, therefore, to candor and to the amicable relations existing between the United States and those powers to declare that we should consider any attempt on their part to extend their system to any portion of this hemisphere as dangerous to our peace and safety. With the existing colonies or dependencies of any European power we have not interfered and shall not interfere. But with the Governments who have declared their independence and maintained it, and whose independence we have, on great consideration and on just principles, acknowledged, we could not view any interposition for the purpose of oppressing them, or controlling in any other manner their destiny, by any European power in any other light than as the manifestation of an unfriendly disposition toward the United States...

It is impossible that the allied powers should extend their political system to any portion of either continent without endangering our peace and happiness; nor can anyone believe that our southern brethren, if left to themselves, would adopt it of their own accord. It is equally impossible, therefore, that we should behold such interposition in any form with indifference.

Indeed with several exceptions no European country established new colonies in the hemisphere after 1823. President Monroe's statement to the Congress was barely noticed outside the United States at the time. It was the 1850s before it was called the Monroe Doctrine. Historians agree European powers were deterred "not by the paper pronounced of Monroe but by Britain's powerful fleet."[5] More important prospectively than Britain's navy, however, was the forewarning faithfully followed, that the United States intended dominion over this half of the globe.

While the history of the hemisphere would have been the same had President Monroe never announced his doctrine, because the U.S. conduct and the policies it implied would have been the same, chronologically the pronouncement of the doctrine came after Spain's vast empire in the Americas collapsed and as U.S. domination and exploitation of the hemisphere began its ascendancy. Thereafter the young nation expanded its territory and increased its military and economic power over the region.

From 1820 to 1860, U.S. population growth continued each decade at an average rate of more than 33%—from 9.6 million in 1820 to 31.4 million in 1860. Its land area, still all contiguous, increased from 1,798,000 square miles to 3,022,000 square miles. The lands taken were nearly three times the size of Colombia. They included more than half of Mexico: all of the present states of Texas, California, Arizona and New Mexico and parts of four other states-to-be.

Texas declared independence from Mexico in March 1836, secured it in April by force of arms and joined the United States by annexation in January 1845. It added a slave state to the Union and seceded to join the Confederate States of America in 1861. Cuba was invaded four times by interests in the United States between 1850 and 1860 in desperate efforts to secure additional territory for slavery and political power in the Union to prevent its abolition. Jefferson Davis was asked and considered leading one invasion.

Only during the U.S. Civil War did European nations attempt to establish new colonies in the Americas. Both were near the United States and hostile to U.S. intentions. For four years, Spain fought the Dominicans and yellow fever, only to withdraw in 1865 as the Civil War ended. Spain re-established its dominion over the Dominican Republic on its first colony of Hispaniola founded by Columbus.

A French-backed, pro-Confederacy European intervention in Mexico— claimed to be justified by Mexico's default on foreign loans—placed Archduke Ferdinand Maximillian of Austria on the throne of Mexico in 1863 after defeating Mexican forces and driving Benito Juárez from the presidency. The enormous cost of maintaining the Maximillian monarchy against the guerrilla warfare of Juárez caused France to withdraw its promised support and in June 1867, the monarchy collapsed and Maximillian was executed.[6]

After the Civil War, U.S. assertion of power in the hemisphere became more open and demanding. By 1895, the United States dared to confront Great Britain directly in a border dispute between British Guyana and Venezuela. In a "swaggering, even belligerent" note to Lord Salisbury, who was both prime minister and foreign minister of Great Britain at the time, U.S. Secretary of State Richard Olney wrote of South America, "Today the United States is practically sovereign on this continent, and its fiat is law upon the subjects to which it confines its interposition."[7]

With war fever rampant, the United States, relying on an unsupportable interpretation of a unilateral policy—the Monroe Doctrine—surpassed Great Britain, establishing its superior authority over Venezuela and the Caribbean and foreshadowing further dominion over the hemisphere, a course that has continued to this day. In 1898, U.S. asserted itself more boldly by waging wars against the people of the Phillipines, Cuba and Puerto Rico. To this day, Puerto Rico continues to be the only U.S. colony in the hemisphere.

VI. THE MANY MEANS OF INTERVENTION

Intervention has many faces. Seen in a good light, none is pretty, however skillful the cosmetology. Direct military invasion, or threat from outright war to low intensity conflict to bluff, is as old as history. It has been employed by the United States in the hemisphere on scores of occasions—occupying territory, killing people, exacting demands.

Indirect violence has been employed through support for revolutionary, insurgent or exile groups, by encouraging or aiding a *golpe* or coup d'etat, through bribery or coercion of national leaders and assassination. William Sidney

Porter, writing as O'Henry, describes the early practices of intervention in Central America in "Cabbages and Kings," written in 1904 after his years in Honduras, a text that has been required reading for U.S. foreign service officers.

Elections can be influenced, disrupted or stolen by funding selected candidates—an effective means of intervention cloaked in the innocence of democracy which it corrupts. This has become a frequent method of the United States. While it demands "democratic elections," it then seeks to determine their outcome. Political parties can be influenced or coerced to select candidates chosen by the United States. Money can be pumped into the campaign coffers. Candidates can be demonized through the U.S.-controlled media and the media controlled by ruling oligarchies. Candidates can be bribed, coerced, or assassinated.

Constitutions and other legal standards have been forced on many countries. Franklin D. Roosevelt, while a young assistant secretary of the Navy, boasted while campaigning for the vice presidency in 1920 that he drafted the 1916 Constitution of Haiti from the deck of a U.S. destroyer in Haitian waters.

Congressional legislation, executive policies and treaties drafted in Washington have been major means of intervention, often more important to the lives of the peoples in the Americas than acts of their own governments. Always cloaked in benign, if not benevolent, garment, their substance speaks of U.S. domination and exploitation. Consider the Monroe Doctrine and its corollaries: too many tariff acts to mention; the Platt Amendment—that forced Cuba to acknowledge the right of the United States to send troops into Cuba on its sole discretion; the Good Neighbor Policy; the Alliance for Progress and NAFTA.

Most pervasive, a major purpose behind most other interventions and ultimately most damaging to the standard of living in a victim country are economic interventions. They include foreign ownership or control of key industries; major utilities; lands and businesses of all types; the exploitation of natural resources; human labor; surplus wealth and opportunities for profit and power. Single U.S. companies have often been the dominant political and economic power in whole nations and not just "banana republics." Exploitation by U.S. capital of foreign labor at desperately low wages through direct U.S. ownership and lucrative contracts for local businesses has been a common experience throughout the hemisphere.

Any decent person who has read B. Traven's *Trozas* describing conditions he witnessed in Chiapas in the 1920s would never dine at a mahogany table or sleep in a mahogany bed made from logs cut in the Chiapas rain forest by men torn from their families to die in indentured servitude. The logs, or trozas, were shipped to New Orleans, where cheap African American labor made expensive furniture for wealthy Americans.

Today millions in Latin America labor in *maquiladoras* for U.S. companies and local companies contracting with them at survival wages, pennies an hour, so that a profit of many dollars can be made from the sale of a pair of Mickey Mouse pajamas for children of the poor in the United States.

Another result of the exploitation of foreign labor is the destruction of organized labor in the United States and more arbitrary power in the hands of corporate executives protected by, or beyond the control of, U.S. laws and government.

In contrast, control of government, industry, business, the entire economy of a nation is obtained through indebtedness to U.S. banks, the International Monetary Fund, the World Bank and other U.S. controlled financial institutions.

Economic policy, national choices of development, investment, trade, agricultural policy, companies to be awarded valuable contracts and local businesses themselves are coerced by U.S. financial power through debt. Latin American governments are forced to take food from the mouths of their hungry children to repay loans to wealthy foreign banks that primarily benefited foreign interests in the first place.

Simón Bolívar, a Venezuelan, but the major hero in history for Colombians and other South American nations, experienced the pain of foreign debt. "I abhor debt more than [I abhor] the Spanish. That is why I warned Santander that any good we would do for the nation would be worth nothing if we accepted debt, because we would continue to pay interest for centuries and centuries. Now we see it clearly—the debt will end up defeating us."

Blockades, economic sanctions, embargoes, U.S. tariffs, coerced trade agreements and unfair business arrangements are means of dominion and exploitation by the United States and U.S. economic power. They have reaped enormous wealth from every country in the hemisphere, created and maintained subservient oligarchies, contributed to the enormous gaps between rich and poor and left the masses impoverished.

Collectively, such interventions by the United States and its major corporations and businesses have been the dominant fact in the lives of the people from Tierra del Fuego to the Bering Sea at most times during the past century.

U.S. interventions experienced by any country are not only instructive for all other countries; they are often more harmful to the country seemingly let alone. Whose bananas get to markets in rich countries determines the poor country whose children eat. U.S. policy in the Philippines forced hunger and malnutrition on the inland of Negros which has produced as much as 60% of Philippine sugar for export. Negros workers on vast plantations, owned by a handful of families, could not find a patch of land to grow vegetables or staples for their families.

These rich farmlands could feed all the people of the Philippines and export food for others. Sugar from these farms kept international prices low and excluded some countries from sugar export.

The United States, by market power alone, can force low prices for goods it purchases by creating price competition among poor countries producing the goods. The oligarchies which own the land can still profit, but the poor pay in sweat and malnutrition.

Intervention can be even more destructive by embargo, sanctions or blockade. The U.S. blockade of Cuba for more than four decades is one of the great international crimes of the modern period, punishing 11 million Cubans for resisting U.S. exploitation. That Cuba, against such adversity, has developed among other things the best health care and educational systems in the hemisphere shows resistance is not only possible, it can prevail over intervention and provide a better life than submission to the United States, but at a terrible human cost.

Iraq is the most extreme example of the devastation sanctions can cause. U.S. sanctions have reduced per capita income by 75%, life expectancy by more than 20 years, killed more than a million and a half people, mostly children under 5, and left a physically weakened population. They have impoverished a whole people in the presence of vast oil riches.

U.S. arms sales to governments that misuse them, often against their own people, like Argentina, Chile, Ecuador, Colombia, El Salvador, Nicaragua, Peru and others, not only deprives the people of needed food, shelter, education and health care, but subjects them to violence and repression by their own government and the threat of war and hostility with neighbors.

The cruelest form of intervention within a country may be the knowledge and skills taught at the U.S. School of the Americas and U.S. Special Forces training bases. There, favored police and militaries from submissive governments learn the arts of torture, intimidation, destruction of privacy and civil liberties, death squad deployment and assassination.

Mexico has suffered military invasions from the United States by such worthies as Zachary Taylor, Winfield Scott, Ulysses S. Grant, Robert E. Lee and General John Joseph Pershing, among many others. It has been forced to surrender more than half its land to the United States. In his classic *Democracy In Mexico*, Pablo Gonzalez Casanova, former rector of the National University of Mexico, reports on economic intervention in Mexico since 1960:

> Among the four hundred largest enterprises—with incomes amounting to 77 percent of the total national income—the percentages (of ownership) are 54.06 percent (foreign): 21.09 percent (independent private sector); 24.85 percent

(government). The foreign enterprises and those with strong foreign participation earn more than 50 percent of the total income...[8]

Mexicans must ask, whose country is it anyway? U.S. businesses and citizens hold the great majority of all foreign investment in Mexico. In 1998, in foreign trade, imports by Mexico from the United States were 75.7% of the total imports of $89.6 billion. Japan was a distant second with 4.4%. Exports to the United States were 84% of the total exports of $97.6 billion with Japan a more distant second with 1.4%.

U.S. sources dominate foreign news published in Mexico's many newspapers. González Casanova found in the early 1960s: In general, between 63 and 75 percent of the foreign news items in the Mexican press are derived from United States agencies.

In time, NAFTA may prove to be the most devastating economic intervention Mexico has experienced. It has destroyed much of Mexico's agriculture, made it dependent on the United States for corn and other food, and driven millions to urban poverty and joblessness. Mayans believe they are made of corn. For them corn is more than the national average of 60% of total calories consumed. The million Mayans in Chiapas knew what NAFTA meant for them before January 1, 1994. They greeted the first day of NAFTA with effective non-violent resistance and demonstrations that captured widespread international support, but they could not stop U.S. corn from coming in.

The whole Mayan culture, which had survived centuries of European intervention, was threatened. They could no longer maintain their native lifestyle by selling their surplus corn because the market price dropped 60% that first day. U.S. agribusiness, subsidized by the U.S. government, flooded Mexico with surplus corn. Sixteen-wheel, tractor-trailer trucks were lined up for seven miles at Laredo, Texas, on New Year's Eve 1993, waiting to dump corn on Mexico and take over the market.

Now the price of U.S. corn has risen and Mexico, trapped by dependency on it, pays the price. Today, President Fox and Mexican business leaders can see that NAFTA is relegating Mexico to even greater economic servitude.

Cultural intervention can alter a whole society, destroying traditions, customs, values and mores developed over centuries. In cultural intervention carried by globalization and the media, parents see their children ignoring, abandoning, ashamed, even contemptuous of the life and ways they always lived. Music, films, magazines, clothes, hairstyles, automobiles, radio, TV, guns, foreign fast food, architecture—a whole new array of consumer goods and foreign words, phrases, slang, language flood countries. Far beyond its economic exploitation, cultural intervention destroys the aspects of life that best identify a whole people from all their history, imagination and character. To the extent the intervention succeeds, the people no longer know who they are and can be quickly assimilated and easily manipulated. Once gone for a generation or two, a culture cannot be recaptured as those who lived in it knew it. Pindar's truth that "culture is lord of everything" could not have imagined how globalized commercialism and omnipresent media could wipe away a culture developed over centuries.

Psychological intervention invades the mind, telling its subjects what they are to believe and be. The conquistadores and the priests and colonial scholars and teachers taught Indigenous and African slaves and those with mixed blood they had no history, no culture, that they were inferior to the European and must obey their masters.

What has been perceived by many as an attack on the greatest hero in South American history, Simón Bolívar, by Gabriel García Márquez in his historical fiction *The General In His Labyrinth*, was a wise writer's powerful demonstration that Bolívar was a real American of his time with Indian, African and Spanish blood, not the Spanish aristocrat that those who write history had presented. Garcia Marquez wanted to humanize Bolívar, then show the people that he was like them, that they could be like him. This is a lesson no conquistador, colonial administration or oligarch would tolerate. Garcia Marquez also wanted to illustrate the meaning of his Argentine soulmate Jorge Luis Borges' observation that "fame is a form of incomprehension, perhaps the worst." He wanted to set his people free from the illusion that only the famous matter, and help them see that only they can free their country. The man on horseback is imperious and dangerous. Bolívar had said, "My element is war."[9]

VII. U.S. INTERVENTIONS AND COLOMBIA

Colombia has experienced virtually every form of intervention employed by the United States, at a tragic cost to its people.

In 1846, the decade following Bolívar's death, Benjamin Bidlack, the U.S. charge d' affairs in Bogotá, negotiated a treaty with New Granada in which the United States secured the exclusive right to transit across the Isthmus of Panama by any mode of "communication" in exchange for the U.S. guarantee "positively and efficaciously" of New Granada's sovereignty over the Isthmus.[10] The United States would exploit and abuse the Bidlack treaty for 150 years and its effect on the region would continue beyond that time. The U.S. Senate ratified the Bidlack treaty in 1848, five months after the discovery of gold in California. President Polk saw the railroad as the precursor of a canal across the isthmus.

Both the Panama Railroad and the French effort to construct a Panama Canal four decades later were under the authority of the Bidlack treaty. Like the hundreds of treaties the United States made with its own Indigenous peoples, the Bidlack treaty was honored in the breach.

Work on the railroad began in 1850. It was completed in five years. Costly in lives and money, it was the first transcontinental railroad and proved to be a gold mine. Fortunes were made. Annual dividends on shares of the New York corporation that built and owned the railroad averaged 15% and rose as high as 43%. It became the highest-priced stock on the New York Stock Exchange. Upward of 400,000 passengers crossed the 50-mile-wide isthmus on its tracks between 1856 and 1866.

Colombia received nothing but death, mostly of ethnic Africans, and a small share in income from the railroad.

Many of those who died were without identity other than a first name, without known address or next of kin, rather ghoulish, but thriving trade developed in the shipping of cadavers, pickled in large barrels, to medical schools and hospitals all over the world. For years, the Panama Railroad Company was a steady supplier of such merchandise, and the proceeds were enough to pay for the company's own small hospital at Colón.[11]

In 1879, under the leadership of Ferdinand de Lesseps, the driving spirit in the successful construction of the Suez Canal which was completed in 1869, a company of French investors was created. It obtained the conditional "exclusive right" from Colombia for 99 years to construct a canal across the isthmus. In return it was to make a cash deposit and pay Colombia 5% for the first 25 years, 6% for the next 25 years and 8% of the gross revenue for the remaining 49 years. Colombia retained full sovereignty over the isthmus.

The company was required to reach "some amicable agreement" with the Panama Railroad, that is with the United States, before undertaking construction. The canal was to be completed within 12 years. The railroad company was paid $17 million by the French interests, more than twice the cost of its construction, and the Bidlack Treaty was recognized. This meant a U.S. military presence, with rights to act, would remain at Colón on the Caribbean and Panama City on the Pacific. This U.S. military presence created friction and violence as the French struggled to complete the canal. Many blamed the United States for major difficulties that interfered with completion of the project.

The French effort to build the canal was a famous financial and human tragedy. The railroad ran a "regular funeral train out to Monkey Hill each morning." The dead were buried there on high ground formally named Mount Hope. An American, S.W. Plume, who spent years on the canal projects, testified before the U.S. Senate in 1906 about the failed French effort between 1883 and 1885 to construct a canal: "...bury, bury, bury, running two, three and four trains a day with dead Jamaican 'n-------' ... They die[d] like animals."[12] In 1889, the French company collapsed.

Before the turn of the century, interest in completing a canal across Central America was again high. Colombia was determined to have the canal on its soil in Panama. Its primary concern in negotiating for U.S. construction of the canal was to retain sovereignty over the proposed "canal zone."

In 1902, to show his authority under the Bidlack treaty, President Theodore Roosevelt sent Marines into Panama to protect the railroad, without receiving the consent of Colombia, as required by the treaty. When a treaty for a canal was finally agreed upon between Colombia and the United States, Colombia, uncomfortable with the assurances of its sovereignty over the Canal Zone, failed to ratify it. Impatient with delay, the United States looked for better ways to proceed.

On October 10, 1903, President Roosevelt met with Phillipe Bunau-Varilla, a Frenchman with technical training and long experience in Panama. In the meeting, Bunau-Varilla suggested that Panama might revolt and secede from Colombia and asked whether, if a revolt occurred, the United States would prevent Colombia from sending troops to Panama. Roosevelt gave no direct answer, we are told.

Within three weeks, a small group that would soon stage an apparent revolt met in Panama City. The group included the U.S. consul general and two Army Corps of Engineers officers at its first meeting. It agreed that Manuel Amador would be president of Panama. Born near Cartagena, Colombia, far from Panama, Amador was a medical doctor who later served as chief physician for the Panama Railroad. He was 70 years old and once had been designated president of the Department of Panama by the government of Colombia.

On November 2, 1903, in Panama City, this small group announced Panama's secession from Colombia and the USS Nashville arrived in Colón from Kingston, Jamaica. Orders dated November 2 to the U.S. naval command from acting Secretary of the Navy Charles Darling were explicit: "...prevent landing of any armed force with hostile intent, either government or insurgent. ... Government force reported approaching Colón in vessels, prevent their landing. ... Darling, Acting."

Colombian troops were prevented from traveling from Colon to Panama City. In all, 10 U.S. warships arrived at Panama, including the USS Dixie from the U.S. "refueling station" at Guantánamo, Cuba. The "revolution" succeeded without firing a shot.

In celebration, Manuel Amador, the new and first president of Panama paraded "between two U.S. flags. ... As he passes, Amador shouts *viva's* for his colleague Roosevelt."[13]

The United States recognized Panama immediately.

Four U.S. secretaries of state—beginning with William Seward in 1865, then

Hamilton Fish, William Evarts and James G. Blaine—had determined that the Bidlack treaty did not give the United States authority to intervene in Colombia in a civil war or internal dispute. Nor did an internal dispute or insurrection involving Panama occur.

Bunau-Varilla was immediately appointed Panama's representative to Washington. The Hay-Bunau-Varilla Treaty was signed on November 18, 1903-39 days after President Roosevelt met with the French citizen Bunau-Varilla.

Under the treaty, the United States was empowered to construct a canal. The zone would be 10 miles wide. The United States had the right to appropriate additional land or water areas "necessary and appropriate" to the canal's operations or defense. The United States guaranteed the independence of Panama.

Panama granted the United States sovereignty over the zone in perpetuity "to the entire exclusion of the exercise by the Republic of Panama of any such sovereign rights, power, or authority."

Thus ended Simón Bolívar's dream of a canal between the great oceans on Colombian soil. By 1827 Bolívar had been "thinking about it for some time." In 1828 he ordered "that priority should be given to geographical engineers in the Isthmus" to complete their reports on locations and feasibility for the canal by 1829.[14] By 1829 Bolívar had gone to fight the civil war that threatened the federation of New Granada.

The *New York Times* attacked President Roosevelt for his "act of sordid conquest." Roosevelt asked Attorney General Knox to prepare a defense of the U.S. military intervention and installation of its president of Panama. Knox is said to have remarked, "Oh, Mr. President, do not let so great an achievement suffer from any taint of legality."[15]

Colombia had lost an invaluable resource and a department of the nation. The United States had incurred the enmity of two nations: Colombia and Panama.

In a 1911 speech at the University of California at Berkeley, Roosevelt, in academic gown, stated: "The Panama Canal would not have been started if I had not taken hold of it...I took the isthmus, started the canal, then left Congress not to debate the canal, but to debate me." Panama was stolen by force and deception.

The United States began its turn at construction on the largest engineering project ever attempted in 1904. From the French experience, it learned the necessity of combating yellow fever and other threats to the lives of workers. Doctors made possible what death had defeated.

The canal across the isthmus was completed a decade later, shortly before the outbreak of World War I. It has dominated the lives of Panamanians since.

The United States tried to overcome the ill will of Colombians in 1922 with a belated payment of $25 million for its theft of the territory on which the canal was built. By that time annual tolls, a small part of the wealth generated by the canal, exceeded $25 million.

The people of the new Republic of Panama were no happier about the U.S. intervention against Colombia and the canal treaty that followed than the rest of the people in Colombia. The Panamanians have fared worse than Colombia as a result. The Canal Zone cut the new country in half, with an omnipresent U.S. military and political influence, the silent parade of ships from all over the world passing through, but out of reach; the foreign banks rising on their soil; all as remote as the foreign capital that controlled them. The people remained poor, became more dependent and were soon protesting. Long after Colombia viewed the theft of the isthmus as an ancient wrong, the former Colombians in Panama lived with it as a daily fact.

After World War II, anger spread. Riots against the U.S. control of the canal broke out in the 1950s and 1960s. A treaty modifying the unacceptable perpetual sovereignty of the United States over the Canal Zone was Panama's goal.

In 1964, 18 Panamanians were killed in rioting in the Canal Zone. The following year, President Lyndon Johnson announced that a fairer treaty would be negotiated. A draft was completed but did not appear before a military coup, headed by General Omar Torrijos, took control of the government of Panama in 1968.

By 1977, a treaty had been negotiated. Graham Greene attended the signing ceremonies in the Organization of American States building in Washington, D.C., as a member of the Panamanian delegation headed by General Torrijos.

Greene describes how Torrijos began his speech, "The treaty is very satisfactory, President Carter, vastly advantageous to the United States, and we must confess not so advantageous to Panama." Torrijos, bitter and ironic, was quoting Secretary of State Hay's words at the signing of the Hay-Bunau-Varilla Treaty in 1903.

Torrijos, who had endeavored to free Panama from the Hay-Bunau-Varilla Treaty for years and who personally negotiated the final terms, signed with great reluctance in order to save the lives of "young Panamanians," according to Greene. "Two clauses of the Treaty particularly stuck in his gullet: the delay till the year 2000 for complete Panamanian control of the Canal and the clause which would allow the United States to intervene even after that date if the Canal's neutrality were endangered."[16]

All the dictators of the hemisphere came for the event, including Pinochet of Chile and Stroessner of Paraguay. Only the most embattled, Duvalier of Haiti and Somoza of Nicaragua, were absent. President Carter asked General Torrijos how to deal with the dictators and received a simple answer: "Just refuse them any arms."[17]

Torrijos was a fierce opponent of Pinochet, Stroessner and all dictators in the hemisphere. He provided substantial support to the Sandinistas in Nicaragua and the Farabundo Marti National Liberation (FMLN) in El Salvador during their struggles for freedom. Powerful interests in the United States wanted to remove Torrijos from power.

Torrijos believed his principal service to his country was completed with the Panama Canal Treaty. As reported in the Encyclopedia Britannica, Torrijos sought the transfer of the Canal "to offset the economic woes of Panama and provide the base for a more aggressive role among nations for his small country."[18] In other words, to end exploitation and become an independent nation.

Torrijos stepped aside as head of government, surprising everyone and assuring an orderly transfer of power to an elected president. Later, in words reminiscent of Bolívar's near the end of his life, he told Greene, "I don't even know if I have done good or bad."

Torrijos was dead by 1981, within seven months after Ronald Reagan was first inaugurated president, killed in a plane crash that many believe was caused by a bomb placed by the CIA.

Before the 1980s were over, the successful Sandinista revolution was stolen in the election of a coalition candidate chosen and financed by the United States. During the campaign the United States threatened Nicaragua with more contra attacks, more war for the weary nation. The Salvadoran revolution was lost in peace negotiations, with the oligarchy firmly in control.

Panama was invaded by the United States in December 1989. Thousands of Panamanians were killed. The Panamanian police and military forces nationwide, organized by Torrijos, were the direct object of attack. Panamanian police, military and political leaders were killed or imprisoned to create forces and leaders reorganized and chosen by the United States.

President Manuel Noriega, who as a Panamanian Army officer had been corruptly paid $200,000 a year by the United States, more than President Reagan was paid at the time, was tracked down at the papal offices in Panama City where he sought sanctuary and was taken to the United States. In Miami, Noriega was tried and convicted of various criminal charges, including drug trafficking, in a federal court in Miami. He remains a prisoner of the United States in south Florida.

Years before the U.S. invasion of Panama in 1989, a new invisible and invincible form of U.S. intervention—the demand for drugs within the United States—challenged Colombia's ability to govern itself. In the late 1970s, a prominent group of Colombians came to the United States to plead for effective drug control measures here. The group came from the oligarchy. The group told me that the wealth generated by the production and sale of drugs destined for the United States, overwhelmingly cocaine, was so great that it was too powerful to control within Colombia. Government forces and the oligarchy's wealth combined were unable to cope. Only elimination of the vast demand for drugs in the United States could contain this powerful drug empire and enable the government to protect and serve its own people. Drug cartels with large paramilitary forces and enormous new wealth were beyond the control of the government of Colombia.

Even before the drug cartels became too powerful for Colombia to control, a strong popular movement came alive in Colombia after World War II, ignited by the widespread and growing awareness of the vast social and economic inequality and injustice in the country.

The young democratic movement was arrested with the assassination of Jorge Eliécer Gaitán in 1948, which was followed by widespread violence. Many believed that the United States was involved in the assassination, a belief reinforced in recent years.[19]

Between 1948 and 1958, a period called "La Violencia" ensued where some 300,000 people died in the struggle for political freedom and social and economic justice. In 1958, the two old political parties—Conservative and Liberal—agreed on a bipartisan government that they called a "qualified democracy."

The United States addressed similar struggles in other Latin American countries in various ways. In 1954, the democratically-elected government of Jacobo Arbenz in Guatemala was overthrown by force. Since then authoritarian Guatemalan governments have systematically eliminated leadership of Indigenous Mayans, who are 70% of the population, with U.S. complicity and awareness.

In 1958, Vice President Richard Nixon was met with violent demonstrations in South America. In 1959, the Cuban revolution overthrew the corrupt Batista government and was met with a major U.S. effort to isolate it politically, socially and economically.

In anticipation of the Punta del Este conference in Uruguay in 1961 and the charter to be agreed on by participants, which was designed to strengthen capitalist economic power during the Cold War, the United States announced the Alliance for Progress: "the first continental effort to show that U.S. and Latin American governments were actively organizing and learning from the success of the Cuban revolution."[20] The Alliance was seen in Latin America as a counter-revolutionary program to support and strengthen reactionary and conservative economic and political forces in the hemisphere—a program more focused and aggressive than the Good Neighbor Policy of the 1930s. A month after the Alliance for Progress was launched, the invasion of Cuba failed at the Bay of Pigs.

Colombians were as aware of the U.S. programs, as Mayan Indians were of

NAFTA three decades later. With hope for economic justice fading, revolutionary opposition to the government of Colombia grew. Both the National Liberation Army (ELN) and the Revolutionary Armed Forces of Colombia (FARC) were founded in the first half of the 1960s. Their struggle expanded and intensified quickly. Government forces were unable to either destroy or contain the revolutionary movement.

Even under these conditions, the United States has continued to dominate Colombian foreign trade—both imports and exports, in good times and bad. In 1998 Colombia's imports from the United States were 39.1% and exports to the United States were 34.9% of all Colombia's foreign trade. Venezuela was second in imports by Colombia with 9.8% and Germany second in exports from Colombia with 7.3% of the total foreign trade.

Elsewhere in the hemisphere, by the 1970s the United States was deeply involved in direct efforts to maintain governments protective of its interests and to change governments that it believed threatened them. In the southern cone, after September 1973, Argentina, Uruguay, Paraguay and Chile were engaged in violent repression of their peoples. Many thousands were arrested and disappeared by governments with strong U.S. support.

Chile had twice elected a socialist government headed by Salvador Allende. ITT and other transnational companies urged the United States to prevent Allende's first inauguration in 1970 and offered to help finance the operation.

Nixon's Secretary of the Treasury John B. Connally, who consistently supported the interests of U.S. investors in South America, lamented in the July 10, 1971, issue of *Business Week*, "We have no friends left there [in Latin America] anymore." It was a truth that could have been uttered at nearly any time in the 20th century. It helps explain why the worst dictators, like Peru's Alberto Fujimori, would publicly attack the United States to gain popular support in their own country while secretly serving U.S. interests.

In September 1973, a U.S.-supported *golpe* overthrew the Allende government in Chile. Thousands were summarily executed and disappeared. A military dictatorship headed by General Pinochet overthrew a constitutional system dating from 1824. The fiction of a Chilean "economic miracle"—propaganda to support the policies of conservative U.S. economist Milton Friedman adopted there—collapsed with the recognition two decades later that a brutal regime had not only murdered and imprisoned tens of thousands of its citizens, it had impoverished the nation.

The few reformist governments that emerged in Latin America seeking to reduce poverty and exploitation were overthrown or isolated. Any government that seized or threatened U.S. property or investments was subjected to economic, political, sometimes military interventions or covert actions.

The Dominican Republic, which elected a leftist government, threatened U.S. economic interests in the region and was crushed by a U.S. military intervention in 1965.

Cuba was able to consolidate its successful revolution and offer medical services and other assistance to poor countries struggling for independence on several continents. On occasion it provided military assistance. Cuban extended range missiles saved Angola from a South African invasion that had driven more than halfway to the capital.

By the late 1970s, Central America was a focus of U.S. concern as revolutionary movements in Nicaragua and El Salvador threatened governments with their struggle for independence and economic and social justice. Support groups for these countries in the U.S. worked hard to change U.S. policy, but were never able to approach the size, unity or effectiveness of the peace movement during the Vietnam war.

In Colombia in the 1980s, paramilitary forces created by the Colombian military with U.S. aid altered the life of the country. While created to combat revolutionaries, they engaged in drug trafficking and terrorized the public. Kidnappings, summary executions and armed violence became nearly a way of life in the cities and most rural areas. This forced greater efforts to meet revolutionary demands. In 1982, President Betancur signed an amnesty in the ongoing struggle with revolutionary movements in Colombia. In April 1984, a ceasefire was agreed on with the FARC. It proved to be one of a number of failed efforts to settle differences within the country.

In November 1985, a group called M-19, seized the Palace of Justice, taking hundreds hostage. More than 100 civilians were killed when the government bombarded the palace. Eleven of the 24 members of the Supreme Court died. Colombia's inability to govern was exposed to a startled world.

In 1999 a large area, nearly the size of Switzerland, was created to be governed by the FARC-EP during negotiations with the government with its center at San Vicente de Caguán. It became a large peaceful island in the turmoil of Colombia.

The fall of the U.S.-supported authoritarian government of Fujimori in Peru in 2000 and the election of the popular government of Hugo Chávez in Venezuela caused alarm in the U.S. government and greater commitment of resources to consolidate U.S. control.

In 2002, just before the election of U.S.-backed President Uribe, the government of Colombia abandoned the peace process and announced plans to destroy the revolutionary groups. Colombian Army forces trained by the Untied States occupied San Vicente without resistance.

VIII. PLAN COLOMBIA AND THE 'WAR ON TERRORISM' REVEAL U.S. POLICY TO DESTROY REVOLUTIONARY MOVEMENTS, STRENGTHEN OLIGARCHIES AND CONSOLIDATE U.S. CONTROL OF SOUTH AMERICA

President Clinton and Colombia's President Pastrana, announced Plan Colombia—"for peace, prosperity and strengthening of the state" in September 1999. Its purpose is to eradicate the four-decade-old revolutionary struggle of the poor in Colombia, bring drug cartels under government control and reinforce small oligarchies subservient to U.S. economic and political interests in Colombia, Ecuador, Peru and Venezuela.

Plan Colombia is the largest, most comprehensive and direct U.S. intervention in the hemisphere in the long history of U.S. interventions. It threatens Colombia, Peru, Ecuador and Venezuela—countries with over 100 million people—with more than a "war on terrorism." Plan Colombia places the political and economic independence of this huge region at risk.

It will directly affect the other countries in South America, including Brazil and Argentina, which are burdened with staggering international debt and facing further defaults. Tens of billions of dollars in new debt were arranged for Brazil in the face of the election of Luiz Inacio "Lula" da Silva, making any program to alleviate poverty and improve conditions for the people extremely difficult. Argentina has announced default on its international loans. Bolivia and the other southern cone countries are too small to offer serious resistance.

The economic collapse of the Soviet bloc has been followed by a decade of U.S. military, political and economic attacks on socialist and contrarian governments. The overwhelming military power of the United States, with its devastating destructive capacity, and the vast economic power of transnational corporate America have created unique conditions for the domination and exploitation of the hemisphere, and beyond, by those who seek a New World Order led by the United States.

The "war on terrorism"—announced as the solution to terrorism after September 11, 2001—along with the older "war on drugs," provides the excuse to use extreme military means to establish domination.

Multi-billion-dollar funding has already been provided for Plan Colombia. Hundreds of U.S. military advisors are in place, directing the Colombian military, which was already dependent on U.S. support. Hundreds of Colombia's elite military troops have been trained by the U.S. 7th Special Forces Group and other elite forces in Colombia, at Fort Bragg, N.C., and elsewhere. Key Colombian officers are graduates of the School of the Americas—with degrees in death-squad operations, mass murder, search-and-destroy tactics, torture, assassination and counterinsurgency against their own people.

The United States coordinates with the military and political leadership in Ecuador and Peru, and maintains contacts with officers in Venezuela.

Plans include a major assault to destroy the FARC-EP, the ELN and other revolutionary forces and bring the treacherous paramilitary forces created in earlier times under control.

The United States has used illegal claims to extra-territorial jurisdiction to indict leaders of the FARC-EP and paramilitary groups in U.S. courts—destining them for U.S. prisons or perhaps Guantánamo if they are caught. It can threaten others with prosecution.

The priority and magnitude of military action in Colombia and support for Plan Colombia forces by the United States will depend on other military demands in places like Iraq, Afghanistan, the Persian Gulf region, Sudan, the Horn of Africa, North Korea, the Philippines. But President Bush's policy in Colombia is as clear as his determination to attack Iraq and change its regime.

His National Security Strategy statement to the Congress, like his speech at West Point in June 2002, proclaimed:

> We will defend the peace by fighting terrorist and tyrants, [We cannot let our enemies strike first.] We will preserve the peace by building good relations among the great powers. [America has, and intends to keep, military strength beyond challenge.] We will extend the peace by encouraging free and open societies on every continent [LAFTA, NAFTA, FTAA, the Free Trade Area of the Americas].

Plan Colombia will support repressive oligarchies in Colombia, Ecuador and Peru, while requiring them to repay foreign debts, protect U.S. investments and trade within their countries. It will seek to destabilize and remove President Hugo Chávez from power in Venezuela, contain and undermine the administration of newly elected President Lula da Silva in Brazil, and work toward Cuba's return to U.S. domination and the end of its revolution, the most successful of the 20th century. For countries like Brazil, Argentina and Mexico that have faced bankruptcy and obtained enormous loans, the United States will support oligarchies under the same conditions of Plan Colombia, and their economies, independence and poor will suffer for years.

The new U.S. plans will be far more direct and intensive than its role in the struggle in Nicaragua and El Salvador. The policies of exploitation will further increase the gap between rich and poor and the numbers living in poverty.

If Plan Colombia and the "war on terrorism" are not stopped by the people of the United States, there will be decades of violence, suffering and poverty before the consequences of U.S. emergence as the one superpower on earth are overcome.

The Colombian people's struggle for freedom and dignity, for independence from both foreign exploitation and domestic repression, will shape the future of Latin America for decades to come.

This is one of the great human struggles of our time. Everyone who wants peace and economic justice for all must join in the efforts to assure a just future for the beautiful, beleaguered people of Colombia.

[1] *Encyclopedia Britannica,* 1999 Book of the Year, Colombia, Major Causes of Death, p.578

[2] *Memory of Fire,* Eduardo Galeano, Vol. I, Genesis, p.58-59

[3] Id., p.59

[4] *The Making of the Monroe Doctrine,* Ernest May, Belknap Press, 1975, p.3

[5] *A Diplomatic History of the American People,* Thomas A. Baily, 3rd Edition, Appletion-Century, Crofts, p.482

[6] Bailey, Id., p.191

[7] Bailey, Id., p.482

[8] *Democracy by Mexico,* Pablo González Casanova, Oxford University Press, Second Edition, 1970

[9] *Labyrinths,* Jorge Luis Borges, Pierre Menard, Author of Quixote, New Directions, 1964

[10] *The Path Between The Seas,* David McCullock, Simon and Schuster, 1977, pp.32-33

[11] McCullough, op. cit., p.37

[12] McCullough, op cit., p.173

[13] *Memory of Fire, Century of the Wind,* Eduardo Galeano, Vol. III, Pantheon Books, 1998, p.8

[14] *Bolívar,* Salvador de Madariaga, Pellegini and Cudaly, 1952, p.585

[15] McCollough, Op. cit., p.383

[16] *Getting to Know the General,* Graham Greene, Lester and Orpen Dannys, 1984, p.123

[17] Green, op. cit., p.116

[18] *Encyclopedia Britannica,* Year Book, 1980, p.565

[19] See chapter "Gaitán and U.S.: Head to Head," in this book

[20] *Latin America and the United States, Part One, Imperialism and Diplomacy in Inter-American Relations* by Octavio Ianni, Brazilian Center of Analysis and Planning. Stanford University Press, 1974, p.27

DEMONIZING RESISTANCE

TERESA GUTIERREZ

Plan Colombia has placed U.S. intervention in Colombia on the front burner for the progressive and anti-war movement in this country. Even though the U.S. government's strategy is still being formulated, the struggle in Colombia and how the anti-war movement in the U.S. relates to it is crucial now.

The Colombian struggle has become one of the most important in Latin America, along with the critical situations in Venezuela, Argentina and Vieques, Puerto Rico. As a result, stepped-up actions against Plan Colombia by the solidarity and anti-war movement become ever more urgent.

In fact, solidarity with all the people of Latin America and the Caribbean is more important than ever as the continent as a whole seethes with both struggle and repression, becoming a cauldron ready to boil over with revolutionary turbulence at any moment.

Colombia has the distinct dishonor of being the hemisphere's number-one recipient of U.S. aid. Washington will spend over $2 billion in the Andean nation by the end of 2005, through Plan Colombia and its successor, the Andean Initiative.

When Plan Colombia was first initiated, the U.S. government attempted to sell it to the people of this country as a "war on drugs." When that phony campaign is failing and the pundits talked about "nation building," for instance strengthening the Colombian judicial system.

Is that what the $2 billion is really for? And is it meant to resolve the problem of the 2 million displaced Colombians? Will it be spent to bring down the more than 20-percent unemployment rate?

This vast sum is solely for U.S. military intervention in Colombia.

Money robbed from poor and working people in the U.S.—money that could be spent on education or health care—is to be used instead against those who are fighting for social change in Colombia.

Plan Colombia will do nothing to eradicate the decades-long conflict in Colombia. In fact, it will exacerbate it.

It is not known if or when the Pentagon will send combat troops to Colombia, but the stakes are high nonetheless as the United States prepares in various ways for all-out domination of not only Colombia but the entire region.

GOALS ARE SAME AS IN VIETNAM

When Colombian President Andrés Pastrana traveled to Washington for the umpteenth time in February 2001, he stated that U.S. intervention in his country was not going to be like the war in Vietnam.

In fact, while there are many important historical differences, U.S. intervention in Colombia is very much like what Washington tried to do in Vietnam. The aim is the same: to suppress a movement by a people struggling to free themselves from the yoke of imperialism.

One of the techniques used in Vietnam is also being used in Colombia. An intense disinformation campaign organized by the U.S. government is being propagated by all the corporate media.

DISINFORMATION CAMPAIGN HATCHED IN PENTAGON

What is the real U.S. role in Colombia? Who are the players? What are their interests? And what do they want? The purpose of this intense disinformation campaign is to obscure the answers to these questions.

The word "narco-guerrilla" does not appear in any dictionary. Yet it has come into vogue.

The Pentagon coined the term to confuse people about the issues in Colombia. As they have done so often elsewhere, the military's public-relations people invented it to discredit the movement there.

In every U.S. news account, the term "narco-guerrillas" is used to describe the movement in Colombia, specifically the insurgents. People are told that the Revolutionary Armed Forces of Colombia-People's Army (FARC-EP) and the National Liberation Army (ELN) are narco-guerrillas.

These forces are described as drug traffickers, a charge the United States has failed to prove. Even Pastrana said in 2001 that there's no evidence to sustain this charge.

Yet the slander continues.

The media distort the situation in Colombia in other ways as well. Whenever there is an incident, they immediately blame the rebels. They becomes the judge and jury with a single mouse click, long before any evidence has been gathered.

This kind of disinformation points to the Vietnamization of Colombia. No one who remembers Vietnam should think it far-fetched to accuse the Pentagon of being responsible for this campaign against the Colombian people.

THE REAL TERROR: U.S./PARAMILITARY ALLIANCE

Hardly anything is written about the real horror going on in Colombia today and who is responsible for it.

A war of repression and terror—a war of horrifying proportions—rages in Colombia. The terror is institutionalized. It is state-sponsored. It has gone on for decades.

For over 100 years, the Colombian people have waged a heroic battle against this repression. They have struggled to free their country from domination by U.S. capital and themselves from the resulting poverty and exploitation.

The 20th century was filled with mass resistance, but mass repression as well. By the late 1950s, over 300,000 people had been killed in Colombia. In the 1980s, when the insurgent movement put aside its weapons temporarily to participate in the electoral process, the U.S.-backed government and right-wing paramilitaries responded by killing more than 4,000 activists, including mayors and other officials who were among the thousands of Patriotic Union (UP) candidates who had been elected.

This kind of terror continues. Gustavo Gallón, director of the Colombian Commission of Jurists, says his organization estimates that from October 1999 to October 2000 there were 160 separate massacres in which 1,084 people were killed.[1] Eighty-two percent of the deaths came at the hands of the paramilitaries, specifically the so-called United Self Defenses of Colombia (AUC).

Winifred Tate, writing in the Feb. 16, 2002, issue of *Foreign Policy in Focus* magazine, asserted that the precise number of people who have died at the hands of the right-wing paramilitaries will never be known. But it is known that over the past decade more than 35,000 Colombians have been killed, the vast majority at the hands of the death squads operating in collusion with the Colombian military. The military provides the intelligence, personnel and logistics to the paramilitaries and blocks human-rights activists from reporting the situation.

THE REPRESSION OF DAILY LIFE

The repression is incredible, but daily life is also a grind. International banks, big business and the Colombian oligarchy have brought untold misery to the Colombian people.

From 1990 to 2000, unemployment in Colombia nearly doubled. It went from 10.5 percent to over 20 percent, according to official figures. Austerity policies imposed by the International Monetary Fund have deepened the suffering.

An April 4, 2002, *Baltimore Sun* report revealed how draconian IMF and World Bank economic measures have devastated the Colombian economy. *The Sun* cited a report by the Medellín-based Global Policy Network (ENS). This agency documents how so-called globalization ushered in a series of economic "reforms" that began in 1990, resulting in increasingly dire conditions for Colombian workers.

After accepting an infamous IMF structural-adjustment loan, the Colombian government began to privatize industries and public services. Not only did unemployment rise, but Colombia became more dependent, more dominated by multinational corporations.

Opening the nation's economy to so-called world competition meant that Colombia would now import more than it exported. The once-healthy agricultural sector was devastated.

The Sun reported, "Colombia now imports more than 6 million tons of food annually while 2 million acres of arable land lie idle." It continued, "Between 1997 and 2000, the percentage of Colombians living in poverty rose from 50.3 percent to 60 percent."

National Trade Union School (ENS) analyst José Luciano Sanin Vásquez pointed out, "When people have a choice of seeing their family starve or breaking the law, laws against drug cultivation mean nothing and some people will take up arms."

The March 6, 2001, issue of *Hoy*, a Spanish-language newspaper published in the United States, reported that Colombia spends $134 million every month to pay just the interest on its huge foreign debt.

FUMIGATION: AN ACT OF WAR

Aerial fumigation is another act of war. Supposedly a measure to eradicate coca plants, the chemical spraying is used against the peasants and their rights to the land.

Meager plots of land worked by thousands of Colombian peasants are being eradicated by deadly myco-herbicides. Food crops in many areas of the country are being destroyed.

Florida's Department of the Environment has deemed some of these chemicals too dangerous to use in that state. But the myco-herbicides were sent to Colombia anyway, to be sprayed in areas where there is believed to be guerrilla activity, just as the Pentagon used Agent Orange and other herbicides in Vietnam.

EXPLOITATION BREEDS RESISTANCE

Over 2 million Colombians have been displaced by the internal conflict. Decades-long repression, miserable economic conditions, massive unemployment abound. Who are the culprits? Certainly not the FARC-EP or the ELN.

Is it any wonder that Colombia has produced the oldest guerrilla movement in Latin America? Exploitation and the people's refusal to reconcile themselves with this exploitation explain why Colombia has become such a hot spot in the world today.

History shows that as long as dire conditions exist for the vast majority of poor people, workers and peasants, they will take up all forms of struggle. The real terrorists—the Pentagon, with the biggest arsenal ever arrayed placed at the service of the banks, transnational corporations, big landowners—leave ordinary people no option but to fight back.

The FARC-EP has been in existence since 1964. The ELN was formed not long after that. The FARC-EP controls over 40 percent of Colombian territory. The ELN controls about 10 percent.

A U.S. disinformation campaign about the Colombian army and the AUC seeks to legitimize and prettify these forces. The ugly truth is that although the horrific war in Colombia began long before Plan Colombia, the U.S. government's infusion of $2 billion for military hardware is intensifying it, strengthening repression and bringing new misery to the people at the hands of the Colombian army and the AUC.

The money is going to a military that, according to Jack Nelson-Pallmeyer, author of *School of Assassins*, was trained in the art of killing at the Pentagon's School of the Americas: "More than 100 of the 246 Colombian officers cited for war crimes by an international human rights tribunal in 1993 are SOA graduates."

AFTER SEPTEMBER 11, 2001

On February 20, 2002, Pastrana broke off talks with the FARC-EP.

Pastrana, backed by the U.S. government, shut down the "zona de despeje," a demilitarized zone about the size of Switzerland where the FARC-EP could carry out talks without paramilitary or government intervention. The zone was set up in 1999 as the place to conduct dialog between the FARC-EP and the Pastrana government. It was not a gift from Pastrana—the zone was already under the FARC-EP's control.

The breakdown of that dialog and the entry of troops into the demilitarized zone reflected a hardening of the Colombian government's position. Washington was pressing Pastrana, and the oligarchy as a whole, as result of the new political climate. President George W. Bush's "war on terrorism" required the Colombian government to ratchet up its war against the people's struggle.

The Feb. 20 decision to shut down the dialog zone resulted in an escalation of the war in Colombia—which is exactly what the Bush administration wanted.

The Washington Post reported on March 27, 2002, "U.S. lawmakers are deciding whether more help from the U.S. could tilt the balance toward Colombia's armed forces. The additional aid would result from a U.S. rule change allowing the Colombian military to use 80 transport helicopters donated for use only against the drug trade to be employed directly against the guerrillas. It would also entail additional electronic intelligence sharing with Colombian forces."

The U.S.-funded Colombian government campaign will not be directed against the Colombian death squads, although they have committed the most vile, despicable atrocities.

This is another reason the U.S. movement against Plan Colombia is so critical. Every day the situation in Colombia becomes more polarized. The decades-long civil war is escalating. The horrid death squads, particularly the AUC, are becoming more active.

They operate with impunity. They carry out murders, rapes, massacres, suffocations, tortures and terror. Human-rights groups report that 92 massacres were carried out in the first 10 months of 2001, primarily by the death squads.

But the death squads don't operate on their own. Neither the Colombian nor United States government can be let off the hook. The Colombian military is known to be in cahoots with the fascist thugs from the AUC.

Human-rights organizations from Colombia and abroad have documented that the Colombian military not only turns its back while atrocities are carried out. Many of its number directly carry out the atrocities themselves. It has been repeatedly shown that death squad members are in the military.

This same military that has the blood of the Colombian people on its hands is growing by leaps and bounds. The *Los Angeles Times* reports that between 1999 and 2002, the military grew from 20,000 to 50,000 troops. And the government plans to add 10,000 more soldiers by 2004.

WASHINGTON CALLS THE SHOTS

In Colombia, as around the world, developments since Sept. 11, 2001, have meant that those fighting for social change are labeled terrorists by the powers that be. Pastrana invoked the word almost as many times as Bush.

Trying to drive a decisive wedge between the Colombian people and the rebels who are the main targets of the "terrorism" diatribe, Pastrana repeatedly announced large bounties against the rebels. Indeed, he adopted the same belligerent, bellicose language issuing from the White House and the Pentagon.

The Bush administration has hypocritically used the events of Sept. 11 to denounce certain groups for allegedly financing themselves through the drug trade. In March 2002, the Bush administration had a U.S. federal grand jury indict three members of the FARC-EP on drug trafficking charges. This was the first time the United States had indicted Colombian rebels on drug charges.

Earlier in the same month, in an interview with the Mexican daily *Reforma*, Pastrana said the so-called peace initiatives in Colombia were now on a totally new footing. Why? Because of the U.S. call for total war. But what he said was that the Colombian rebels were discredited at home and abroad.

"I believe that any new start to talks in Colombia will set off from a totally different perspective because politically the FARC-EP are defeated, and this generates a new space to be able to consolidate a peace process,"[2] Pastrana told *Reforma*.

THE RIGHT TO FIGHT

From the centuries-long history of the struggle between oppressed peoples and their oppressors, rich lessons can be drawn about peace processes.

Peoples that have endured occupations, genocide, massacres, economic exploitation and domination have had to carry out every form of struggle. None yearn for peace more than those who bear the brunt of colonial and neocolonial aggression.

For example, the sisters and brothers who carry out heroic actions with their bodies alone in Palestine surely hunger for peace. But decades of struggle that have taken many tactical forms have shown that real peace can only be won if it is accompanied with real justice. Vieques, Puerto Rico, is another example. Although the U.S. Navy continues to use this beautiful island for military practices, the people of Vieques have not been deterred from carrying out civil-disobedience actions.

In Colombia, the movement for progressive social change has gone through some staggering experiences that influence the forms of struggle used today.

Most striking was what occurred in the 1980s when the armed movement declared a ceasefire to participate in the electoral arena through the Patriotic Union. A bloodbath against the people's movement ensued over the next decade. More than 4,000 activists were killed. Mayors, presidential and other candidates were assassinated. The U.S. government did not condemn the terror. On the contrary, the bloodbath helped strengthen the U.S. hand in Colombia.

This experience weighs heavily on the movement today.

Clearly, the Colombian people want an end to violence. It has gone on for so long. It has been horrific. But the real purveyors of violence are deeply wedded to the very conditions that give rise to all forms of struggle.

The U.S. establishment and its puppet Colombian oligarchy are inherently opposed to fundamental social change. They will do anything to defend the interests of the haves against the have-nots, to defend their own economic interests against the claims of Colombia's suffering millions. U.S. imperialism will encourage the atrocities carried out by the AUC or slap its wrists with a wink, while at the same time demonizing the left-wing movement. It will do this because the AUC death squads serve the interests of the banks, the transnational corporations and the Pentagon, while the FARC-EP and the ELN defy them.

Whether in Colombia, Palestine or elsewhere, the task of the anti-war and solidarity movement in the United States is to support the struggle of the oppressed against the oppressors.

SUPPORT RESISTANCE TO INJUSTICE

In the face of the destruction of human life and the environment in Colombia, it is long overdue for the anti-war movement to raise its powerful voice in mass protest against not just one aspect of Plan Colombia but every aspect. Whether taken piece by piece or altogether, the plan is an act of war.

Fortunately, the movement against Plan Colombia is growing. Organizations and individuals in this country are holding forums, conferences and demonstrations. But much more must be done.

One of the most important tasks ahead is to raise the level of understanding of what is happening in Colombia today, and about the U.S. role. The avalanche of disinformation about the struggle in Colombia must be turned back by an avalanche of resistance against Plan Colombia and in support of the struggle there.

One way resistance can be built is by uniting to support the rebels and all who are fighting back in Colombia. The Pentagon and Wall Street would prefer to see the movement in this country confused and paralyzed on this issue. It would prefer that we put an equal sign between the right and the left or put "all the armed actors" in the same basket.

TWO SIDES IN A STRUGGLE

Whenever a union is on strike or in an intense organizing drive, the bosses turn up the anti-union rhetoric to a fever pitch. They put the union under a microscope, distorting or falsifying this or that incident in order to break solidarity. Union leaders become targets of scrutiny. They are slandered as corrupt or sellouts, as if the bosses really cared about that. The anti-union rhetoric aims to confuse the workers, to make it look as if there are many sides, when there are really only two: the side of the workers and the side of the bosses.

Unfortunately, the disinformation campaign sometimes works. Workers get confused, start questioning the union, support is derailed and unity dissolves. They start turning away from the union instead of defending it to make it stronger.

What the U.S. government is trying to do with regard to Colombia is not so different.

When the media talk about the civilian population being caught in the middle between the right and the left, the Pentagon is elated because it blurs the distinction between the two sides in the struggle. When the media equate the institutionalized state terror of the paramilitaries and the Colombian military with the acts of those defending themselves from that state terror, it means to confuse the issue.

In the case of Colombia, no matter what Bush says, it is clear that the U.S. government is on one side: the side of the paramilitaries and the Colombian government. The Colombian people being terrorized by them are on the other.

It is understandable that the people of Colombia do not want war. They are exceedingly tired of the repression.

That makes it even more urgent for the movement in the U.S. to unite and turn its full attention to the real source of war in Colombia: the Pentagon, Wall Street, Washington and the oligarchy in Colombia that does their bidding.

That's why a mass movement to stop Plan Colombia is urgently needed. So we can raise our voices loud and clear to demand that the United States get the hell out of Colombia. So we can demand self-determination for the Colombian people so that this devastated nation can finally win the peace it yearns for.

The Colombian people must finally be left alone to build the kind of society they want, free of IMF and Pentagon interference.

---

[1] *New York Times*, March 4, 2002
[2] *Reforma*, March, 2002

THE ORIGIN AND EVOLUTION OF PLAN COLOMBIA

ANDY MCINERNEY

U.S. intervention in Colombia is not a new phenomenon. One need only recall the U.S.-organized secession of Panama from Colombia in 1903, two months after the Colombian Senate refused to give the U.S. control over the isthmus.[1] In fact, U.S. intervention has been a constant feature of Colombian political history for the past hundred years.

In the post-World War II period, successive Colombian governments pledged themselves part of the U.S. anti-communist camp in Latin America. Any political force that challenged that relationship, like the popular movement headed by Jorge Eliécer Gaitán in the 1940s, was confronted by the full violence of the U.S.-backed Colombian state.

While U.S. intervention has been constant, the political situation in Colombia has changed dramatically.

The vast majority live in poverty, whether the traditional rural poverty or the more modern urban shanty life, while a small fraction of Colombia's 42 million people live lives of luxury based on their ties to the United States This elite is in a precarious situation that is becoming increasingly untenable. As class conflict intensifies, its needs have expanded and evolved.

Plan Colombia, a $7.5 billion program presented in 2000 by Colombian President Andrés Pastrana with the enthusiastic backing of the U.S. Clinton administration, reflects increasing reliance on the U.S. government by the Colombian government and the political and economic elite it represents. They are relying on Washington not simply to improve the efficiency of the Colombian state. On the contrary, Plan Colombia is designed, more or less explicitly, to shore up Colombia's elite against growing waves of popular discontent at decades of poverty, social misery and exploitation.

SITUATION IN 1990: BUSH'S ANDEAN INITIATIVE

To understand Plan Colombia and its continuation, the Bush administration's Andean Regional Initiative, it is worth stepping back 10 years earlier, to 1990.

The socialist camp in Eastern Europe was collapsing. The world's political battle lines and balance of forces were being redrawn. Without the counterweight of the socialist camp, U.S. intervention went all but unchecked. Opponents of U.S. imperialism and advocates of national self-determination alike became military targets at the very time when political disorientation was highest.

The effects were felt immediately in Latin America. In December 1989, U.S. forces invaded Panama. In February 1990, the Sandinistas in Nicaragua stepped down from power after years of U.S.-financed civil war. Civil war in El Salvador continued for two more years before the FMLN liberation movement agreed to lay down arms as part of a U.S.-brokered peace accord.

The retreat of large sectors of the Latin American left following the collapse of the socialist camp did not, however, mark an end to U.S. military aid to the region. On the contrary, in February 1990 U.S. President George Bush announced the so-called Andean Initiative. The Andean Initiative was a five-year $2.2 billion economic and military aid package to Bolivia, Colombia and Peru.

For the first time, a major U.S. aid package was justified in terms of the "war on drugs."

A major target of the 1990 Andean Initiative was the Peruvian insurgency led by the Communist Party of Peru (PCP), known in the Western media as the Shining Path. Unaffiliated with, indeed, hostile to, the pro-Soviet left, the PCP did not experience the same political disorientation that had afflicted most of the left. Peru's Indigenous and super-exploited peasantry formed a fertile recruiting ground for the PCP insurgency, which was launched in 1980. By 1992, one Pentagon opponent of the Andean Initiative described the "backdrop of the nation of Peru coming apart at the seams."[2]

The impact of intensified U.S. intervention along with the PCP's inability to forge alliances with wider sectors of the working-class movement in Peru proved disastrous for the revolutionary movement there. In 1992, Peruvian President Alberto Fujimori staged a "self-coup," assuming dictatorial powers in an effort to smash the PCP and the smaller Tupac Amaru Revolutionary Movement insurgency. The same year, Peruvian military intelligence captured PCP leader Abimael Guzmán with the aid of the U.S. CIA.

While Peru was the original focus of the first Bush administration's Andean Initiative, concern about Colombia was never far away. In fact, according to the George Washington University-based National Security Archive, "the Andean Strategy developed largely in response to events on the ground in Colombia."

An influential March 1988 cable from U.S. Ambassador Charles Gillespie set off alarm bells in Washington, warning of escalating levels of violence from guerrilla groups and drug cartels, and the seeming inability of the Colombian security forces to do anything about it. These concerns about the internal threat to Colombian stability triggered an interagency review of Colombia policy, coordinated by the National Security Council.[3]

BACKGROUND TO PLAN COLOMBIA: NAFTA, THE 1996 OFFENSIVE

Two specific events set the stage for the massive escalation of U.S. military aid and intervention in Colombia that would become known as Plan Colombia. The first was the implementation of the North American Free Trade Agreement (NAFTA) in 1994. With NAFTA, the U.S. government announced what would become a major policy goal toward the Western Hemisphere: a continent-wide pool of cheap labor for U.S. corporations and consumers for U.S. products. NAFTA itself only opened the markets of Canada and Mexico, but the longer-term goal was clear and often explicitly stated.

"NAFTA is the defining issue in American foreign policy not just toward Latin America, but toward the world over the next several years," stated Lawrence Summers, a Treasury Department official in the Clinton administration. "If you look toward the end of this century, you will see a much closer relationship between the U.S. and other Latin American countries," prophesied Commerce Department official Jeffrey Garten.

President Bill Clinton made the goal explicit. The day that NAFTA passed Congress, he pledged to "reach out to the other market-oriented democracies of Latin America to ask them to join this great American pact."[4]

The opening of NAFTA had another impact beside announcing U.S. foreign policy in Latin America. On Jan. 1, 1994, the day NAFTA took effect, the Zapatista National Liberation Army (EZLN) burst onto the world scene by taking over towns in Chiapas in southern Mexico. The EZLN insurgency, whatever its limitations, became a lightning rod for opposition to U.S. economic domination of Latin America. It was a signal that U.S. designs on the continent would not go unchallenged.

The second major event that set the stage for Plan Colombia was a dramatic change in the balance of forces within Colombia itself that took place in 1996. In the years before 1996, the political climate in Colombia was characterized by a rise in right-wing, death-squad terror, accompanied by a decline in mobilizations by the unions, peasant organizations, and other popular sectors. Many of these forces had participated enthusiastically in the Patriotic Union (UP) political movement, which arose in 1985 out of the talks between the Colombian government and the Revolutionary Armed Forces of Colombia-People's Army (FARC-EP). But after the talks collapsed in 1987, UP activists became targets of right-wing terror. More than 4,000 were killed in the next decade, laying a pall of fear over Colombia's progressive movement.

Two parallel events in 1996 reversed this climate of fear. The first was in August, an unprecedented military offensive by the FARC-EP. Actions were carried out in over half of the country's 32 provinces. The offensive was unprecedented in terms of both its nationwide scope and the extent of damages inflicted on government troops. Rebel troops completely overran a government military base at Las Delicias in the province of Caquetá, capturing 60 troops. This offensive marked the beginning of a series of victories for the FARC-EP, to the extent that one year later the *New York Times* ran a headline describing a report by advisers to Colombian President Ernesto Samper, "Colombia Aides Indicate Rebels Are Winning War."[5]

At the same time as the rebel military offensive, Colombia's mass movement took to the streets again after decades of repression. In early September 1996, tens of thousands of peasants staged blockades of major roads across Colombia to protest Samper's defoliation campaign. This campaign, carried out as part of the U.S.-backed anti-drug effort, was indiscriminately destroying crops in the countryside, leaving peasants without their livelihood. Also in September, unions staged mass protests against economic austerity measures and cutbacks in social services. For example, on Sept. 17-18, 1996, tens of thousands of workers took to the streets of Facatativa, near Bogotá. They set up barricades and took over buildings to protest utility price hikes. At least one person was killed, 25 injured, and several government offices were destroyed.[6]

These demonstrations set the stage for a new wave of protests that would shake successive Colombian governments in the coming years. In February 1997, Colombian unions launched their first major general strike in a decade. Since then, up through September 2002, the unions have carried out at least five other general strikes. Each involved hundreds of thousands of workers.

This increased mobilization came despite continued death-squad activity against union activists. In 2001, for example, 185 trade unionists were assassinated. Another 2,000 had received death threats between 1997 and 2001.[7] But the paralyzing cloud of fear had lifted.

THE PLAN

José Noe Ríos and Daniel García Peña, the two advisers to President Ernesto Samper who warned of the growing threat the insurgency posed for Colombia's regime, presented only one option for the Colombian government: "There is no instrument other than dialog to overcome" the insurgency.[8]

By 1998, there was wide agreement within Colombia's ruling circles that the Colombian military could not defeat the insurgency. Newly elected President Andrés Pastrana moved quickly to open a dialog with the FARC-EP. He went so far as to pull back police and troops from five municipalities in central Colombia—an area the size of Switzerland—to guarantee the safety of the FARC-EP delegation.

It was against this backdrop—a string of guerrilla military victories, growing mass opposition to the government's pro-International Monetary Fund economic policies, open talks with the FARC-EP—that Plan Colombia was born. Like its predecessor, the Andean Initiative, Plan Colombia was originally couched in the language of the "war on drugs."

The plan was most remarkable for the comprehensive U.S. intervention foreseen in every facet of the Colombian government and economy.

Andrés Pastrana first proposed Plan Colombia to Colombia's Congress in 2000. But the original conception for the plan can be traced to 1998.[9] By 1999, the process was well under way. According to Professor Manuel Salgado Tórres, a former vice president of Ecuador's Congress, "The Plan circulated in Washington in September 1999. It was discussed first in the U.S. Congress, and its contents were first made known through the U.S. press."[10]

A "fact sheet" prepared by the U.S. State Department, entitled "Is Plan Colombia a Colombian Plan?" issued on February 20, 2001, reveals how sensitive the issue of the plan's origin was. The "fact sheet" admits that "the Colombian government did consult extensively with the U.S. government as it refined its strategy," but insists that Plan Colombia was prepared by the Colombian government.[11]

While the official rhetoric is phrased in the language of the drug war, the opening sentence of the actual 47-page document points starkly to the real purpose of Plan Colombia. "We are faced with the historic challenge of establishing and securing a society where the Colombian state can exercise its true authority and fulfill its essential obligations,"[12] The plan's preface identifies the problem to be addressed, "There is no question that Colombia suffers from the problems of a state yet to consolidate its power: a lack of confidence in the capacity of the armed forces, the police, and the judicial system to guarantee order and security; a credibility crisis at different levels and in different agencies of government and corrupt practices in the public and private sectors."[13] The source of the problem, the document claims, is drug trafficking. But the problem itself is a state apparatus unable to carry out its historic role of defending the interests of the country's political and economic elite.

How does Plan Colombia envision solving this problem of a crisis in the state? Pastrana described it as a sort of "Marshall Plan" for the Colombian state: a vast $7.5 billion infusion of aid into the state apparatus, including $4 billion to be raised by Colombia itself and $3.5 billion from the international community. The Clinton administration initially pledged $1.5 billion over three years.

The document describes 10 elements of the plan falling into five basic categories: the peace process, the economy, counter-drug strategy, reform of the judicial system, and social development. Some of these elements were inherently tied to the immediate needs of the Pastrana administration, most notably the dialogs with the FARC-EP (that were canceled in 2002). Other elements, however, clearly have a broader scope. For example:

• The Colombian government will continue the pro-International Monetary Fund policies of austerity and privatization, outlined under stabilization measures. "As part of budget cutbacks, money going to the military, police, and judicial system has been reduced dramatically (20 percent). Outside [financial] assistance is essential if the government is to be able to consolidate its economic reforms and at the same time increase the flow of resources to finance the military effort and address social needs."[14]

• The Colombian government will "combat illicit cultivation through continuous and systematic actions of both the military and police forces, especially in the Putumayo region and in Southern Colombia."[15] Both of these areas are in the traditional base of support for the FARC-EP.

MYTH VS. REALITY

When Plan Colombia was first announced and the U.S. Congress appropriated $1.3 billion for a two-year period in July 2000, many researchers and human-rights groups carefully analyzed the official rhetoric of Plan Colombia to expose the reality behind it. In the words of one report, "It is clear that Plan Colombia's intent is to combat the principal threat to the nation's political and economic elite: the FARC."[16]

This conclusion is further supported by the Plan's actual implementation. The Colombian government never put up the $4 billion in social spending it had pledged, as the country remained mired in the worst economic depression of the century. Nor did European countries contribute much to the effort.[17] Plan Colombia essentially became synonymous with U.S. aid, which totaled some $2 billion between 1999 and 2002.

Of this $2 billion, 80 percent went to military aid. A big part went directly to U.S. military contractors in the form of 18 Blackhawk helicopters and 42 Huey combat helicopters. Other aid went to counterinsurgency training for three special elite battalions of the Colombian Armed Forces. More aid went to increased intelligence-gathering capacity. Only about $364 million of the aid went to ostensible social programs, most of which are related to incidental costs of the war like costs related to Colombians displaced by the war.[18]

The Bush administration dropped any effort to hide behind the fig leaf of the "war on drugs" in the wake of the Sept. 11, 2001, attacks on the United States. Under the terms of the original Plan Colombia legislation passed by the U.S. Congress, military aid was to be restricted to supporting the anti-drug effort.

While this distinction was largely fictitious,[19] it did require the Colombian military to keep up appearances. Now, as part of the $29 billion Anti-Terrorism Package, military aid to Colombia "shall be available to support a unified campaign against narcotics trafficking and designated terrorist organizations."[20] The FARC-EP and the smaller National Liberation Army (ELN) are both listed as "terrorist organizations" by the U.S. government.

WIDENING THE WAR

Plan Colombia began at a time when the Colombian government was being battered on the one side by an insurgency that was growing both numerically and militarily and on the other by an increasingly assertive movement of workers and peasants. Accompanied by the 1999-2002 dialog process with the FARC-EP, it was an effort on behalf of the Colombian government to tilt the balance of forces back in its favor. Since the talks collapsed in February 2002 and Álvaro Uribe Vélez was subsequently elected president of Colombia, the Colombian military and backers in the Pentagon apparently believe that they are again ready for battle.

Technically, the Clinton-Pastrana Plan Colombia framework has been replaced by the Bush administration's Andean Regional Initiative, a name harking back to George W. Bush's father's policy. But the aid package's outlines remain the same: a reliance on military aid to the Colombian military and police to shore up the Colombian elite against popular opposition. The expectation, in turn, is that the Colombian government will prove loyal to the U.S. government's greater goals in the region, like the Free Trade Area of the Americas.[21]

---

[1] See for example Díaz Espino, Ovidio, *How Wall Street Created a Nation.* Four Walls Eight Windows, NY, NY, 2001.

[2] Lt. Commander C.D. Bott, U.S. Navy, "Counternarcotics in Peru: High Risk, Low Return." Globalsecurity.org, 1992. Commander Bott argued for more counterinsurgency training and less direct military aid to Peru.

[3] "War in Colombia: Guerrillas, Drugs and Human Rights in U.S.-Colombia Policy 1988-2002," National Security Archive Electronic Briefing Book 69, May 2002.

[4] "NAFTA's Sequel: Moving Free Trade Farther South," *Christian Science Monitor*, Nov. 29, 1993.

[5] *New York Times*, Sept. 11, 1997.

[6] See for example "Colombia: Anti-inflationary Social Pact Wages a Losing Battle," *Inter Press Service*, Sept. 25, 1996.

[7] "Colombia: Annual Survey of Violations of Trade Union Rights," International Confederation of Free Trade Unions, 2002.

[8] Quoted in "Colombian Aides Indicate Rebels are Winning War," *New York Times*, Sept. 11, 1997.

[9] Oficina Internacional de Derechos Humanos Acción Colombia, "Plan Colombia: A Strategy Without a Solution," reprinted by Equipo Nizkor, February 2000.

[10] Salgado Torres, Manuel, "Falacias y Verdades Sobre el 'Plan Colombia,'" Quito, October 2000.

[11] "Is Plan Colombia a Colombian Plan?" Bureau of Western Hemisphere Affairs, U.S. Department of State, Feb. 20, 2001.

[12] "Plan Colombia: Plan for Peace, Prosperity and Strengthening of the State," Bogotá, Colombia, Presidency of the Republic, 1999.

[13] "Preface," ibid.

[14] "Approach to the Colombian Economy," ibid.

[15] "Counter-Drug Strategy," ibid.

[16] "Plan Colombia: A Closer Look," Information Network of the Americas, July 2000.

[17] In October 2000, the European Union pledged $321 million toward Plan Colombia, but restricted the aid to non-military spending.

[18] "U.S. Aid Can't Fix Drug War Setbacks," *Houston Chronicle*, Sept. 29, 2002.

[19] Between 1998 and 2002, at least 12 U.S. government personnel have been killed in Colombian combat zones. See "U.S. Casualties in Colombia's Civil War," New Colombia News Agency (ANNCOL), Aug. 28, 2002.

[20] "Shifting Colombia's Aid: U.S. Focuses on Rebels," *New York Times*, Aug. 10, 2002.

[21] In the words of Colombian economist Hector Mondragon, "If neoliberalism came to Latin America on the boots of General Pinochet, the FTAA will arrive in the helicopters of Plan Colombia." ("Plan Colombia: Throwing Gasoline on the Fire," 2000).

RIGHT-WING TERROR AND DRUG LORDS

GARRY M. LEECH

Many of Colombia's nearly 200 years of independence have been marred by violence. This includes civil wars during the 19th century, the "Thousand Days War," at the turn of the 20th century, and "La Violencia" in the mid-20th, out of which evolved the civil conflict that continues today. The Colombian military's inability to control the entire national territory has led to the creation of vigilante groups during times of conflict. Many of these groups were formed by the country's landed elite. They frequently functioned under the moniker "self-defense groups." While these militias often worked in conjunction with the Colombian Armed Forces, they were usually temporary organizations with limited numbers and scope of operations.

Over the past two decades, however, these paramilitary forces have established a permanent presence throughout Colombia in order to wage a dirty war against leftist guerrillas and their suspected sympathizers, with support from the U.S.-backed Colombian military.

An unforeseen consequence of the cocaine boom that began in the late 1970s was a dramatic growth in the military strength of leftist rebels and right-wing paramilitary forces. This resulted in a dangerous escalation of the civil conflict. The enormous wealth garnered by drug traffickers, especially the Medellín and Cali cartels, was often invested in land. The drug barons soon became Colombia's dominant land-owning class. These narco-landowners' new status as members of the country's landed elite placed them in the ranks of the guerrillas' traditional enemy. Leftist rebel groups, especially the biggest and oldest guerrilla force, the Revolutionary Armed Forces of Colombia-People's Army (FARC-EP), rapidly increased their military strength as a result of the income garnered by levying war taxes on coca growers. They began kidnapping drug traffickers and their relatives for ransom. In 1981, Colombia's narco-landowners responded, in conjunction with traditional landowners, wealthy business owners, the military, and U.S. advisers, by forming militias to defend themselves and their families from the escalating rebel attacks.

These regional paramilitary forces worked hand in glove with the Colombian military. The military routinely provided the paramilitaries with the intelligence, weapons, and transportation that allowed them to effectively target guerrillas and anyone they deemed to be a potential rebel sympathizer, including labor leaders, community organizers and human-rights activists.

In the early 1990s there were an estimated 850 paramilitary fighters in Colombia. Ten years later that number had increased to approximately 12,000. In 1997, Carlos Castaño, a former associate of notorious drug lord Pablo Escobar and leader of the biggest militia force, the Peasant Self Defenses of Córdoba and Urabá (ACCU), oversaw the merging of the regional paramilitary forces into one national organization, the United Self Defenses of Colombia (AUC).

The AUC launched an offensive in guerrilla-controlled regions of southern Colombia that was marked by massacres of the civilian population. During one operation in the initial phase of the offensive, paramilitaries flew into a military-controlled airstrip in July 1997 and went on a five-day rampage that left 49 peasants dead in the town of Mapiripán.

Many of the victims were decapitated and mutilated with machetes, a trademark tactic of the paramilitary death squads.

The AUC routinely entered rural Colombian villages and induced fear by massacring some of the residents and ordering the rest to abandon their homes and lands. By forcibly displacing the rural population, the paramilitaries hoped to eliminate local support for the guerrillas. This strategy has aggravated the already grossly inequitable distribution of arable lands as large landowners, as well as multinational corporations interested in oil, coal, and natural gas resources, have seized the abandoned farms.

More than 2.5 million rural Colombians have been displaced by the conflict in the past 15 years. Many fled to the impoverished shantytowns that are rapidly encircling Colombia's cities.

Responding to international criticism and seeking political legitimacy, the paramilitaries have begun implementing a strategy of selectively assassinating two or three victims at a time over a prolonged period instead of perpetrating a single large massacre. Because a massacre is defined as more than three people killed at the same time in the same place for the same reason, this tactic means a smaller percentage of Colombia's massacres is attributed to the paramilitaries. It has also resulted in less negative coverage by news organizations that often only deem mass killings to be newsworthy.

In June 2001, Carlos Castaño resigned from his position as military commander of the AUC in an attempt to distance himself from the atrocities the group regularly committed. He would remain as political head of the organization. One year later, in another apparent public-relations ploy, Castaño announced he was dissolving the AUC, citing the national command's inability to control the drug trafficking activities and kidnappings committed by regional paramilitary units. He would, however, continue to head Colombia's biggest regional paramilitary force, the ACCU.

Several months later, the paramilitary leader announced that a revamped AUC, minus two regional militias, would focus on combating the guerrillas. He said it would not tolerate its members being involved in drug trafficking and kidnapping. It is clear that limiting massacres, Castaño resigning as the AUC's military chief, and supposedly cleansing the AUC are all steps in an ongoing process intended to present the paramilitary leader as a legitimate political figure capable of participating in future peace negotiations between the rebels and the government.

This legitimization process for Castaño and the AUC has coincided with the sudden rise to power of President Álvaro Uribe Vélez on an anti-guerrilla platform. There are many questions regarding possible links among the new president, drug trafficking and paramilitary groups. Uribe's presidential campaign manager and close advisor, Pedro Juan Moreno Villa, owner of GMP Chemical Products, was Uribe's chief of staff when Uribe was governor of Antioquiá between 1995 and 1997. During those years, GMP was Colombia's biggest importer of potassium permanganate, an important precursor chemical used in processing cocaine. During 1997 and 1998 in U.S. ports, the U.S. Drug Enforcement Agency seized three ships GMP was using to illegally transport enough potassium permanganate to Colombia to manufacture 500,000 kilos of cocaine. Under U.S. law, advance notification has to be given for all shipments of cocaine precursor chemicals passing through U.S. ports. GMP repeatedly failed to provide the necessary notification.

Uribe has also reinstated retired army Col. Alfonso Plazas and appointed him as head of a counter-narcotics department. Plazas is a U.S.-trained soldier with, to put it mildly, a troubling human-rights history. He was the commander of the Colombian army unit that destroyed the Palace of Justice in 1985 after M-19 guerrillas seized it. In an act of callous disregard for human life, Plazas ordered tanks to level the massive building; in the ensuing bombardment 128 people, including 11 Supreme Court justices, died. An investigation by the Colombian attorney general's office revealed that Plazas helped establish and was an active member of paramilitary death squads during the 1980s, and also linked him to Cali cartel drug lord Gonzalo Rodríguez Gacha. As a result of his human-rights record, both the German and U.S. governments have refused to accept his being posted to their countries as a Colombian consul. The fact that Uribe has appointed Plazas to a high-ranking counter-narcotics position is especially troubling in light of his past connections with Rodríguez Gacha.

Uribe's lack of concern about paramilitary activities is clearly evidenced by his plans to establish a nationwide network of civilian informers. As governor of Antioquiá, Uribe oversaw a program that established civilian self-defense groups known as Convivirs (Cooperatives for Surveillance and Private Security). The president has now begun implementing a nationwide version of this program—even though the Convivirs were outlawed in 1999 because of human-rights violations and because at least two of them evolved into full-fledged paramilitary groups. Human-rights organizations have criticized the new civilian informer program, which calls for more than a million citizens to report on suspected members of the armed groups and their activities, because it will inevitably make participants military targets in a conflict in which civilians already constitute a huge majority of those killed.

The civilian spy program is clearly a strategy to combat the leftist rebel groups. Most informers will be located in areas where there is a military or police presence, which also means a paramilitary presence. Consequently, they will primarily snitch on guerrilla infiltrators in these regions because turning in paramilitary suspects would be akin to committing suicide. Furthermore, while the military may need the information provided by civilian spies in order to flush out guerrilla operatives, the security forces do not need help locating paramilitary fighters. The paramilitaries often control towns and villages containing military and police bases; their whereabouts are common knowledge to officials and the local population.

Uribe's Minister of Defense Marta Lucía Ramírez has also announced a government plan to provide up to 20,000 peasants with arms to defend themselves. It is simply a matter of time before those peasants who aren't slaughtered by the guerrillas—they can legally be considered military targets under international law—evolve into full-fledged paramilitary groups. In short, the plan is simply a means to help boost the ranks of the country's illegal paramilitary forces.

While Uribe's warlike rhetoric has targeted guerrillas, drug traffickers, and paramilitaries, it is clear from his history and the steps he has so far taken as president that his agenda is to continue working hand in glove with right-wing death squads in order to combat the rebels. To this end, the Bush administration has lifted conditions on U.S. aid that restricted the use of U.S.-trained counter-narcotics battalions and helicopter gunships in counter-narcotics operations.

Washington's escalating military involvement in counterinsurgency operations under the guise of the "war on terrorism" will inevitably increase the collaboration between U.S.-trained troops and right-wing death squads. Targeting leftist armed groups that attack U.S. political and economic interests in Colombia under the guise of the "war on terrorism," the Bush administration is willing to support a government and military that are closely allied with an even more brutal right-wing terrorist organization. The old saying, "the enemy of my enemy is my friend" has never been more applicable.

SOLDIERS FOR THE BANKS

PARAMILITARIES IN COLOMBIA

CARL GLENN

The Bush administration is prosecuting a secret war in Colombia that yearly takes the lives of thousands of Colombians, primarily impoverished campesinos. This secret policy has been conducted systematically and continuously by previous U.S. administrations for at least 40 years.

In Colombia this policy is carried out by Special Operations units of the Colombian Armed Forces trained by U.S. soldiers and acting under the supervision of U.S. Southern Command officials. These Special Operations units are most frequently referred to as "paramilitaries" and are the direct instruments of U.S. statecraft. Members of the National Police also participate in "death squad" activities.

The crimes of the paramilitaries and their role as a covert extension of the Colombian Armed Forces and National Police are extensively documented by human-rights organizations and corroborated by investigations carried out by agencies of the Colombian government itself. Here is a brief example of dozens of such reports that are readily available, "Last year, Colombia's Public Advocate recorded over 400 massacres. [A massacre is defined here as the killing of four or more civilians at a time.] Most massacres were perpetrated by paramilitaries working with the total acquiescence or open support of the Colombian Army,"[1] states the record of the United Nations Human Rights Commission in Geneva, citing Colombian government reports.

> Government investigators have described direct collaboration between the Medellín-based Fourth Brigade and paramilitaries. Repeatedly, paramilitaries killed those suspected of supporting guerrillas, then delivered the corpses to the Army. In a process known as 'legalization,' the Army then claimed the dead as guerrillas killed in combat while paramilitaries received their pay in Army weapons. Together, evidence collected so far by Human Rights Watch links half of Colombia's 18 brigade-level Army units to paramilitary activity.[2]

While these reports are valuable in documenting the complicity of the Colombian Armed Forces in the crimes of the paramilitaries, they fail to observe that these are not "abuses" of authority but deliberate manifestations of policy. Official, if secret, United States policy. This is why, to the consternation of the human-rights organizations that are duly consulted during the charade of "human-rights certifications," their recommendations are routinely ignored.

How can we know that these actions are part of a systematic United States policy? Fortunately, we have the words of some of the authors of this policy. One is Charles Maechling Jr., who was staff director of the National Security Council's special group for counterinsurgency during the Kennedy and Johnson administrations. He was also a staff member for the Joint Chiefs of Staff and a naval attaché in Latin America. Here is how he describes the original formulation of this policy, which is still in effect:

> President Kennedy moved quickly to establish the institutional framework for a global crusade against Third World revolution. ... Gen. Maxwell Taylor was instructed to prod the Pentagon into building up the Army's counterguerrilla capabilities. As a result, the Special Forces training center at Fort Bragg, N.C., was given added responsibilities and the secretary of defense appointed a special assistant for unconventional warfare...
>
> Kennedy authorized the formation of a new Cabinet-level body, the Special Group (Counter Insurgency). ... After being approved by the Special Group, the Overseas Internal Defense Policy (OIDP) ... was made official policy by President Kennedy in a secret directive, National Security Memorandum No. 182.[3]

The similarities between these Kennedy administration efforts in the Cold War context and George W. Bush's "war on terrorism" are striking.

Shortly after the Fort Bragg Special Forces training center was set up, its commander, Gen. William P. Yarborough, visited Colombia. After his two-week visit in February 1962, he wrote a secret supplement to his report to the Joint Chiefs of Staff. In it he recommended that a concerted effort "should be made now to select civilian and military personnel for clandestine training [and] development of a civil and military structure for exploitation in the event the Colombian internal security situation deteriorates further. This structure should be used to ... execute paramilitary [operations], sabotage and/or terrorist activities against known communist proponents. It should be backed by the United States."[4]

He further recommended "exhaustive interrogation ... to elicit every shred of evidence."

Michael McClintock, who is regarded as the leading authority on this subject outside of the repressive apparatus, comments that this recommendation was "a paramilitary prescription, a virtual blueprint for the Colombian Army 'death squads' that are still active."[5]

The Reagan and first Bush administrations employed the same methods in Central America.

During the course of protracted civil wars in El Salvador and Guatemala, "death squads," as the U.S.-guided Special Operations units were known, were responsible for the murders of hundreds of thousands of rural villagers, farmers, farm laborers and urban poor.

This same policy had been applied in Vietnam, guided by the CIA. It was known there as the "Phoenix Program." Estimates of the number of suspected civilian sympathizers of the National Liberation Front tortured and murdered under this program range between 20,000 and 40,000 people.[6]

One of those responsible for overseeing the Phoenix paramilitary murder campaign in Vietnam was a man named John Negroponte, the CIA political officer in the U.S. embassy in Saigon. Soon after Ronald Reagan took up residence in the White House, his administration began to build a terrorist counterrevolutionary army, the "contras," in Honduras to attack the Sandinistas of Nicaragua. The Reagan administration needed someone to direct covert counterinsurgency operations in Honduras. Honduras is situated strategically between El Salvador and Nicaragua. John Negroponte was named ambassador to Honduras in 1981.

During Ambassador Negroponte's tenure, from 1981 to 1985, the secret counterinsurgency unit Battalion 316 was formed within the Honduran Armed Forces. This unit was responsible for the torture, murder and disappearance of hundreds of Hondurans.[7]

In 2001, President George W. Bush named John Negroponte to be U.S. ambassador to the United Nations. While his appointment was being debated in Congress, the United States delegation was for the first time voted off the U.N. Human Rights Commission panel.

In a move that may be directly related to the U.S. role in Colombia, the Bush administration is acting strenuously to exempt only the United States from prosecution by the new United Nations International Criminal Court. Article 7 of the "Rome Statute" establishing the court expressly prohibits crimes against humanity, including "widespread or systematic attack directed against any civilian population" resulting in murder, torture, the forced displacement by coercion, and the "disappearance" of people.

Washington's political need to obscure the true nature of its objectives leads it to mask direct and indirect military intervention with counterfeit policy imperatives such as the "war on drugs" and the "war on terrorism."

A brief comment on the question of drug trafficking is needed here. The evidence is straightforward.

The paramilitaries freely incriminate themselves in drug trafficking. Carlos Castaño, until recently the leading spokesperson for the paramilitaries in Colombia, has said openly that up to 70 percent of the financing for paramilitary operations comes from cocaine trafficking. On the opposite side of the war, leaders of the Revolutionary Armed Forces of Colombia-People's Army (FARC-EP) do not deny protecting the peasants who grow the coca leaf. They explain that these campesinos are forced to grow the coca plants as a cash crop to feed their families because the government has consistently refused to assist them in the cultivation of alternate crops. Klaus Nyholm, the director of the United Nations Drug Control Program (UNDCP) in Colombia, corroborates this. "The guerrillas are something different than the traffickers," he said recently. "In some areas they're not involved at all. And in others, they actively tell the farmers not to grow coca."[8]

Before the Colombian government seized the zone granted to the FARC-EP to permit secure peace negotiations, Nyholm said that the FARC-EP were cooperating with a $6 million UN project to assist small farmers raise alternative crops.

In 2001, Donnie Marshall, administrator of the Drug Enforcement Agency, testified to the U.S. Congress Subcommittee on Criminal Justice, Drug Policy and Human Resources, "At present, there is no corroborated information that the FARC-EP is involved directly in the shipment of drugs from Colombia to international markets, although we are always watchful for such developments."[9]

In addition to the special paramilitary Army units, there is a history in Colombia of privately financed terror groups formed to ensure the protection of the interests of urban and rural capitalists, including cattle ranchers and narcotics traffickers. Groups of this nature appeared in Colombia during a period known simply as "La Violencia," which began around 1948 and lasted more than 10 years. These private-interest terrorists are estimated to have murdered about 300,000 people during this period—in part to clear the land of poor campesinos and thereby extend their land holdings. Some 2 million people were displaced, fleeing for their lives. A scholar, Mary Roldán, writing in Medellín about this period, observes another dimension to the violence. In common with the current violence, she writes, there is a "disproportionate presence [among the displaced] of individuals of Afro-Caribbean and Indigenous descent." Thus, she discovered that racism has played a statistically significant role in the violence, both then and now.[10]

The war has continued to intensify. Noting this, on March 27, 2001, Marine Gen. Peter Pace, commander in chief of the U.S. Southern Command, revealed an important strategic shift when he told the Senate Armed Services Committee, "Many drug-trafficking organizations provide financial support to the insurgents and illegal self-defense groups to secure protection from counter-drug operations conducted by the Colombia National Police and the Colombian Military."[11]

After making the matter-of-fact and outlandish assertion that drug traffickers support the revolutionary movement, Pace used the word "illegal" to distinguish between the supposedly clandestine paramilitaries and "legal" self-defense groups. This has tremendous significance. In so doing, he was setting the stage for implementing legitimized paramilitaries openly sanctioned by the state, using the same method employed by U.S. counterinsurgency policy in Guatemala with the creation of murderous "Civil Defense Patrols."

This is precisely what the recently-elected president of Colombia, Álvaro Uribe Vélez, plans to do. President Uribe has promised to create his "Civil Self-Defense" units with upwards of 1 million members, in a nation of 42 million people.

Another issue Price raised in his congressional testimony reflects other deep strategic concerns. He pointed out that Colombia is now the seventh largest exporter of oil to the United States, where demand for oil continues to rise and domestic production continues to decline. The U.S. Department of Energy reported in 1999 that the increase in Colombian oil production compared to the early 1980s, was a leap of 750 percent, to 844,000 barrels per day. In a presidential national security report in 1997, President Bill Clinton wrote that the United States was "undergoing a fundamental shift in our reliance on imported oil away from the Middle East. Venezuela is now the number one foreign supplier, and Venezuela and Colombia are each undertaking new oil production ventures."[12]

If we strip away the deceitful and confusing rhetoric about drugs and terror, we discover the simple fact that there is a civil war raging in Colombia. The two sides in this civil war represent the two basic interests in the country.

On one side are the guerrilla movements, the rural and urban poor, the workers, the Indigenous peoples and the millions of displaced people. Although the war was forced on them and they continue to suffer punishing blows—approximately 40,000 people have been murdered during the last decade, and the daily average is now about 20 per day—the revolutionary armed forces grow stronger and stronger.

On the other side are the Colombian military—regular and special operations forces, paramilitaries, the Colombian government, the wealthy landowners and business owners including the cocaine entrepreneurs, the Pentagon, international private banks and the International Monetary Fund.

Despite great natural wealth, Colombia was forced to accept "structural readjustments" demanded by the IMF. As a result, Colombia sold off its most valuable possessions to foreign investors and banks. It is now deeply in debt. Foreign investments, rather than laying the basis for development of national industries, have done just the opposite. They have stripped the country of its best chances to gain economic independence. For example, Colombia, once self-sufficient in food production, now annually imports 6 million tons of agricultural products it formerly produced and exported. Domestic industrial production has suffered the same fate.[13]

As a consequence, unemployment is now nearing 20 percent by official count. And as the economic squeeze produces labor resistance, trade union leaders have been murdered in record numbers. In 2000, 129 trade union leaders were assassinated and in 2001, 159 more were struck down.[14]

The nation's teachers have become a special target. This is because the teacher's unions have given leadership to resistance to the IMF-demanded restructuring. On May 15, 2001, the Colombian Federation of Educators (FECODE) went on strike for 48 hours to protest budget cuts they predict will deprive 500,000 students, out of a total 7 million, of an education. Three million people signed protest petitions. FECODE President Gloria Inés Ramírez said, "We will not allow the government to make budget cuts for two of the most important necessities for our poorest sector simply to pay interest on the foreign debt."

Between 1986 and 2001, 418 educators were murdered.

Thus, it is no exaggeration to say that the "paramilitaries" objectively function as hit squads for private banks and the International Monetary Fund.

---

[1] Human Rights Watch. Oral Intervention: 56th Session UN Commission on Human Rights. March 20-April 28, 2000, Geneva [Online]; Available:http://www.hrw.org/campaigns/geneva/colombia-oral.htm.

[2] Ibid.

[3] Klare, Michael T. and Kornbluh, Peter. *Low Intensity Warfare.* (New York: Pantheon, 1988), 25-28.

[4] McClintock, Michael. *Instruments of Statecraft.* (New York: Pantheon, 1992), 222.

[5] Ibid., 223.

[6] Ibid., 192. See also: McGehee, Ralph. *Vietnam's Phoenix Program.* Vietnam War Internet Project [cited October 13, 2002]; available from: http://www.vwip.org/articles/m/McGeheeRalph_VietnamsPhoenixProgram.htm

[7] Thompson, Ginger and Cohn, Gary, "A Carefully Crafted Deception," *The Baltimore Sun,* June 18, 1995. "A 14-month investigation by *The Sun,* which included interviews with U.S. and Honduran officials who could not have spoken freely at the time, shows that Negroponte learned from numerous sources about the crimes of the unit called Battalion 316. The Honduran press was full of reports about military abuses, including hundreds of newspaper stories in 1982 alone. There were also direct pleas from Honduran officials to U.S. officials, including Negroponte."

[8] Stokes, Doug. June 7, 2002 "Perception Management and the U.S. Terror War in Colombia," *ZNet Colombia Watch*; available from http://www.zmag.org/content/Colombia/stokes_perception-management.cfm

[9] Ibid.

[10] Roldán, Mary. *Blood and Fire: La Violencia in Antioquiá, Colombia,* 1946-1953. (Durham: Duke University Press, 2002), 290.

[11] U.S. Congress Senate Armed Services Committee, Testimony of Gen. Peter Pace, commander in chief, U.S. Southern Command, March 27, 2001, available from http://www.ciponline.org/colombia/032701.htm.

[12] Klare, Michael T. "Shadowplay-The Reason Behind the Reason for $1.6 Billion Colombia Aid Package," Pacific News Service, April 4, 2000, available from: http://www.pacificnews.org/jinn/stories/6.07/000404-colombia.html.

[13] Avirgan, Tony. "World Bank/IMF Threw Colombia Into Tailspin" *Baltimore Sun,* April 4, 2002, available from http://www.epinet.org/webfeatures/viewpoints/colombia.html.

[14] Bacon, David. "Teaching Peace in a Time of War; Colombian Teachers Try to Separate Children from Guns," *ZNet Colombia Watch*; available from http://www.zmag.org/content/Colombia/bacon_teaching-peace.cfm.

THE BLURRING OF THE LINES

U.S. OVERT AND COVERT ASSISTANCE IN COLOMBIA

STAN GOFF

The official narrative on Colombia is a morality play, in which a drug-financed communist insurgency is tearing at the fabric of an otherwise peaceful Colombian society. This has provoked right-wing "aberrations" like death squads, and threatens U.S. society with the scourge of cocaine. The United States Departments of State and Defense, in response to this threat, have intervened to protect both Colombian and American society. So the story goes.

Events in Colombia show some of the contradictions in the U.S. government and corporate media's ideological construction of the situation in Colombia.

For example, on July 13, 2001, elements of the Revolutionary Armed Forces of Colombia-People's Army (FARC-EP) successfully attacked a right-wing paramilitary group for the second consecutive time in Vereda de Papaya, Antioquiá. The paramilitary base not only held units of the so-called United Self Defenses of Colombia (AUC), the biggest right-wing paramilitary group in Colombia, but also members of the Colombian Army's 11th Brigade.

Eighteen members of the Army-paramilitary unit were killed. Money, goods, and livestock that the unit was suspected of having stolen from peasants in Peque and Ituango were recovered and returned to those who said they were robbed.

Thirteen assault rifles of various makes, one Soviet machine gun with five extra barrels, two 60 mm mortars, and 200 sets of military personal load carrying equipment were recovered. So were unspecified quantities of ammunition.

It is worth considering the background to that battle. On July 8, FARC-EP guerrillas had launched a surprise attack on the AUC-Army unit in Vereda de Papaya, disorganizing the unit and forcing survivors to flee in disarray. On July 11, paramilitary forces, reorganized and re-integrated with elements of the 11th Brigade of the Colombian Army, entered the town of Ituango, Antioquiá, where they killed five peasants and robbed a number of others.

This appeared to be the same combined group that had robbed and threatened peasants in Peque on July 4, in response to a FARC-EP assault on an AUC-Army camp that killed over 20 government and paramilitary forces and captured substantial amounts of military materiel.

The military-paramilitary operations appeared to be designed to force peasants to flee the town and abandon their land. A November 2000 paramilitary attack designed for that purpose had displaced approximately 400 people from Ituango.

Depopulation has been central to the AUC strategy. AUC commander Carlos Castaño called it "emptying the sea," an ironic reference to Mao Zedong's comparison of guerrillas to the fish and the people to the sea. Over 2 million Colombians have been displaced by this strategy.

Depopulation is also being accomplished with U.S. aid—using myco-herbicides that have been outlawed in the United States to kill crops and contaminate water sources. These spraying operations have been conducted by both Colombian and U.S. pilots. The latter are mercenaries with DynCorp, a private military outfit on contract with the Pentagon.

The claim has been that the spraying is targeted on coca fields. But reports from within Colombia dispute any attempt at precision targeting. These myco-herbicides do not stay in one place. They travel on air and water, and percolate into water tables.

A central demand of the FARC-EP in the dialogs with the regime of Colombian President Andrés Pastrana was that spraying cease. The FARC-EP also called for a rural program that includes land redistribution, price supports for agricultural products, and crop substitution for coca growers.

Some of the Antioquiá peasants displaced in the November 2000 attacks appealed to the commanders of the José María Córdoba Bloc (BJMC) of the FARC-EP for protection and assistance. And they provided information on AUC-government forces' composition, strength, and disposition. In the wake of the FARC-EP attack, which was based on this intelligence, uniforms of the AUC-government casualties confirmed that the unit combined AUC and the 11th Brigade regulars.

In 2001, in response to dramatic increases in paramilitary activity, the BJMC began expanding combat operations, formerly concentrated in the South, into Antioquiá. The FARC-EP delivered a string of tactical defeats to paramilitaries from January through March. Then direct Army support was reported to suddenly increase, first as intelligence and air support, then as actual integration with paramilitaries for ground combat operations, which included a series of massacres.

Peasant allegations of an integrated AUC-Army force were further supported by the fact that Colombian Air Force helicopters, under the direct control of the Colombian Armed Forces, apparently transported these units. The helicopters appeared to be based in the regional capital of Monteria, also the headquarters of the 11th Brigade.

In the past, the Army avoided direct participation in operations directed against local peasants in Antioquiá, many believe, to maintain "plausible" denial with regard to massacres and other abuses. It was a case of the Army letting the AUC take care of the "wet work."

WHAT IS THE MILITARY SIGNIFICANCE OF A STAFF?

The staffs of the AUC and the Colombian military were integrated as early as 1991, with assistance and training from the U.S. Department of Defense and the Central Intelligence Agency. The U.S. press consistently ignores this documented fact. Yet the fact flatly gives the lie to claims by the governments of both the United States and Colombia that the Colombian Army is being employed to stop paramilitary operations.

The integration of a military staff, the very organ of command, coordination, communication, and control for a military organization, explicitly makes all elements operating under that integrated staff parts of the same organization.

The Colombian Armed Forces, now thoroughly dependent on U.S. financing and assistance, have become a virtual subset of the Pentagon. The Pentagon, having been forced to resort to a cover story about a drug war to maintain congressional approval, funding, and oversight, circumvents that oversight by employing private mercenary outfits. These include MPRI, recently ejected from Colombia for incompetence, and DynCorp, still there and active in combat operations against peasants and guerrillas.

These companies are on contract with the Pentagon, in other words spending appropriated funds, but not subject to congressional oversight because they are private corporations. Nor are they subject to restrictions placed on the 7th Special Forces, the primary U.S. trainers of the Colombian Army. Special Forces activities are restricted to avoid direct combat and the visibility that might bring. But they are all accountable to U.S. military authority.

The Colombian Armed Forces and the AUC, as well as DynCorp and 7th Special Forces contingents (while on station), are effectively one organization. The Colombian and U.S. governments' claims that the Colombian Armed Forces are now or ever will be employed against the paramilitaries is absurd on its face. Military organizations do not attack themselves.

The (para)military violence has escalated with the introduction of the funds from Plan Colombia. These funds are used not only against guerrillas, whom the army and paramilitaries are still somewhat reluctant to engage, but against civic leaders, progressive political figures, unprotected villages perceived to be sympathetic to the FARC-EP and other insurgent groups, and unions. This appears to be a strategy to undercut elements within the Pastrana government who wanted to find a way out of the civil war.

Why? A straight line can be drawn from Washington, D.C., to Fort Bragg, North Carolina, to Colombia.

The principal advisory and assistance unit in Colombia is the 7th Special Forces Group. Elements of the 7th Special Forces have been training the Colombian military for decades. They maintain a constant presence there. When they are in Colombia, they fall under the control of the Theater Command, SOUTHCOM.

SOUTHCOM coordinates and supervises all U.S. military activity in Latin America, most of which originates from the U.S. Army Special Operations Command (USASOC) in Fort Bragg.

These units also fall under the control of the U.S. embassy in Bogotá. The U.S. embassy includes a section called the Military Group, or MilGroup for short. Its main responsibility is to maintain a constant liaison with the Colombian military.

SOUTHCOM coordinates the deployments and missions of U.S.-based units to Latin America. MilGroup directly supervises and supports Special Forces teams in Colombia.

USASOC provides. SOUTHCOM coordinates. MilGroup links.

Gen. Peter Pace is the SOUTHCOM commander. He visited Bogotá in January 2001, and conferred with the Colombian General Staff. On Jan. 18, he held a news conference at the Ministry of Defense describing the role of new U.S. attack helicopters bought by Colombia under Plan Colombia. When asked who would be in charge of these new military assets and their employment, he indicated Gen. Mario Montoya Uribe.

Montoya is a very sinister character. A graduate of the School of the Americas, later a guest instructor there, Montoya is a former member of the right-wing death squad known as the American Anti-Communist Alliance (AAA), who specialized in bombings. He has also been implicated in a number of massacres, not only as a commander, but also as a direct participant.

The Pastrana government appeared unwilling or unable to purge the Armed Forces of these elements at every level of command. This makes the human rights situation essentially intractable. Pastrana needed the military to ensure his political survival, but he was under intense pressure from every other sector to find an accord with the FARC-EP. This is precisely why both the Clinton and Bush administrations have found it necessary to waive any requirement that Colombia show progress on human rights before sending military aid, even though such progress was mandated by the U.S. Congress.

Colombia is incapable of implementing any "human rights" agenda with the current balance of economic, military, and political power there. And the United States is committed to fighting the insurgency there in order to gain and maintain control over Latin America's natural resources, particularly petroleum and cheap labor.

This leaves only one unambiguous decision-making force in Colombia: the

U.S. military, which responds directly to the U.S. executive branch, embodied in Bogotá as the U.S. ambassador and in the United States as the National Command Authority (NCA). The latter consists of the president, the secretary of defense, and the national security advisor, two of whom, along with the vice president, are themselves in the oil business.

My own personal experience as a military advisor in Colombia in 1992 leads me to conclude that the "war on drugs" is simply a propaganda ploy, a legitimizing story for the American public. We were briefed by the Public Affairs Officers that counter-narcotics was a cover story for curious journalists, friends, and family that our mission, in fact, was to further develop the Colombians' capacity for counterinsurgency operations.

The other experience I take from the military, having worked directly under U.S. embassies on a couple of occasions, is related to covert operations. Influence on the ground in foreign countries is based on the quality and quantity of relationships. The CIA contingent in any country is based out of the political section of the embassy, and is limited. Moreover, the CIA spends very little of its budget on actual intelligence operations, having been long ago eclipsed for intelligence gathering by the high-tech National Security Agency. Over the last couple of decades, though many on the left still see it as a powerful bogeyman, the CIA has proven an incompetent embarrassment more often than an asset. The number of their actual relationships on the ground in a country like Colombia is very limited. The U.S. military, on the other hand, has nurtured relationships with countless Colombian military officers over the past decades.

Thus, the Department of Defense is a far more influential player in Colombia than Central Intelligence. The CIA's incompetence at military covert operations is legendary by now, and the NCA has come to depend more and more on Special Operations military, as well as former Special Operations military now employed in private companies, to conduct covert operations. In the case of the latter, there is no compelling reason to make the operation terribly covert, because it is already free from official oversight, and described as private "security." Central Intelligence has even seen the military begin training "agent handlers" in the last few years, to collect human intelligence, formerly the exclusive domain of the CIA.

Replacing the old Cold War secrecy, which sometimes classified everything down to dry cleaning receipts, is the active, energetic, and highly sophisticated collaboration of the corporate media. Through innuendo, lie, and repetition, they can create an overwhelming impression about the reasons for various U.S. foreign policies. As a result, grotesque distortions like "narco-guerrillas," Serbian war crimes, and North Korean missile programs are taken by most people in the United States almost as articles of religious faith.

My own belief, however, is that all this chicanery, expert and effective as it has been, is still an attempt to pursue a policy that, though certainly the most cynical kind of predatory imperialism, is just as certainly doomed to fail. The central miscalculation of both the Pentagon and the Colombian (para)military seems to be that intensifying the war and repression will quell a popular rebellion that has been going on and gaining strength for 40 years. In the short term this has created more havoc among civilians, swelling the ranks of the FARC-EP and other armed resistance groups. In the long run, it will further destabilize the fragile and divided Colombian government.

DEFOLIATION IS DEPOPULATION

SARA FLOUNDERS

The "war on drugs" packaged under the name Plan Colombia is really a U.S. war on a growing popular resistance movement. The vast defoliation program under way in southern Colombia is a mechanism designed to uproot and drive the poor peasant population out of an area where guerrilla forces hold wide popular sympathy.

The millions of dollars allocated for coca eradication must be seen as part of a larger war against a growing people's movement in Colombia. Aerial eradication programs and the deployment of thousands of U.S.-trained soldiers to the region are displacing hundreds of thousands of peasants. This is no accident. Nor is it simply a by-product of eliminating coca, the plant that is the source of cocaine. This is the way U.S. defoliation programs have worked in the past. It is the way that they are intended to work now.

More than 3 million liters of the dangerous fumigation chemical known as Roundup Ultra have been sprayed on hundreds of thousands of acres in Colombia as part of a U.S. government plan to defoliate coca fields. The defoliant chemicals sprayed on the fields don't just kill coca. They kill yucca, plantains, corn and other subsistence crops. A field withers and dies within three days of fumigation. If farmers can't plant or grow, they can't feed their families.

In the face of environmental warnings, health alerts, international outcry, U.S. congressional restrictions and strong internal Colombian opposition, the U.S. government has announced the biggest, most aggressive aerial spraying of defoliants to date. Colombia's right-wing president Álvaro Uribe Vélez has approved Washington's latest plan, which calls for more crop dusters, operating more hours. The limited restrictions on fumigation that had been won in past campaigns have also been lifted.

The goal is to spray at least 300,000 acres in 2002 and double that by 2003. According to the September 4, 2002, *New York Times*:

> President Uribe is allowing U.S. officials to plan missions wherever and whenever they see fit, and there is no pretext that small farmers will not be hit. American planners say they intend to cover as much acreage with defoliant as possible to stop the replanting of coca.

The U.S. government supplies Colombia with the technical advisors and the planes, along with the escort helicopters, reconnaissance flights and the pilots.

OPPOSITION IN COLOMBIA

In Colombia in the southern state of Putumayo, 58 Indigenous groups are among those affected by the aerial fumigation. Their territory covers almost half the region. Emperatríz Cahuache, president of the Organization of Indigenous Peoples of the Colombian Amazon, said: "Fumigation violates our rights and territorial autonomy. It intensifies the violence of the armed conflict and forces people to leave their homes after their food crops have been destroyed."[1]

The United Nations Drug Control Program agrees with this view. Klaus Nyholm, who oversees the program in Colombia, said, "Fumigation has an effect, but we would argue it's an effect of displacement."

Opposition to widespread use of the herbicide is growing in Colombia. Small farmers whose crops were destroyed by the spray have allied with Indigenous groups, environmental advocates, human-rights workers and local politicians to develop a grassroots movement. This pressure galvanized the governors of four southern provinces: Putumayo, Narino, Cauca and Caquetá. They traveled as a group to Europe and to the United States to lobby for a halt in the spraying and consideration of alternatives.[2]

"The fumigation program doesn't take into account the human being. All it cares about are satellite pictures," said Putumayo Gov. Iván Gerardo Guerrero.[3]

Prominent officials, like Eduardo Cifuentes, the Colombian Human Rights Ombudsman who has files confirming many spraying complaints by individuals and whole communities, oppose use of the herbicide. Carlos Ossa, the general comptroller, also called for spraying to be suspended. There have been calls for hearings in the Colombian Senate over the issue. In Bogotá, Judge Gilberto Reyes had the spraying suspended. His ruling was appealed.

In July 2001, the UN Drug Control Program called for international monitoring to determine the safety of spraying and the extent of inadvertent spraying of legal crops. Almost all opponents of spraying call for a program of voluntary coca eradication that would provide subsidies for farmers who replace coca and poppies with legal crops.[4]

One of the most outspoken advocates of increasing spraying is Anne Patterson, the U.S. ambassador to Colombia. She and other U.S. officials say fumigation is central to the "war on drugs." Patterson dismissed other proposals as "too dangerous and, frankly, it is too expensive."[5]

UN Commission on Human Rights advocates, who were exposed to the chemicals, said the spraying caused "gastro-intestinal disorders, severe bleeding, nausea, vomiting, testicular inflammation, high fevers, dizziness, respiratory ailments, skin rashes and severe eye irritation." The State Department responded that the herbicide is not toxic even when people are sprayed directly.[6]

GLYPHOSATE—A DANGEROUS TOXIN

In news releases and public statements, U.S. State Department officials blandly assure everyone that vast aerial fumigation is not a problem worthy of consideration. A January 17, 2001, State Department news release actually stated that the chemical glyphosate—the main ingredient of the sprayed herbicide Roundup—is less toxic than common salt, aspirin, caffeine, nicotine or vitamin A.

These reassuring statements are at odds with the findings of another arm of the U.S. government, the Environmental Protection Agency. A 1993 EPA study ranked glyphosate third in a list of 25 chemicals that cause harm to humans.[7]

The 1993 report noted that glyphosate caused a "high number of injuries to agricultural workers in California. It required a standard precaution that workers generally not be allowed to enter areas that have been sprayed for 12 hours."[8]

A provision inserted into a $15.4 billion spending measure for U.S. government operations abroad requires that the program to eradicate coca crops in Colombia must meet the same health-and-safety standards that would apply to herbicides sprayed in the United States. The EPA must certify that aerial spraying of the herbicide does "not pose unreasonable risks or adverse effects to humans or to the environment."

Given the EPA's own 1993 study listing glyphosate as a dangerous chemical, and other similar studies, it would be difficult for the EPA to certify that there are no adverse effects. In announcing the expanded program the State Department simply refused to say whether it had considered or even received the required EPA report. The State Department simply asserted that the herbicides "do not pose unreasonable risks or adverse effects to humans or the environment."[9]

Sen. Patrick J. Leahy, a Vermont Democrat who chairs the appropriations subcommittee that finances the operation, froze the money needed to buy the herbicide earlier in 2002. Leahy said: "Spraying a toxic chemical over large areas, including where people live and livestock graze, would not be tolerated in this country. We should not be spraying first and asking questions later."[10]

Freezing the funds does not seem to have stopped the U.S. spraying program.

Just how dangerous is the aerial spraying program in Colombia? The label on a container of the milder form of Roundup—commercially available at Home Depot, K-Mart, Wal-Mart or any garden store in the Unite States—cautions that it is a deadly threat to plants, pets, aquatic life, birds and people. Grazing animals must stay clear of the area for two weeks after limited use of the mild form of Roundup. Studies have shown that Roundup destroys aquatic life and substantially affects the growth of the most common worms found in farming soil.

Roundup is considered a non-selective herbicide. This means it kills the entire root system and stops regrowth of any plant exposed to the chemical in sufficient quantities. It is strictly for controlled use in limited areas. It should be applied using protective clothing. The manufacturer, Monsanto, specifically warns against aerial spraying. It is illegal to aerially spray Roundup in the United States.

In a 1996 out-of-court settlement Monsanto withdrew claims that Roundup is "safe, nontoxic, harmless or free from risks," and signed a statement that absolute claims that Roundup "will not wash or leach in the soil" are not accurate.[11]

The Roundup used for chemical spraying in Colombia is called Roundup Ultra. It is far stronger and more lethal than the herbicides used in the United States under careful control. Not only are the herbicide concentrations far stronger. The glyphosate is mixed with other ingredients that are potentially even more toxic.

The formula used in the Colombian Aerial Spray Program contains two adjuvants: Cosmoflux-411F and Cosmo-In-D. There are no toxicological studies regarding the effects of mixing these ingredients with glyphosate. Roundup Ultra also contains other ingredients that are not even listed.[12]

The Bush administration has further fueled suspicion about Roundup Ultra by refusing to disclose the precise ingredients or discuss how the final product is prepared. Officials say they do not want to divulge trade secrets.

AGENT ORANGE IN VIETNAM

There is good reason for the people in Colombia to be suspicious of the U.S. defoliation program in Colombia. It is remarkably similar to the widespread use of Agent Orange in Vietnam. Washington also claimed that was relatively harmless to humans.

From 1962 to 1971 in a program called Operation Ranch Hand, approximately 18 million gallons of Agent Orange, which contained dioxin, were sprayed from UC-123 aircraft, helicopters, trucks and jeeps.

The herbicides were used to destroy thick jungle vegetation under which the guerrilla forces could hide. They were also meant to destroy the food crops that sustained the entire population, and with them the resistance movement.

Agent Orange was sprayed over the jungle canopy, over rice paddies, lakes, rivers and ponds. Lush green vegetation shriveled over vast tracks of land.

Large areas of Vietnam were depopulated as agriculture was systematically destroyed. The population was herded into "strategic hamlets" in an effort to break the resistance.

Vietnam has still not recovered from the systematic destruction of hundreds of thousands of acres of fertile land and fragile jungle. Over 50 percent of the mangrove forests and at least 14 percent of all the other forests in Vietnam were destroyed.

The health consequences for the Vietnamese peasants and for U.S. soldiers involved in spraying or based in the sprayed areas have been devastating. Birth defects, neurological and psychological damage, and rare cancers affect tens of thousands. According to a study in Vietnam, over 400,000 Vietnamese were killed or disabled by the chemicals and 500,000 children were born with birth defects.[13]

The Vietnamese found that more than 30 years after the U.S. use of these chemical weapons, their impact is still felt. Many diseases appear years later. For example, now there are very high rates of cancer. This creates a long-term burden on the whole society. High rates of birth defects continue to appear in the second and even third generation, even when the first generation children were unaffected.

The agro-conglomerate Monsanto, which markets Roundup, is the same corporation that produced Agent Orange. Monsanto and the U.S. government's line on both spraying Agent Orange in Vietnam in the 1960s and now spraying Roundup in Colombia is that only the immediate plants are affected.

WAR AGAINST WHOLE POPULATION

Historically, each time the U.S. military machine targeted its mighty engine against a struggle of an entire people, the battle quickly became a war against the environment that sustained the population. U.S. history is replete with examples of military offensives against poorly armed opponents that expand into war against civilians, the infrastructure and the entire environment. A few examples will help put the U.S. policy of defoliation spraying in Colombia in perspective.

The 200 years of westward expansion within the North American continent were marked by a series of genocidal wars against the Indigenous population. Along with outright military carnage, other key tactics included targeting the environment that sustained life and forcing removal of the entire population. In the single four-year period from 1866 to 1870, the enormous buffalo herds of the Great Plains were hunted almost to extinction in order to defeat and remove the Native nations of the Plains. This opened the lands to white farmers, and to super-profits for the railroad barons.

From 1899 to 1906, more than 1 million Filipino people died in the U.S. war to seize the Philippines. The U.S. troops were in combat against a popular insurgency demanding independence. The U.S. generals' systematic policy was to have those troops burn foodstuffs and harvests and uproot thousands of villages.

Other U.S. wars fought in Asia used the same brutal tactics. In World War II after Japan's anti-aircraft defenses were totally destroyed, the U.S. military firebombed Tokyo and 100 other Japanese cities. Then the US unleashed nuclear destruction against Hiroshima and Nagasaki.

The U.S. assault on Korea killed over 4 million Koreans and laid waste to the entire country. Saturation bombing of the north destroyed every city, town and village. U.S pilots complained that they had run out of targets.

The images of burning Vietnamese villages and the lunar landscape created by hundreds of thousands of bombs dropped by B-52s created revulsion and mass opposition among a whole generation in the United States and around the world.

The 1991 U.S. bombing of Iraq targeted the water supply. Water purification plants and the sewage and irrigation infrastructure were destroyed. Bombing petrochemical and industrial plants created massive pollution. U.S. weapons made with depleted uranium left behind over 600,000 pounds of radioactive waste. This has leached into the soil, water and air, contaminating the entire region.

In 1999, the United States and its NATO allies bombed 23 petrochemical plants, oil refineries and fuel depots in Yugoslavia along with 120 major industrial plants. This released thousands of tons of highly toxic chemicals into the air, water and soil. The contamination spread to European countries far beyond the Balkans. NATO has admitted to firing at least 31,000 rounds of radioactive depleted-uranium rounds. Throughout Europe the major media have carried articles on NATO soldiers' health problems since the war.

In Vieques, Puerto Rico, the U.S. Navy has carried out military excercises for over 60 years. The island is inhabited by over 9,400 people. In its efforts to depopulate the island and derail the struggle against U.S. colonial rule, the U.S. defies international laws by continuing to bomb a civilian population.

Increasingly, U.S. troops, told they are invincible, suffer far more casualties from the side effects of the weapons they used than in the battle itself. In 1984 the U.S. Congress acknowledged that 250,000 GIs were due compensation for chronic illness, high cancer rates and birth defects in their children due to radiation exposure from nuclear testing programs in Utah and the South Pacific from 1945 to 1963. Tens of thousands of Vietnam veterans today suffer from the effects of Agent Orange, and there are abnormal rates of birth defects in their children. Over 150,000 of the roughly 500,000 Gulf War veterans are today chronically ill with Gulf War Syndrome derived from the radioactive depleted-uranium weapons they used.

A campaign to oppose the continued defoliation programs in Colombia is urgently needed. This is a campaign that can draw in all those concerned with environmental and health issues. Activists who have opposed past U.S. wars have an important role. Because only by understanding the devastation wrought by past U.S. wars is it possible to see the real scale of the danger of Pentagon involvement in Colombia.

---

[1] *New York Times*, July 30, 2001
[2] *New York Times*, July 11, 2002
[3] *New York Times*, July 30, 2001
[4] *New York Times*, July 30, 2001
[5] *New York Times*, July 11, 2002

[6] James Ridgeway, *Village Voice*, August 1, 2001

[7] *New York Times*, July 11, 2002

[8] *New York Times*, September 6, 2002

[9] *New York Times*, September 6, 2002

[10] James Ridgeway, *Village Voice*, August 1, 2001

[11] www.usfumigation.org

[12] *Mother Jones Magazine*, January/February 2000

[13] "Agent Orange in the Vietnam War: History and Consequences," Prof. Le Cao Dai, MD, Vietnam Red Cross Society, 2000

THE NEW TERRORS OF THE PHONY 'WAR ON DRUGS'

IMANI HENRY

Every president since Ronald Reagan has used the code phrase "war on drugs" to justify spending more money for prison construction and police at home, while allocating enormous resources for military intervention abroad.

The late 1990s ushered in greater public awareness of the racist and anti-poor character of this so-called "war on drugs." National movements against racial profiling and police brutality helped expose state repression against communities of color. One of the most high-profile cases was the 1999 killing of Amadou Diallo by New York police officers. Diallo, a 22-year-old West African immigrant, was shot 19 times, from 41 rounds of ammunition, by four white officers of the New York Police Department. The four cops, who were never convicted for this brutal murder, were part of the NYPD's anti-narcotics division, the Street Crimes Unit.

By 2000, the U.S. prison population had grown to over 2 million. The U.S. government was beginning to come under harsh criticism for its use of the death penalty. Terms like "Prison Industrial Complex" spread from the progressive movement to the mainstream media and public opinion.

Then came Sept. 11, 2001. The drive for war and the call for patriotism took over the political climate. Suddenly the NYPD, previously seen by many as ruthless killers, were lauded as heroes. President George W. Bush launched his "war on terrorism." An insidious campaign to justify a new offensive in the "war on drugs" was part of the package.

Soon after Sept. 11, new anti-drug commercials began to air on network television. Teenaged spokespeople not only apologized for their recreational drug use, but took personal responsibility for supplying "terrorists" with money and weapons, leading to the deaths of innocent people.

During the 2002 Super Bowl broadcast, commercials sponsored by the National Office of Drug Control Policy claimed that "money to purchase drugs likely ends up in the hands of terrorists and narco-criminals." These ads cost nearly $3.5 million apiece.[1]

By linking drug use to "terrorism," the Bush administration played on people's fears in the wake of the Sept. 11 attacks. This tactic was part of the overall pro-war propaganda to win support for increased U.S. funding for repression-both inside the United States and in other countries, like Colombia.

The primary international target of Bush's phony drug war has been the insurgent movement of Colombia. Although the U.S. government had referred to the FARC-EP and the ELN as "terrorists" in the past, a new campaign of vilification began in the aftermath of the Sept. 11 attacks.

On Oct. 16, 2001, State Department counter-terrorism head Francis Taylor told the Associated Press that the FARC-EP and the ELN would receive "the same treatment as any other terrorist group." He said that the U.S. would fight terrorism in Latin America using "all elements of our national power as well as the elements of the national power of all the countries in our region."

Again, on Oct. 25, 2001, U.S. Ambassador to Colombia Anne Patterson warned that leaders of the FARC-EP and the ELN would be subject to extradition to the United States. In addition, on November 2, 2001, she added the FARC-EP and the ELN to groups whose funds would be investigated and seized by the U.S. government.

By April 18, 2002, during Colombian President Andrés Pastrana's trip to the United States, President Bush chimed in. Bush said, "these aren't 'so-called' terrorists, these are terrorists, in Colombia. ... We've put FARC on our terrorist list. We've called them for what they are. These are killers ... And we want to join, with Plan Colombia's billions of dollars, to not only fight them, and by fighting narco trafficking, by the way, we're fighting the funding source for these political terrorists. And sometimes they're interchangeable. And we've got to be strong in the fight against terror."

The Bush administration's desire to increase U.S. involvement in Colombia's civil war is at the heart of the attacks on that country's insurgent movement. According to a Feb. 4, 2002, report in the *Washington Times*, "The Pentagon and State Department are debating the size and scope of a follow-up to the Clinton administration's Plan Colombia, which is consuming $1.3 billion in U.S. aid. The new program would be dubbed 'Colombia: The Way Ahead' and would earmark up to $1 billion for training Colombian security forces and eradicating the coca crop from which cocaine is processed. The plan could be sent to Congress later this month."

This new phase of the war on drugs not only reaches beyond Colombia's borders into the rest of Latin America, it poses a new danger for people of the United States as well.

THE 'WAR ON DRUGS' AT HOME BEFORE SEPT. 11

In March 2001, "Traffic," a movie about Washington's war on drugs, won four Academy Awards, including Best Adapted Screenplay and Best Director. This racist film, which depicted Latin Americans as ruthless drug lords, had also been considered a serious contender for the Best Picture award.

In 2000, the year "Traffic" played in theatres, the Federal Bureau of Investigation's Uniform Crime Reports (UCR) estimated that there were 1,579,566 state and local arrests for drug use violations in the United States: "Prisoners sentenced for drug offenses constitute the largest group of Federal inmates (57%) in 2000, up from 53% in 1990. ... On Sept. 30, 2000, the date of the latest available data in the Federal Justice Statistics Program, Federal prisons held 73,389 sentenced drug offenders, compared to 30,470 at year end 1990."[2]

And who exactly is a drug offender? "The average 'dealer' holds a low-wage job and sells part-time to obtain drugs for his or her own use."[3]

According to the Federal Household Survey, "most current illicit drug users are white. There were an estimated 9.9 million whites (72 percent of all users), 2.0 million Blacks (15 percent), and 1.4 million Latinos (10 percent) who were current illicit drug users in 1998."

> And yet, Blacks constitute 36.8 percent of those arrested for drug violations, and over 42 percent of those in federal prisons for drug violations. African Americans compose almost 58 percent of those in state prisons for drug felonies. Latinos account for 20 percent.[4]

The war on drugs systematically targets young Black and Latino males. Harsher sentencing guidelines, such as the "three-strikes-you're-out" laws, have meant these young men of color are likely to be imprisoned for life even if they are guilty of little more than a history of untreated addiction and several prior drug-related offenses.

With institutionalized racism at the core of the justice system, billions of dollars are allocated to build new prisons instead of schools. Many prisoners will never be released, but will be warehoused until they die of old age.

As has been widely documented, federal spending for prison construction has increased while funds for education and social programs are on the chopping block. A study released in May 2002 by the Charlotte, N.C.-based organization Grassroots Leadership revealed,

> Mississippi built 16 new correctional facilities, including six for-profit private prisons, in the 1990s alone. By contrast, the state has built no new four-year colleges or universities in over 50 years. There are almost twice as many African American men in prison (13,837) as in four-year colleges and universities (7,330). The state spends more to incarcerate someone ($10,672) than to send them to college ($6,871).

Also targeted are women, who have become the fastest-growing prison population. The vast majority—approximately 85 percent—of women entering state and federal prisons were sentenced for non-violent crimes of survival such as petty theft and drug-related offenses.[5]

Over a five-year period, the incarceration rate of African American women increased by 828 percent.[6] An African American woman is eight times more likely to be imprisoned than a white woman. African American women make up nearly half of the nation's female prison population, with most serving sentences for non-violent drug- or property-related offenses. Latina women are incarcerated at nearly four times the rate of white women.

According to an Amnesty International USA Women's Human Rights fact sheet, state and federal laws mandate minimum sentences for all drug offenders. This takes away the judges' option to refer first time non-violent offenders to drug treatment, counseling and education programs, which in any case are scarce and financially strapped. Racial disparities, starkly revealed in sentencing for charges involving crack vs. powder cocaine, ensure that more African American and Latina women will land in prison. In 1994, eighty-four percent of defendants convicted of crack cocaine possession were African American.[7]

Crack is the only drug that carries a mandatory prison sentence for first-time possession in the federal system.

The following is the story of Christine Taylor, a white woman in prison on a 20-year sentence for drug conspiracy:

> I have been incarcerated since I was 19 years old. I am now 30. I was convicted for conspiracy to manufacture methamphetamine and attempt to manufacture methamphetamine When I was 19, my boyfriend asked me to go to a chemical store in Mobile, Alabama, to pick up a shipment of chemicals.
>
> The Drug Enforcement Agency (DEA) was working with the chemical store in a reverse-sting operation. The DEA sold me the chemicals and then arrested my boyfriend and me, not for possession or purchase, because to do one or both is not illegal. We were arrested for the intent to manufacture instead. My trial judge had never handled a federal trial, nor had my attorney or my co-defendant's attorney. The prosecutor had the upper hand and the experience that the rest lacked.
>
> I went to trial, lost and was sentenced to 20 years. I was a drug user—I admit that. I was not a 'cook' or 'trafficker,' even if my co-defendant was. Women come to prison with 20, 30, 40 years and even life sentences. These women are not kingpins or queenpins! They were low-level dealers or their husbands or boyfriends were dealers, and some did not even know. The stories are so sad.[8]

So why is the U.S. government imprisoning young people of color, women and men at such an alarming rate? Why not provide the resources for drug treatment or jobs instead of warehousing people in prisons?

The Prison Industrial Complex supplies U.S.-based multinational corporations with not only cheap but free labor. Prisoners' labor is used for a range from manufacturing computer parts to constructing roads and buildings—but prisoners have no power to form unions or to strike. The vast majority of these prisoners turned to selling drugs because of lack of jobs and education, and now they are forced to work for free under the most heinous conditions.

According to a fact sheet produced by the California-based prisoner rights group PrisonActivist, "The actual wage of a California prisoner is as high as $1.15 an hour." Out of this wage, prisoners must pay for everything from toothpaste to telephone calls to medical treatment. As a result, most prisoners actually make less than 20 cents per hour. Many don't make any money at all for the work they do.

The fact sheet also states:

> The conditions for working prisoners are among the worst in the industrialized world. There are no benefits, no vacation, no decent health care, no safety standards, and prisoners are not allowed to form a union. Severe repression and longer sentences result from a refusal to work. Prisoners are beaten, put in solitary confinement, or both. There is no oversight of prison labor conditions, and no accountability, so prison officials have no incentive to provide safe working conditions or treat prisoners humanely.

The corporations that exploit prison labor in the United States include IBM, McDonald's, Motorola, Compaq, Toys R Us, Texas Instruments, AT&T, Dell, Revlon, Kaiser Steel Corporation, Eddie Bauer, Microsoft, Boeing, Victoria's Secret, Honeywell, Pierre Cardin, Nordstrom and MCI.

For these and other U.S. corporations, the drive to profit off prisoners' backs does not stop there. For U.S. big business, the real money lies in the billions of dollars that are made from investing in the Prison Industrial Complex itself.

It is estimated that private companies spend billions of dollars annually investing in prison construction and prison-related contracts. This includes some of the biggest architectural and construction firms, along with Wall Street investments banks.

> Investment firm Smith Barney is a part owner of a prison in Florida. American Express and General Electric have invested in private prison construction in Oklahoma and Tennessee. Correctional Corporation of America, one of the largest private prison owners, already operates internationally, with more than 48 facilities in 11 states, Puerto Rico, the United Kingdom, and Australia.[9]

U.S. multinational corporations and banks are involved in another of the most insidious aspect of the phony "war on drugs." Many have been accused of profiting from the drug trade through money laundering. In June 1999, the Justice Department met with CEOs of some of the biggest corporations—General Electric, Phillip Morris, Hewlett Packard and others—to discuss their involvement with laundering drug profits.[10]

On Feb 2, 2000, the *Miami Herald* reported that Bank of America, Citibank and Chase Manhattan were among those cited for facilitating the laundering of money from drug trafficking.

While thousands of young men and women of color languish behind prison walls for small-time drug offenses, the real drug king-pins are the criminals within corporate America who profit from laundering drug money and exploiting the prisoners of the U. S.

Between January 1 and October 13, 2002, in the United States, 1,244,646 people were arrested for drug violations. By the end of 2002, arrests for drug law violations are expected to exceed the 1,579,566 arrests of 2000.

Currently, 186,593 people are incarcerated for drug violations. The FBI and Justice Department expect approximately an additional 23,680 people to be incarcerated for drug law violations in the United States in 2002.

Six hundred forty-eight people are locked up every day for drug-related violations in the United States. This means that someone is arrested for a drug law violation every 20 seconds.[11]

This is the legacy of the United States' "war on drugs."

BUSH SAYS MONEY FOR DRUG WAR, NOT FOR PEOPLE'S NEEDS

With the signing of the Anti-Terrorist Bill on Oct 26, 2001, President George W. Bush could now launch, in his words, a "two-front war—one overseas, and a front here at home."

This has meant increased military spending in the name of fighting terrorism, and providing more muscle for police agencies by funding the new Department of Homeland Security. Part of homeland security, Bush stated, is "to keep drugs and other unwanted goods from coming into the U.S. by land, sea or air."

How will his drug war play out against the people of the United States? The Homeland Security budget includes $3.5 billion—a 1,000-percent increase—for local police and emergency personnel. Seven hundred million dollars are slated to improve intelligence gathering and information sharing between agencies and throughout all levels of government. Another $11 billion will go toward "border security." This $2 billion increase to border security includes a significant boost for the Immigration and Naturalization Service, the Coast Guard and the U.S. Customs Service, along with funding to develop a new entry-exit visa database and tracking system.

What is Bush's plan for the war on drugs abroad, especially against Colombia? According to a Feb. 4, 2002, report in *The Washington Times*:

> The United States would help establish a second Colombian anti-narcotics
> brigade and also train local troops in protecting the country's vital—and often

targeted—oil pipelines. The U.S. plan also calls for increased intelligence-sharing with Bogotá. This would include intercepted communications and satellite photographs, U.S. officials said.

Already, 46 percent of the 2003 federal budget—a whopping $776 billion—is earmarked for military expenditures. That is a $115 billion increase from 2001. Only 32 percent of the federal budget is allocated for drug rehabilitation, unemployment insurance, housing subsidies, food stamps, Social Security and education combined.

Meanwhile, living conditions for people inside the United States have worsened as the economy slides downward. More than 2 million people lost their jobs in 2001.

Yet Bush boasts about pushing unemployed workers off welfare. In a White House statement, Bush gloated that "4.7 million fewer Americans were dependent on welfare within three years after welfare reform was first passed in 1996. The percentage of the population that is dependent on welfare fell from 5.2 percent to 3.3 percent during this time."

In a directly related development, 798,000 people are homeless in the United States, according to Department of Health and Human Services figures.

Cuts to social programs and lack of jobs and education force people into drug-related crimes of survival. If George W. Bush were really interested in fighting drugs, why not put more money into drug treatment on demand? Why not take the billions of dollars being spent on the "war on terrorism" and use that money to insure everyone has a job, housing, education, healthcare and all the services they need to survive and thrive?

The truth is that Washington's war on drugs is, in fact, a war on working and poor people in the United States and a war against those struggling for justice in Colombia and other countries. By linking the issues of poverty, joblessness and lack of health care at home with the fight for freedom and self-determination abroad, those opposed to racism and war can expose the truth behind the smokescreen.

---

[1] *Washington Post*, Feb. 3, 2002

[2] Harrison, Paige M. & Allen J. Beck, Ph.D., U.S. Department of Justice, Bureau of Justice Statistics, Prisoners in 2001 (Washington, D.C.: U.S. Department of Justice, July 2002)

[3] Reuter, P., MacCoun, R., & Murphy, P., "Money from Crime: A Study of the Economics of Drug Dealing in Washington, D.C." (Santa Monica, CA: The RAND Corporation, 1990).

[4] Substance Abuse and Mental Health Services Administration, National Household Survey on Drug Abuse: Summary Report 1998 (Rockville, MD: Substance Abuse and Mental Health Services Administration, 1999). Bureau of Justice Statistics, *Sourcebook of Criminal Justice Statistics* 1998 (Washington DC: US Department of Justice, August 1999). Beck, Allen J., Ph.D. and Mumola, Christopher J., Bureau of Justice Statistics, "Prisoners in 1998" (Washington DC: US Department of Justice, August 1999). PhD, and Paige M. Harrison, US Dept. of Justice, Bureau of Justice Statistics

(Washington, DC: US Dept. of Justice, August 2001).

[5] John Irwin, Ph. D., Vincent Schiraldi, and Jason Ziedenberg, "America's One Million Nonviolent Prisoners" (Washington, DC: Justice Policy Institute, March 1999).

[6] "NAACP LDF Equal Justice," Spring 1998.

[7] www.amnestyusa.org/women/fact-sheets/women_in_prison

[8] Updated-3/29/01 Excerpted from the website of the November Coalition, an organization to support families and prisoners of the U.S. government's "war on drugs". www.november.org

[9] "The Prison Industrial Complex and the Global Economy," Eve Goldberg and Linda Evans, pamphlet produced by Prison Activist Resource Center

[10] *New York Times*, Oct. 10, 2000

[11] "Drug War Clock" www.drugsense.org

HUMAN RIGHTS WATCH COVER UP

HEATHER COTTIN

> The United States plays an important role in Colombia and can contribute to the defense of human rights and international humanitarian law. We support U.S. engagement when it furthers these goals. ... The critical thing, Mr. Chairman, is that the assistance under consideration today should be used to combat all sources of terror in Colombia. That includes the guerrillas known as the Revolutionary Armed Forces of Colombia (FARC).[1]

So said José Miguel Vivanco, executive director of the Americas Division of Human Rights Watch, to the U.S. Senate on April 24, 2002. With this testimony, Vivanco gave the U.S. government his organization's approval for millions of dollars of additional military appropriations for Plan Colombia.

This was not the first time Vivanco endorsed a bill to beef up Colombia's military. In 2000, he lent the prestige and support of Human Rights Watch to President Bill Clinton's request for the original Plan Colombia military aid package. While the whopping $1.3 billion military-aid package was under consideration by Congress, Vivanco had concluded that the only strategy "was to install in the [appropriations] bill language ensuring that the Colombian military would be forced to respect human rights." Vivanco said the Colombian military has cleaned up its act and is responsible for only 2 percent of all human-rights violations.[2]

This pro-intervention lobbying role may seem strange to activists who rely on HRW for documenting human-rights abuses. But Human Rights Watch-Americas Watch's support for U.S. policy in Colombia is consistent with HRW's global role as a putatively, privately-sponsored non-governmental organization that has backed U.S. interventionism all over the world. With its stable of foreign-policy institutions and "experts," many of whom are connected to the U.S. government foreign policy establishment, Human Rights Watch has a specialized mission. It disseminates propaganda that creates support at home for U.S. foreign policy and neoliberal economic "reforms." For example, Human Rights Watch justified the U.S./NATO war on Yugoslavia. It accepted the validity of U.S. war and embargo on Iraq that has cost close to 2 million lives.

HRW has international recognition and unlimited resources. It has published reams of documents purporting to analyze the situation in Colombia. But the analysis is tainted with the neoliberal establishment's prejudice and philosophy. As a neoliberal institution, HRW has consistently opposed every nation, every group that challenges the right of the United States to dictate the terms of their economic and political life.

José Miguel Vivanco is Americas Watch's ideological bellwether. In 2000, the Cuban government reported to a United Nations Economic and Social Council conference:

> "It is important to note that [U.S. State Department Head of Cuba Bureau Charles] Shapiro proposed that the Cuban counter-revolutionaries should use Mr. José Miguel Vivanco, Regional Director for the Americas for the so-called NGO 'Human Rights Watch' to facilitate their access to the Latin American presidents. ... The United States special services have for many years been channeling substantial sums of money to Human Rights Watch through foundations and private donors, with the aim of promoting propaganda campaigns to discredit a group of countries which for one reason or another constitute an obstacle to the goals of global hegemony espoused by United States foreign policy."[3]

HUMAN RIGHTS WATCH AND CONGRESSIONAL VOTES

Human Rights Watch has been following events in Colombia for a long time. With the inception of the Clinton administration's Plan Colombia and later the evolution of the Andean Initiative, HRW has become more intrusive and useful for the U.S. foreign-policy apparatus.

In the summer of 2001, HRW opened a campaign of accusations against the Revolutionary Armed Forces of Colombia-People's Army (FARC-EP) to discredit the guerrilla group. In doing so, HRW gave ammunition to pro-intervention elements in the U.S. House of Representatives, helping them to pass a $676 million military-appropriations bill for Plan Colombia.

In a 20-page letter made public on July 9, 2001, the day before the House began to consider the bill, Vivanco wrote the FARC-EP's leader, Manuel Marulanda Vélez. In the open letter, entitled "Rebel Abuses Worsening," Vivanco concluded, "The FARC has an appalling record of abuses."[4]

The Colombian government responded to HRW's letter with glee, "Colombia's military has applauded a new international human-rights report focusing on abuses by leftist guerrillas, calling it a vindication of the charges they have been making for years."[5]

A July 23, 2001, HRW Americas Watch news release responded to Marulanda, who had challenged the fairness of HRW's charges. This highly publicized document denouncing the FARC-EP's "worsening record of abuses"[6] was instrumental in guaranteeing Congressional support for the multi-billion-dollar war in Colombia. The bill passed two days later.

In fact, HRW's July 23 release contained no new charges against the FARC-

EP. Rather, it was full of disinformation provided by the Colombian government, notably Colombia's Fiscalia (attorney general) office. The fact that the charges were aired days before the final passage of U.S. military aid to Colombia shows that the group's professed interest in human rights is secondary to its pro-intervention lobbying role.

In August 2001, and again in November, HRW published dozens of documents noting that "Human Rights Watch ... found overwhelming evidence of the Colombian government's failure to meet the human-rights conditions."[7] These "failures," though well documented, were downplayed. Noting them after the vote to beef up Plan Colombia served to bolster HRW's claims of impartiality.

HRW criticized the connection between Colombia's military and the paramilitary organizations, the United Self Defenses of Colombia (AUC). It noted that the AUC had "significantly expanded its radius of action and troop strength in 2001," and that it grew by over 560 percent between 1996 and 2001.[8]

Yet HRW consciously and deliberately underestimated the enormity of the spree of death-squad murders. HRW stated that "50 percent of the killing of civilians were the work of paramilitary groups."[9] Most human-rights groups find that the actual proportion of murder of civilians attributable to the AUC is closer to 80 percent.[10] Because of HRW's reputation, the lower number, even though inaccurate, was widely publicized. It became part of a false public record, creating the impression that the paramilitary death squads and the insurgency are equally brutal.

A FALSE SYMMETRY

In the Colombia section of HRW's website, the group equates the Colombian paramilitaries' repressive actions with the revolutionary forces' resistance. The website urges readers to get involved: "What You Can Do to Stop Abuses by the Paramilitary: ... Write the U.S. Congress and President Bush" and the Colombian president. The second half of the page suggests: "What You Can Do to Stop Abuses by the FARC-EP: Write to Commander Marulanda."[11]

HRW notes, "The Colombian government has failed to suspend members of the Colombian Armed Forces credibly alleged to have committed gross violations of human rights or to have helped paramilitary groups."[12] Acknowledging this, however, did not move HRW to oppose Plan Colombia or the Andean Initiative.

HRW, U.S. INTERVENTIONISM AND THE NEOLIBERAL AGENDA

Why would a professed human-rights group take such an active role in lobbying for U.S. intervention?

Human Rights Watch began as Helsinki Watch in 1978. It has close ties to billionaire currency speculator and hedge-fund manipulator George Soros. For example, Aryeh Neier served from 1978 to 1981 as director of Helsinki Watch, and then from 1981 to 1993 as head of Human Rights Watch. Soros was a member of both organizations and later tapped Neier to be president of Soros' Open Society Institute in New York City.[13]

There is barely a story in the Western press about "human-rights abuses" in any nation that does not include some mention of a report from Human Rights Watch. Reports of such "abuses" then back up State Department assertions that the United States intervenes around the world for "humanitarian" purposes.

Human Rights Watch's program called "Defending Human Rights Worldwide" has its affiliates writing and criticizing conditions in Africa, Asia, Europe and Central Asia, the Middle East/North Africa, and the Americas. The billion-dollar agency has a presence in 31 countries. It has abrogated to itself the right to determine which countries do and do not fulfill its concept of civil society. Once the organization, made up almost entirely of U.S. citizens, determines a nation is in violation of HRW's principles, HRW goes on the attack.

Actually, Colombia's FARC-EP and ELN are unique in that they are not governments. Still, they have been treated to the same HRW full-court press as have China, Yugoslavia and other states.

WHAT IS HUMAN RIGHTS WATCH?

HRW has tentacles everywhere.

On its website, Director Ken Roth criticized the United States for not opposing China more actively concerning that country's alleged human-rights abuses. Roth's own activities in this regard include creating the Tibetan Freedom Concert, a traveling propaganda project that toured the United States with major rock musicians urging young people to support the remnants of the Tibetan theocracy in its campaign against China.[14]

Roth was also a major supporter of the B92 radio station in Belgrade, which backed the Oct. 5, 2000 coup that overthrew the former leader of Yugoslavia, Slobodan Milosevic.[15] And in March 2002, Roth suggested an international tribunal should be created, dominated by the countries that attacked Iraq in the Gulf War, to indict Saddam Hussein. Similar to the NATO-sponsored kangaroo-court tribunal in The Hague that sits in judgment over Milosevic, such a body could issue an indictment that would "weaken Saddam's support" internationally and "encourage Iraqi officials to overthrow him."[16]

The Board of Directors of Human Rights Watch includes a smattering of liberal names and a very few prominent non-U.S. citizens. HRW is chock-a-block with Cold Warriors and would-be shapers of the New World Order. Paul Goble, communications director of Soros' Open Society Institute, is on HRW's Europe and Central Asia Committee. He was a major political commentator at Radio Free Europe.[17] Herbert Okun, also on the HRW's Europe and Central Asia Committee, was associated with the Committee for National Security. Okun was also executive director of something called the Financial Services Volunteer Corps, part of the United States Agency for International Development, whose purpose was "to help establish free market financial systems in former communist countries."[18]

Kati Marton, who served on the HRW Board until 2002, is married to former U.S. envoy to Yugoslavia Richard Holbrooke. During the U.S.-led campaign to topple Milosevic, Marton, then a journalist with ABC News, made a solidarity visit to the Soros-funded radio station B92.[19] B92 was also a project of the U.S.-funded National Endowment of Democracy, instrumental in directing U.S. propaganda during the anti-Milosevic campaign. Former U.S. Ambassador to Yugoslavia Warren Zimmerman is on HRW's Europe and Central Asia Advisory Board.[20]

George Soros appears twice on HRW's roster, once on the Americas Advisory Committee and again on the Europe and Central Asia Advisory Committee. Soros, who to many symbolizes globalization, is a leading force in the World Economic Forum, the fulcrum of neoliberal economic policy.

The well-paid academics, writers, former government administrators, ambassadors, business executives and policy makers on the Human Rights Watch roster share the same philosophical outlook. HRW is probably among the best funded of the U.S. NGOs, which number in the thousands and receive billions of dollars every year from governments and banks

THE QUINTESSENTIAL NGO

Human Rights Watch is really the quintessential NGO, exemplifying what sociologist James Petras described as,

> a 'grassroots' organization with an 'anti-statist' ideology [organized] to intervene among potentially conflictory classes, to create a 'social cushion.' These organizations were financially dependent on neoliberal sources and were directly involved in competing with socio-political movements for the allegiance of local leaders and activist communities. By the 1990s these organizations, described as 'nongovernmental,' numbered in the thousands and were receiving close to four billion dollars world-wide.[22]

And although there are some NGO's who have bravely taken the side of the oppressed, Americas Watch has never supported the militant demands of Colombia's genuine labor unions even though the death squads have murdered scores of Colombian labor-union leaders. Petras notes:

> NGOs were not part of the trade union resistance. ... Rarely if ever do NGOs support the strikes and protests against low wages and budget cuts. ... While the

neoliberals were transferring lucrative state properties to the private rich, the NGOs were not part of the trade union resistance. On the contrary they were active in local private projects, promoting the private enterprise discourse [self-help] in the local communities by focusing on micro-enterprises.[23]

WATCHING HUMAN RIGHTS WATCH

Many people have accepted the idea that Human Rights Watch is a benign NGO valiantly opposing repression. But genuinely socially-conscious people need to understand the organization's sinister machinations.

These are easier to see in Latin America. Petras notes:

> [I]n Latin America, there do exist Marxist intellectuals who write and speak for the social movements in struggle, committed to sharing the same political consequences. They are 'organic' intellectuals who are basically part of the movement—the resource people providing analysis and education for class struggle, in contrast to the 'post-Marxist' NGO intellectuals, who are embedded in the world of institutions, academic seminars, foreign foundations, international conferences and bureaucratic reports.[24]

The Colombian insurgencies, which are every day growing in size and influence despite the Human Rights Watch campaigns against them, reject HRW's right to dictate how their struggle for justice should be waged. In their response to José Miguel Vivanco's carefully timed and politically charged letter in 2001, the FARC-EP noted:

> ...Mr. José Miguel Vivanco, Executive Director of Human Rights Watch ... [is] part of the interventionist policies that come along with the imposition of the Free Trade Area of the Americas as a mechanism of U.S. economic annexation. Plan Colombia, now known as the Andean Initiative, is the military expression of this project. The so-called transnationalization of North American justice through the United Nations completes the picture, dismantling the sovereign justice systems of individual states...
>
> The executive director, located in Washington, maintained complicit silence in the face of the U.S. invasion of Grenada and Panama, the imperialist attack on Iraq and Yugoslavia, the infamous blockade of socialist Cuba and the state terrorism that is growing in our country. Now it is building smokescreens that hide the responsibility of the United States for the bloodshed [of] that state paramilitary policy that Colombia suffers.
>
> We reject U.S. interventionism. We oppose the transnationalization of U.S. laws. We defend national sovereignty and the right to struggle for peace and reconciliation of the Colombian family.
>
> This type of NGO offers little service to peace, when they try to impose the

agenda of the U.S. State Department on our country. Neither does it help to play politics at the expense of the poor of Colombia. All this in exchange for the dollars provided by proponents of neoliberal globalization ... [dollars that] end up in the pockets of the opportunistic directors of these organizations.[25]

Activists in the United States would be well advised to "watch" the reports coming out of Human Rights Watch.

---

[1] HRW, "Colombia: Human Rights Watch Testifies before the Senate," April 24, 2002.

[2] Alexander Cockburn and Jeffrey St. Clair, "The War Criminal and the Whore," *Counter Punch*, Jan. 23, 2002.

[3] "Note verbale" dated March 8, 2000 from the Permanent Mission of Cuba to the United Nations Office at Geneva addressed to the Office of the High Commissioner for Human Rights, document E/CN.4/2000/131 of the 56th session of the Commission on Human Rights

[4] HRW, "Colombia: Rebel Abuses Worsening", July 9, 2001.

[5] Juan Pablo Toro, "Military applauds human rights report on Colombia guerrillas." Associated Press, July 10, 2001.

[6] HRW, "Colombia: Rebels Trying to Deflect Criticism of Abuses", July 23, 2001.

[7] HRW, "Colombia Human Rights Certification III", Feb. 5, 2002.

[8] Ibid.

[9] Ibid.

[10] See for example Dennis Hans, "Colombia's Right Wing Terror Campaign Easy to Shut Down-If Only the U.S. Had the Will." *Colombia Report*, Oct. 15, 2001.

[11] Accessed Oct., 2002 "Crisis in Colombia," http://www.hrw.org/campaigns/colombia/action/

[12] HRW, "Colombia: Bush/Pastrana Meeting, A Q&A on the Human Rights Situation in Colombia," Nov. 6, 2001.

[13] *Soros on Soros: Staying Ahead of the Curve* (New York: John Wiley, 1995).

[14] http://www.hrw.org/wr2k1/asia/china.html

[15] http://www.hrw.org/campaigns/kosovo98/link.shtml

[16] Ken Roth, "Indict Saddam Hussein." *Wall Street Journal*, March 22, 2002.

[17] Patrin, Radio Free Europe/Radio Liberty News Articles, http://www.geocities.com/Paris/5121/rfe-rl.htm

[18] In the words of Yale's International Security Studies, which lists Okun as a member of the ISS advisory board.

[19] "Serbian Media," Voice of America, Dec. 7. 1996.

[20] As of June 24, 2002.

[21] James Petras, in "Imperialism and NGOs in Latin America" *Monthly Review*, December 1997 estimates that worldwide in the 1990s, NGOs were receiving $4 billion annually.

[22] James Petras, "Imperialism and NGOs in Latin America." *Monthly Review*, December 1997.

[23] Ibid.

[24] Ibid.

[25] General Staff of the FARC-EP, July 2001.

II.

VOICES

FROM

COLOMBIA

GAITÁN AND THE U.S.
HEAD TO HEAD

GLORIA GAITÁN

Jorge Eliécer Gaitán was a popular leader of Colombia's Liberal Party in the 1940s. His 1948 presidential campaign became a focus of millions of Colombian peasants and workers who were attracted to Gaitán's program of social justice and anti-imperialism, a program with clear socialist influences. He was assassinated during the 1948 election campaign, setting off an uprising that began the years known as "La Violencia."

In her article "Gaitán and the U.S., Head to Head," Gloria Gaitán, Gaitán's daughter, traces his political legacy and analyzes the role of the United States in assassinating her father. Excerpts of the article are printed below.

THE NATIONAL OLIGARCHY AND U.S. IMPERIALISM

In May 1929, Jorge Eliécer Gaitán was elected to Congress as a representative in the House. It was there he heard of the massacre of banana workers in the Caribbean region of Magdalena.

The young parliamentarian set off a debate that, up to our times, will be remembered as a classic of criminology put at the service of politics.[1] On that occasion, he pronounced his well-publicized words of protest,

> This case is one of solving a problem of wages by means of the government's machine-gun bullets. Naturally, the government exercised no pressure so that the workers would receive justice. They were Colombians and the company was a U.S. company. And we are painfully aware that in this country, the government has homicidal shrapnel for the children of the homeland and trembling knees on the ground before yankee gold!

His position in the face of the U.S. government and its intervention in Colombian affairs was his constant and permanent political position. It is enough to read a few phrases:

> Neither now nor ever will our nationalist spirit waver. We will defend it today and forever, because we believe that the Latin American nations have a certain danger from imperialism. I know very well that Colombia, like all weak countries, is threatened by a thousand dangers and that it needs the brave ferocity of all its children to defend it against imperialism's avalanche that is passing over above all in the realm of the economy.

THE TROJAN HORSE TACTIC

Confronted by the Liberal Party officialdom and under the label of "Radical Socialist," he formed a dissident group that did not significantly attract Liberal Party members. He made the decision, therefore, to join with a leftist movement then in existence, the Revolutionary Leftist National Union (UNIR), but he knew that the break between the people and the Liberal and Conservative parties was far from coming to pass. It is with this in mind that he declared,

> I join the Liberal Party in the manner of the Trojan Horse, to do with it what I was proposing within the UNIR. The people will take the leadership of the party from the Liberal oligarchy and will give the programmatic orientation that suits its interests. The Liberal Party will then be the party of the people.

THE PEOPLE'S CANDIDATE

From this moment on, Gaitán began building a popular network across the country with determination and extreme consistency. Finally, in 1945, the movement took shape in a popular convention proclaiming Gaitán as the "people's candidate." On May 5, 1946, after Gaitán had been defeated and the Conservative candidate was elected president, the popular leader explained to his supporters,

> The Liberal Party has not fallen, because the Liberal Party is the people, and the people have never been in power. The Liberal Party officialdom has fallen— that is something else entirely. Now we are going to conquer power for the people. The struggle begins today.

On May 16, 1946, the U.S. ambassador in Bogotá, John C. Wiley, composed a report for the State Department in which he made the following observations about Gaitán, "He is a small man of great stature. He is definitely a new political star that has been born in Colombia, and maybe in Latin America."

But the report was not composed as a tribute to Gaitán. On the contrary, it was as a warning to the U.S. government,

> Gaitán wants power. Knowing his own ability to guide the emotions of the dispossessed, he is determined to take the opportunity given to him by people's widespread discontent to take the leadership of the Liberal Party and, if he can, the government. Nevertheless, there is the general belief that his scruples will not prevent him from using other means, if necessary. At this point he believes that his victory is easiest through one of the political parties. As he himself told me, it is easier to sell a new product with an old etiquette. However, it seems to me that Gaitán is farther from the Liberals than President Ospina himself.

THE TAKING OVER OF THE LIBERAL PARTY

In March 1947, elections for Congress and the Departmental Assemblies were held. The popular movement that catalyzed Gaitán suddenly won the elections. "The people are greater than their leaders," he said in his speech at the Municipal Theater after the elections. The newspaper *El Tiempo*, to this day at the service of the right wing current in the Liberal Party, ran a headline, "The Gaitán phenomenon consolidates," and commented, "The Gaitán movement's victory in the March legislative elections, in which the Liberal Party officialdom was defeated, passed to the leader the head of this movement. It defines Liberalism as the party of the people."

The principal columnist of the day, using the pseudonym Calibán, commented:

> The way things are going, Gaitán will kill Liberalism, but without Gaitán, Liberalism dies. This is for the simple reason that Dr. Gaitán has the masses, he moves the electorate, he wins in the elections. We are facing, then, a tremendous dilemma.

The problem was not just for the Liberal Party, the same newspaper said. "The ascendancy of Gaitán over the Liberal and Conservative masses is vast." Before the force of facts, the traditional leaders of the Liberal Party felt obliged to accept Gaitán as the single leader of Liberalism, and they fled the country.

'LA VIOLENCIA'

From the very moment that Gaitán was proclaimed the people's candidate on Sept. 23, 1945, this period in history has became known as "La Violencia." Due to Mariano Ospina Pérez's taking the presidency, the level of terror increased.

Ospina had formed a plutocratic bipartisan government called the National Union, under which persecution, harassment, murders and the growing process of violence was exercised equally by Liberal and Conservative municipal authorities against the members of the dissident Liberal movement. With the parliamentary elections of March 1947 approaching, the number of complaints sent to Gaitán charging harassment inflicted on the followers of the people's movement multiplied.

When Gaitán was proclaimed the single leader of the Liberal Party and he demanded the retirement of the Liberal cabinet ministers, the persecution was extended to Liberalism in general.

Gaitán addressed successive Memoranda of Complaint to President Ospina describing cases of persecution. The responses followed protocol, but the government took no action whatsoever to slow the wave of blood that had covered the whole country.

In February 1948, Gaitán called on the people to carry out a March of Silence. As a show of discipline, the slogan was silence for all participants.

The Plaza de Bolívar in Bogotá was flooded. The multitude overflowed into the neighboring streets, extending as far as the eye could see in an infinite sea of black flags floating amid total silence, that stirred all those who loved peace and frightened the oligarchy and the U.S. government. They were able to see the irrevocable determination of a people that up to that moment they had not believed capable of submitting to any discipline whatsoever.

The head of the U.S. delegation had written in March 1946 in his report to the State Department, "This soil is happily not fertile for foreign ideologies if they imply order and discipline." That demonstration was proof to the contrary.

Gaitán delivered his beautiful "Oration for Peace," addressed to the president of the republic, asking for an end to the violence, "There is a party of order capable of carrying out this act in order to prevent blood from continuing to spill. ... You understand well that a party that achieves this could very easily react under the stimulus of legitimate defense." The oligarchy paid more attention to this warning than to the plea to stop the government violence.

Just two months later, on April 9, 1948, Gaitán was assassinated, raising the spiral of extermination against the most powerful mass organization ever in Colombian history.

A CIA AGENT

A U.S. agent named John Mepples Spirito confessed to having traveled to Colombia in order, initially, to bribe Gaitán. In his filmed and recorded confession, he can be heard saying:

> My name is John Mepples Spirito. I was born in the United States of Sicilian origin. My parents were also both Sicilians, now U.S. citizens. ... In the Houston Center, I was sent directly to Colombia to participate in a 'team way,' that is, with a group of specialists and operatives in the country, to work together with them to carry out an operation called 'Pantomime.' That was how the operation was known from then on. This operation had the fundamental goal of using all means against a lawyer with leftist tendencies, a very popular leader in those times, named Eliécer Gaitán—a criminal lawyer by profession. This individual was already in conflict—according to the reports that they gave me at that time as part of my work—was already in conflict with the embassy of the United States and with various emissaries, that a group leader named Thomas Elliot tried to fix, to make a kind of contract, I could say, with this individual, that is Eliécer Gaitán.

The agent continued:

> After these negotiations failed, this individual was seen as, let's say, difficult to work with within what we had been talking about earlier, within another administration and training, that was through political means, that is, trying to

reach this individual by means of bribery and blackmail. In other words, it was necessary to work with him then in another way.[2]

'OPERATION PANTOMIME'

Later Mepples Spirito says:

> This, naturally, in order to carry this out I had to pass as a student who spoke Italian, due to my background. I worked within the student ranks and so I could know as an exact science its strength, I could know as an exact science who they supported and naturally these studies, along with other studies already made by agents located there, like Thomas Elliot, leader of the group. So we came to an agreement that Eliécer Gaitán, the independence, Liberal and very popular leader, well, that it would be necessary to carry out a physical elimination.

And he adds later:

> ...if we carried out a physical elimination of the individual, sheltered by the U.S. Embassy in Colombia, well it would be necessary to try to do it under some other cover, in another way, so that public opinion would not form some idea like that the U.S. Embassy was behind all this. ... Arriving in Colombia I knew some other people that also worked for the Center linked to the Bogotá Embassy. They introduced me to an individual named Juan Roa Sierra. This individual, a Colombian national with fascist tendencies, was a trustworthy individual that had already carried out programs or other missions for the agents, both for the Center and for the Embassy.[3]

THE ALIBI

Mepples Spirito confirms, in what we have just seen, that it was necessary to give "another cover" to the crime to cover up the fact that "the U.S. Embassy was behind all this." Every plot of the State, throughout time, includes the parallel mounting of a plot that creates the belief that an "isolated individual" committed the crime. The intellectual authors or the ones who cover for them always insist on making the public think that the murderer acted for personal reasons.

It is for this reason, alarming to state that the director of the CIA at that time, Rear Adm. R.K. Hillenkotter, in a secret report on the murder of Jorge Eliécer Gaitán given to the U.S. Congress six days after the crime, would say that the murderer is an individual named José Sierra Galarza, nephew of Eduardo Galarza Ossa, director of the newspaper *The Voice of Caldas*, who was murdered by Lt. Cortés, who Gaitán defended and won his freedom in a defense that ended at one in the morning on the same day as the killing of Gaitán. The explanation given by the Director of the CIA was that Sierra Galarza had been motivated by vengeance.

It is curious to see that the supposed assassin did not figure in any of the file folders. Will it be perhaps from him that the fourth bullet was fired in the attack against Gaitán, whose origin could never be determined?

CONCLUSION

The participation of the U.S. in "Operation Pantomime" is shown by the director of the CIA identifying a supposed murderer that the official investigation never mentioned; by the CIA refusing to open its archives on the case, claiming "reasons of national security;" by the existence of a flesh and blood agent of the CIA who claims to have participated in "Operation Pantomime" in order to eliminate Gaitán and by the fact that in the name of President Clinton, Peter Romero, then secretary for interamerican affairs, in December 1998 offered Gaitán's daughter to arrange a meeting with officials of the State Department with the aim of clarifying the charges of the CIA agent, Mepples Spirito. Taking total responsibility for carrying this out, the presidential secretary remained silent.

It is becoming urgent in order to find the truth, to declassify the CIA archives. It doesn't only interest Colombia, it is also a right of the people of the United States. Gaitán said it well in his time:

> We were nationalists yesterday and we are nationalists today. But we are not nationalists that are enemies of the U.S. people; rather we are adversaries of the imperialist system that has its greatest opponent in that same people that work under the protection of the torch of the Statue of Liberty.

---

[1] Gaitán's formal training was in criminology.-Ed.

[2] The audio of Mepples Spirito's confession, as well as its transcription, can be found at the Center for Audiovisual Documentation of COLPARTICIPAR. The transcription can be requested by email: jega@col1.telecom.com.co.

[3] Gaitán's material assassin.

THE ORIGINS OF THE FARC-EP

THE BIRTH OF THE ARMED RESISTANCE

MANUEL MARULANDA VÉLEZ

Manuel Marulanda Vélez is the founder and commander in chief of the Revolutionary Armed Forces of Colombia-People's Army (FARC-EP). A veteran political leader and military tactician, Marulanda has led the group from a handful of combatants to among the most powerful guerrilla insurgency in the world. The article below is reprinted from his book "Cuadernos de Campaña" (Campaign Notebooks). It was originally two chapters of the book, entitled "Reactionary Action, Popular Response and Some Reflections." The book has not yet appeared in English.

The area that goes by the geographic designation of Southern Tolima is made up of the municipalities of Rioblanco, Ataco, Chaparral, Rocesvalles, San Antonio, Ortega, Natagaima, Coyaima and Purificación, along with two or three others.

The governmental violence in Southern Tolima aimed at Communists and Liberals led to the formation of small groups to confront the police and the armed Conservatives, originally in the munipalities of Chaparral, Rioblanco and Ataco. The specially trained police bands, supported by the Conservatives, were getting 1evenge for what happened on April 9, 1948. On that day the people had risen up in insurrection with great indignation when, during a reactionary attack, the popular leader Jorge Eliécer Gaitán was assassinated in the streets of the capital.

The inhabitants of this area, with a strong Liberal tradition, were identified as responsible by those interested in spreading violence with economic and political aims. Since it was necessary to come up with a pretext and justification, they were accused of arson, murder and rebellion. The accusations of the "April 9" and "chusmeros" death squads provided enough "reasons" to continue with the political persecution in the districts, small towns, and even in the cities. It was enough that a region or a district was identified as having "communist" or "collarejo" residents for the police and the armed Conservatives to destroy it, killing some of the inhabitants, burning their houses, taking prisoners who never appeared again, stealing their livestock and raping women. Conservative gangs organized themselves with the sole intention of spreading terror among the population and taking over the peasants' goods. The police and local authorities supported them. Death was strolling along in the hands of these assassins, with considerable government help.

The drama witnessed by the peasants was really chilling. A massacre today, the burning of an entire district tomorrow, family members taken prisoner and disappeared forever. "La Violencia" touched everyone's door! "La Violencia" was organized and taken advantage of by the government.

The Liberals talked about rising up against the police and the Conservatives who were supported by the right-wing government. Many groups started springing up, although not showing much stability. When one group disappeared, some men and women looked for another one or started a new one. Several of these groups, considering the conditions, were well led. This news was public knowledge, and people joined them in greater numbers.

These groups made their appearance in the Cordillera Central with many natural deficiencies at the beginning: inexperience, inadequate organization, objective limitations, etc. For those condemned to death by the *chulavita* death squads, they were something like a lifesaver. For the peasants who did not want to continue on the unknown road of roaming to the cities, temporarily or permanently abandoning the fruit of many years of hard work, it was the hope of staying, participating and once in a while having a glimpse of their native land to which they were so spiritually and materially attached.

Some veterans leading the groups contributed good knowledge and leadership. They pointed out possible places where the weapons of the "Thousand Days War" could be found. Many of these weapons, largely in bad shape for the long years they were hidden, started coming into their hands.

In the meantime, the Liberal leaders spread the idea that it was possible to buy a great number of arms in the United States and other countries. Naturally, this was a fantasy. Others naively talked about the effectiveness of making demands on the government and the Conservative Party to force them to give back guarantees to the Liberal Party and to re-establish peace.

The national Liberal Party leadership was responsible for spreading deep illusions by starting a wild plan to oust the government among the workers, who were holding back "La Violencia." The party leadership sent emissaries to prepare the details for a "general uprising." They started teaching how to prepare and launch homemade bombs, how to dynamite vital points in roads and bridges, destroy railroad lines, use molotov cocktails, etc. They promised with absolute certainty that everything was ready.

The date to strike the blow arrived, but nobody rose up. Special envoys traveled to Bogotá, and after a few days they came back with a new date and a bunch of other explanations. Meanwhile, time was passing and the waves of violence became bloodier and more frequent.

Those who had already made the decision to go to the mountains to resist were not relying on the Liberal Party leaders. It was known that many of the party leaders were leaving the country. Others were preparing to go into exile, protected by a slogan purposely invented to give the message to the masses that

Liberalism should have "faith and dignity." Between being disappointed and afraid, many people armed themselves with old shotguns, old-fashioned revolvers and anything else they could find. Work in the fields was abandoned due to "La Violencia." People could not work because by doing so they became easy targets of the bandits. A great deal of solidarity grew among citizens, friends in the struggle and those who were persecuted. The first contacts among districts and municipalities were established. The situation was very tense because there were lots of stories going around, all types of gossip that were spreading through the lands where these embryonic groups were helping each other. In some cases, these rumors encouraged people, but in other cases they caused much uncertainty.

The first Liberal actions against the Conservatives took place. Although it was true that these Conservatives identified with the government, in many cases they didn't have anything to do with "La Violencia." Retaliatory police actions followed, and the small groups dispersed or moved to another region. When they regrouped, they became bigger, incorporating new people.

The resistance groups went through the logical and natural process of formation, strengthening and consolidation. It was a process of the emergence of a form of struggle that had no immediate predecessor, rising spontaneously, imprecisely, in which the peasants themselves were protagonists of their own history. The city was far away, contacts were lost, and those who could see the political panorama more clearly were unable to speak out. The process was as complicated as the relationship that generated it was simple: reactionary violence, self-organized resistance, resistance that was led by its principal actors, the peasants.

Many groups organized themselves and dissolved. There was still the hope among workers that the current situation was going to go away. But despite all that, something remained solid: people ready to take all the implicit risks of their decision to resist, and to transform that self-defense resistance into a conscious mass attitude to achieve their goal so that future generations didn't have to experience the scourge of having guns in their hands. These men and women have merited a place in the true "Homeland's History." They formed the nucleus of the determined struggle.

The bourgeoisie wisely knew how to take advantage of these heroic struggles in order to take the leadership in overthrowing the reactionary dictatorship of 1953 and to open a new chapter in governing. This new chapter had slightly different characteristics, but was aimed at preserving the same oligarchic and neo-colonialist interests.

SOME REFLECTIONS

We jump to 1964. In May of that year, official repression began a new stage in the war. This was preceded by a massive U.S. Pentagon-inspired campaign by the reactionary press against the image of "independent republics" to discredit the peasant regions where they were carrying on a life independent of the traditional parties. The first target of this undeclared civil war was Marquetalia; it was then extended to other places like Riochiquito, El Pato, Guayabero, etc.

Against Marquetalia, the military high command deployed a combined force of some 16,000 troops. The air force, artillery, infantry and engineers, trained in the most up-to-date methods of anti-guerrilla struggle, participated. Our combatants fought and continue to fight with an invigorating effectiveness, despite the fact that compared to the monstrous machinery that they successfully faced, they seemed like just a speck.

There are naturally determining causes for this, among which we can point out:

a) We are taking advantage of the valiant experience accumulated in long years of training in this form of struggle;

b) The fundamental nucleus of commanders is made up of combatants who, since 1949, have led diverse and complicated situations of guerrilla warfare, always confronted by an enemy that was more powerful in terms of numbers and technical and military equipment;

c) We receive the widest solidarity from different sources in the revolutionary movement. This solidarity has had many basic forms of expression: material, within the same mass struggle in every area while at different levels; moral, shared by many men, women, and organizations with principles that defend the guerrilla fighters; and economic, in concrete donations by the masses to the struggle of the armed combatants;

d) We are fighting with truth on our side. First, because our guerrilla movements sprang out of nothing else but as a response to an assault against the peasants; later, because the cause we are defending is the cause of the exploited, and our banners of struggle are never raised in isolation from the basic needs of the peasants and of the workers. We form part of the fighters for the national liberation of our homeland;

e) We are guided by a revolutionary ideology. Our political beacon is the theory of socialism, shaped in the practice of communist activity.

When we arrived in Riochiquito after an initial campaign of resisting the enemy, through which we were hoping to fix in the Colombian people's consciousness the justness of our struggle, we encountered the widest solidarity. Thanks to that solidarity in the immediate rearguard, and to national solidarity, we managed to set up a fluid, incisive and highly efficient guerrilla warfare.

For quite a while we continued living and fighting in the very place the enemy was located, giving the impression through our absolute control of the terrain that we were making incursions from other zones. The Colombian military leaders still don't know exactly when we left Marquetalia as the epicenter of our operations. And when we were leaving for a certain time, it was not because—as a French apprentice of the guerrilla fighter believed—of inability, or forced by circumstances. It was because it formed part of the strategy of our military operations. Such an understanding of our tactics is the reason why so many—friends as well as enemies—have many times made mistakes in evaluating our struggle.

When we temporarily chose Riochiquito as a base to organize and deploy several actions, we were in the beginning stages of carrying out a careful plan at the strategic level. We needed to distract and disperse the greatest enemy force possible; we further needed to "re-armor" our small reserve of troops. With them, we would re-establish our supply lines and our working contacts with the masses.

In order to confirm our claims, we can now relate that, in conformance with a series of circumstances, we resolved not to mount a resistance in Riochiquito because, although we would win all the battles, it would have little political repercussion in the country. There are other factors that will continue to remain our military secrets.

We wanted to show the enemy a false preparation for combat. This was not because our plans were heading in another direction, but we needed to attract the enemy and to make the occupation of the region costly and complicated while we were gaining precious time for our plans. We showed ourselves "strong" at points having little importance to us with the objective of drawing the enemy there. Simultaneously we would truly be strong in dominant and advantageous places in order to launch lightning counterattacks and surprise attacks on our part.

The enemy military cordon, designed from inside toward the outer areas with the aid of transports, consisted of simultaneously dropping paratroopers at many points and then forming a ring that would open up. One month later, diversionary actions covered our retreat from this theater of operations.

During our stay in Riochiquito, we carried out the First Conference of the Southern Bloc, which unified our tactics for all the detachments. A series of initiatives was taken toward the creation of the current Revolutionary Armed Forces of Colombia (FARC).

Several other considerations, like the following, will help our enemies understand many of the reasons we state that the Colombian military forces have wasted all their time trying to wipe out our system of guerrilla forces through their path of so-called counter-guerrilla warfare.

The Colombian army counts on an impressive counter-guerrilla apparatus. The public forces are equipped with modern armaments and infinitely superior weaponry, thanks to extraordinary financing for their "preventive war." It is staffed by military officers specially trained and, with the exception of the patriotic officers and soldiers, politically convinced that defending the exploiting class will convert them into administrators of the precarious survival of the current regime. They have enormous forces and resources at their disposal.

Yet a quarter of a century has passed, and every passing day they show themselves more incapable of wiping out the armed insurgency.

Faced with the aggression against Marquetalia, for example, we created a single leadership. We were building a new type of general staff as the supreme political and military authority, taking care that militarism did not overwhelm everything. We set up the military structure that corresponds to an extraordinarily mobile struggle, and we adjusted the tactics to the necessities of that needed mobility. The guerrilla detachments and groupings are deployed in the field with the same versatility as a very small guerrilla unit. If we need to, we establish fixed commands for whatever time is required. Discipline is not imposed; rather, it springs forth in the conscious combatant as a necessity of the struggle. The barracks method modeled on that of the units of troops in the bourgeois army is now but a memory of the first days of the guerrilla force.

However, our military structure is guided by conscious revolutionary military principles, adjusted to our form of guerrilla force. We maintain a critical and self-critical attitude in the face of our own political and military errors, while we are guided by a profoundly respectful conduct in our dealings with the masses and in their interests. We raise and support the immediate and fundamental demands of the masses, who by virtue of our activity are in the fields like us. We were never, and we will never be, a bunch of self-important people trying to dictate the line to everyone else, nor defenders of the absurd thesis that "the guerrilla force creates the party." We go forward guided by the orientation of the only party that has always been with us: the Communist Party. And we will always continue to be so guided.

We have thrown out antiquated aspects of our work and our tactics, with the struggle itself providing us with lessons. We know from life itself that:

a) The armed group, small as it may be, can successfully confront the enemy if it has the support of the masses and a political-military leadership that develops plans, perspectives and political actions that generate solidarity;

b) It can successfully confront the enemy, even in adverse national political conditions, if it has the firm support of the party, as was won in our case by the leadership, displaying the most consistent and comradely efforts;

c) In order for the guerrilla force to establish itself in action and develop in the perspective of prolonged struggle, it needs to know how to join all the other forms and expressions of the struggle of the masses with the armed struggle. The "purist" proposition, declaring all other forms of struggle obsolete in order to make the armed struggle absolute, isolates the guerrilla force, converts it into a sect and wipes it out;

d) The guerrilla force must be in constant activity. That makes it grow, organically strengthens it, projects its presence to the masses so as to maintain their sympathy and establish solidarity. The guerrilla force that vegetates simply disintegrates, and its members fall into banditry;

e) The leadership cadre of the guerrilla force come out of the same social medium that rise to the guerrilla force. But with this cadre as well as with the members of the guerrilla force, educational work needs to be carried out in order to shape them, raising their political-military capability. The needs of the guerrilla struggle increase every day. The demands for correct actions and leadership are greater. For that reason it is indispensable that the growth of the guerrilla force is accompanied by the increased political-military development of its members;

f) The guerrilla force, if it wants to establish and project itself as a prosecutor of the revolutionary conditions permitting it to participate, along with other forces, in the decisive mobilizations for political power, must carry out its strategic goals through a clear program, fostering the type of revolution that the Colombian people is struggling for at the present stage. This program must not oppose fundamental tasks like independence with respect to imperialism and the elimination of large latifundist landholdings;

g) The unity of the armed combatants for the freedom and independence of the homeland is a fundamental element. Within the diversity of tactics, organizational forms and forms of command, within the methods of action and attitudes toward the masses themselves of each movement, there must be unity of action and solidarity. The guerrilla movement that takes the road of absorbing or eliminating the other forces in a sectarian way is digging its own grave.

After some time passed, the conditions were created for carrying out the Constitutive Conference of the FARC. The Conference of the Southern Bloc played a role in unifying the different detachments that arose in Tolima and Huila, as well as in the extreme south of Meta and the north of Cauca, as a result of the government aggression against many peasant regions—regions that the right wing had baptized as "independent republics." That is not to say that these different detachments acted in ways opposing one another. There simply had not been coordination of the guerrilla operations and we lacked a single general staff for all of them.

The general staff that we had created in Marquetalia only had jurisdiction over the guerrilla troops from there. As a result, uniting all the commands into a single general staff and carrying out the plan envisioned for the phase that was opening up became more urgent. The Constitutive Conference of the FARC set out the basis for the work, with the perspective of preparing the organic structure and the subsequent political-military line. We set ourselves a structure governing our internal organization. New detachments were organized, each responsible for a territorial area. Action was widened, with the goal of reaching a national presence. In addition, our tactics were consistently corrected, among many movements, so as to oblige the enemy to confront us in a theater of operations chosen by us, in which we always would try to maintain the initiative.

From that point on, the stage in which the enemy incessantly chased us was past. It was now we ourselves who initiated armed contacts, when and where it was to our favor. The control cordons designed to keep us isolated from the people, the intelligence service to detect our work, and the effects of psychological warfare, all had to be neutralized. The Conference adopted a system of activities to this effect that have continued to yield excellent results.

In the same way, the Conference had to examine our faults, of which there were naturally more than a few. We were still not achieving the necessary synchronization and coherence in our military work and political activities. There were still remnants of indiscipline, displays of caudillismo and blatant contempt for criticism. We were not adequately challenging the political work of the reactionary sectors. We were showing deficiencies in the political-military capabilities of our cadres and rank-and-file combatants. Some cases of bad behavior toward the peasants and friendly political organizations had come up. All this needed to be corrected.

The historical experience of our country has continued to show that the emergence and activity of the FARC, like the other guerrilla groups, correspond above all to a maturation of conditions deriving directly from the national framework of problems coming from before. It came from the first days of the guerrilla movement, in now far-off 1949, the year in which a despotic style of government over the Colombians began, preceded by the state of siege. That guerrilla movement came to take on an element of political transcendence for the whole of the revolutionary movement.

So we bring to the judgment of our readers this first narrative effort of the moments that we consider to be of greatest importance for the appearance and location of a stage in the guerrilla struggle waged by the peasants. In doing so, we are motivated by the hope of making some contribution, however modest, to those who study the phenomenon of "La Violencia," so that with their intellectual gifts they can make an evaluation of the profound damage inflicted upon our homeland by those who continue, after three decades, enriching themselves with this holocaust that still hasn't ended.

A STRUGGLE FOR POLITICAL AND ECONOMIC DEMOCRACY

TRADE UNIONS IN COLOMBIA

JAVIER CORREA SUÁREZ

Our union, the National Union of Food Industry Workers (Sinaltrainal), was born in 1982, a product of a network of a number of workplace-based unions. These unions saw how the struggle of the workers within the factories was sharpening, and the need to take on the process of organizing and formulating proposals dealing with the economic model that is crushing, beating down the workers in the different sectors.

Our union currently has 22 locals spread throughout the different regions of Colombia. This allows us to give very accurate testimony about the situation in Colombia. Being in the middle of zones with a lot of conflict, in zones where the transnational companies have a presence, we see not only how they exploit the natural resources, but also how this level of exploitation causes a very negative impact that brings with it the systematic destruction of the environment and the impoverishment of communities.

It also allows us to testify to the way these transnational companies benefit from state terrorism that is applied against the workers and the trade union organizations. This has also made us feel in the flesh the effects of the war that has been unleashed against the workers who are fighting within the constitution. We are struggling for a true democracy, not only in the political arena but also for the economic, social and cultural rights of the population.

Sinaltrainal is present in the whole national system, primarily in companies like Coca-Cola, Nabisco, Clap, Fruco, Nestlé, the milk sector, as well as in numerous national monopolies that produce soda. Likewise, Sinaltrainal has a presence in the agricultural sector, and we are also making an effort to reach out to workers in small shops.

This allows us to have a very clear idea about what both the economic and production-line problems are for each group of workers taking part in every aspect of the food industry. We also know the effects of the Colombian problem and the international impact of all the neoliberal and globalization policies. We feel the effects of all the accords that are being contemplated as well as the mega-projects like the Free Trade Area of the Americas.

We have a very direct relationship with the peasants through the Agrarian National Coordinating Group, of which Sinaltrainal is a member. Our union is also part of the United Center of Colombian Workers (CUT). Likewise, we continue to be part of the national and international Permanent Campaign Against Impunity, that is, the campaign to stop letting the paramilitaries get away with murdering Colombian workers.

Sinaltrainal is also part of the Social and Political Front, one of the alternatives for building a social movement, a political movement that struggles for transforming the Colombian reality.

BUILDING A SOCIAL MOVEMENT

We have always tried to implement projects to create alternate food distribution routes where the peasants, workers and popular sectors eliminate the intermediaries to make the basic costs to support a family cheaper, and above all to support organic and clean production that protects the health of the human species and the whole environment.

Sinaltrainal is also carrying out some educational projects in Colombia through the leadership school for social and union leaders. We also have the chance to go about building a workers' university, which we are pursuing. Likewise, we have some high schools where we offer the communities with few resources some possibilities for children to study.

We are also initiating a national cooperative in which peasants, all the popular sectors, trade unionists and different sectors of Colombia's oppressed and exploited are involved.

This overall summary of our activities gives the reasons why Sinaltrainal is facing such fierce persecution. The union is struggling amid war. It is constructing its own autonomous thought, expressing the quest for freedom of expression and organization. It is because we are struggling against the penalization of social protest and beyond that fight for the workers' salaries. We have also involved ourselves in the situation of different sectors.

It is also because we do not share the policy that the government is carrying out. We criticize, we question the form of government in Colombia. We criticize the government's corruption. We criticize the lack of democracy, the inability to think, to question or to ask for changes and solutions, not only for the workers but for the whole population.

For these reasons, our union is persecuted, stigmatized, demonized by all sorts of false charges like that we are terrorists, guerrillas and delinquents. This has one purpose: so that they can repress us, murder us, and jail us. It is the justification and the perfect pretext to unleash all the persecution, institutional and para-institutional.

This is the situation in which we are working in Colombia. We are committed to continuing to work despite all the difficulties and all the crimes, abuses and outrages to which we are subjected.

Within the structure of Sinaltrainal, we have statutes governing the internal organization of the union. That is the structure that determines the ways that elections and democratic participation take place in the union. This offers space for elections for the workers affiliated with Sinaltrainal as well as a way to elect those who will speak in the name of all the workers—not only to the bosses and companies, but also to the government. The spokespeople are also the ones to carry out each of the previously agreed upon proposals.

Also in the statutes is the way the workers democratically approve the dues that each must assume. The workers pay 1.5 percent of their monthly salary as dues. These dues make up the common funds of the union. One part of these dues goes toward supporting each of the social projects that the union has. Another part—20 percent of the 1.5 percent dues—is designated for the union's national leadership council to carry out its national and international work.

ORGANIZED LABOR IN COLOMBIA

In the last congress of the CUT, there were 480,000 workers organized in our federation. In the last poll that our union federation carried out, there was a 3.2 percent affiliation rate. From an economically active population of 18,350,000 people, that is a very low rate of unionized workers.

There are reasons for that: the dirty war, the terrorism carried out against workers, the bosses' decertification campaigns, as well as the massive layoffs of unionized workers carried out by the state and private companies. Likewise, there is the displacement and exile of union leaders. There is the stigmatization against the union movement. All that makes the unionization rate in Colombia very low. People are afraid of belonging to a union because they are treated in the most atrocious and criminal way that one could imagine.

The Sinaltrainal union in Colombia currently has 2,300 members. Five to seven years ago, we had 5,400 members. This reduction in members is due to the systematic policy of companies like Coca-Cola and the Colombia state to smash the workers' organizations and disrupt the rights to organize and to bargain collectively.

Here in Colombia, unemployment is 20 percent according to the National Department of Statistics (DANE). But in our minds, it is not true. In Colombia the unemployment rate is higher.

The CUT estimates an unemployment rate of 24 or 25 percent. Take into account that in Colombia, the children and the adults who are displaced and are begging on the streets are considered employed. Those workers laid off from the factories with a severance are considered to be employed. What is true is that the 72 percent underemployment rate, added to the 24 or 25 percent unemployment rate, shows that we have a structural employment problem.

On top of all these figures, another statistic that I recall is that 58 percent of the 42.5 million people living in Colombia live in poverty. That gives us a clear idea of what the real possibilities are for work there.

Another figure that has touched the world and shows the reality in Colombia is that 7 million people are destitute. These are people that one knows are alive, but there is really no explanation, humanly speaking, for how they survive. It is an extremely acute social problem.

GLOBALIZATION AND THE FTAA

What is currently being proposed with the Free Trade Area of the Americas (FTAA) is that the less technologically developed countries will be subservient to the economic powers in the U.S. We in Sinaltrainal are instead talking about an international and independent integration of the people and the nations based on cooperation and mutual respect.

We think that the Colombian government has made some efforts to show that its decision to join the Free Trade Area of the Americas was made in consultation with the people. This is a lie. The social organizations have never been consulted. If they have invited us to some meeting, it was at the last minute when everything was already approved, after the Congress already passed the legislation and the president was already in the international arena making promises on behalf of the whole nation.

We think that the FTAA will bring extremely grave consequences for the population. For example, with respect to the workers, what will happen when we carry out strikes, protests and mobilizations and the transnational corporations present claims on the government for losses? That goes against democracy, against process, and against the right to negotiate.

How is it possible that under the FTAA, all the resources in the country will have to be available to the transnational companies, which will bring them to countries like the United States for processing, because they will be the raw materials for the products that will in turn come back into our country? That will bring with it a greater plundering than the special economic zones for export.

In other words, Latin America will be converted into another *maquiladora* zone where the United States and Canada will come out the winners. Countries like ours—where there is no technology, where there is no industry, where there is no state investment or attention, where there is no legislation to protect the workers and the weakest part of the population—will experience greater impoverishment, not only for the workers but also for elements of the society that are now considered middle class. In other words, we will see a strengthening of the whole financial sector.

We will see the privatization of state enterprises, although under the constitution it is the responsibility of the state to offer some minimum guarantees in these areas. Now they are going to privatize healthcare. They are going to privatize water. They are being privatized on behalf of the transnationals. Seeds are being privatized. All that is left for the people is hopelessness and disorder. That is, there is not a very bright future for most of the population.

We reject outright the onset of the FTAA in 2005, as the government has agreed upon. We believe that many organizations and sectors will protest against the FTAA coming into effect.

The FTAA is part of globalization, part of the current economic model called the neoliberal model. We have characterized that model as a savage model, an inhumane model, a model that doesn't take people into account. It doesn't take the environment into account. It is a model that is going to absolutely destroy anything it finds in its path.

COCA-COLA AND THE PARAMILITARY DEATH SQUADS

We in Colombia have been the victims of a great number of crimes. We have brought these aggressions to the attention of the Colombian authorities, but the authorities have handled any of these reports by unions, by victims or by the workers in the same way—simply, the investigations come up with no result. The cases are archived. They are stalled. They delay them for a long time so that the witnesses get tired and end up abandoning the cases.

With this situation, they try to make it so that no one bothers asking the Colombian justice system to punish the perpetrators. It's another form of impunity, a way to not punish the perpetrators and in that way organize to destroy the union organizations. It is a way to abandon the workers. And since it has been impossible to try and punish the perpetrators in Colombia, we are resorting to the U.S. court in Florida.

A 1889 law makes it possible for foreign citizens to appeal to U.S. courts when they believe that their rights have been harmed by U.S. companies or by U.S. citizens. Based on this law, we have initiated a lawsuit charging the kidnapping or murder of one of our leaders, the extensive detention of five of our leaders, and death threats. That is, we have four charges at this moment. We hope that the U.S. justice system will make an impartial judgment and determine those responsible as well as the reparation for all these damages against the union, the victims and the workers.

ELECTION OF PRESIDENT ÁLVARO URIBE VÉLEZ

Beginning in August 2002, when the Uribe government took office, we think that the human-rights situation in Colombia will get worse. He has already announced that the government is going to take some measures that are not just militaristic—the program of the Uribe government has fascist measures.

He has already announced cuts in various systems, all with the goal of diminishing the state and eliminating its social role. This will bring with it massive layoffs of workers.

They are also announcing a major military escalation in Colombia, searching out more resources from outside the country to finance the war. They are already pushing the possibility that Colombians will have to pay more taxes to directly finance the war, in addition to the ones they already pay.

This government has announced that it will totally privatize the companies that are now state-owned. In the same way, it is trying to put the costs of the whole social component that the state is abandoning on the shoulders of the poorest by announcing a cut in the whole national budget and social investment. This will mean an even greater segment of the population will be shut out of basic services like health care, water, electricity, housing, clothes and education. So the situation will become extremely difficult.

We think that if today there are 2 million displaced people in Colombia, there will be many more. The government of Uribe is going to double that figure. For this reason the Colombian conflict is going to be felt more strongly in the cities. Many discuss how the displaced are going from the countryside to the cities. But few speak of the people who are displaced from their workplace. Few speak of the people who are displaced from their houses because they can't pay for them. Very little is said of those who lose, or who don't have, the right to basic services like water, electricity, or health care. They are excluded because they don't have the money to pay for these services. There is going to be a disproportionate increase in the abandonment and exclusion of the population.

Above all, measures have been announced that bring the civilian population into the armed conflict. The government of Uribe has been one of the sponsors, through the Convivir cooperatives, of the strengthening of the paramilitary groups. At this moment in the National Assembly there is a proposal for a million paid soldiers-mercenaries. It has been announced that the civilian population will have to participate in military intervention on the side of the police and the right- wing.

In Colombia there are two militarily armed opponents. The population is now being grouped by the Colombian state with one of those armed groups, which will forcibly make us into targets like the military targets. They are going to arm the civilian population—another extremely serious problem because they don't want to legitimize the state that wants only to militarize every aspect of national life.

It is a fairly complicated situation because from the perspective of the trade unions, the peasant organizations, the Indigenous organizations and the organizations of the popular sectors, there will be increasing repression against protests, against the right to freedom of thought and the right to mobilize. This will bring with it greater persecution of all who try to question or who don't agree with the system of government that Uribe is implementing. The violation of human rights will increase even more than it is already today.

THE NATIONAL LIBERATION ARMY SPEAKS

ANTONIO GARCIA

Guerrilla leader Antonio Garcia has over-all military command of the National Liberation Army (ELN), Colombia's second largest guerrilla movement. Below are excerpts from an interview with him.

The main objective of the Plan Colombia is to give the Colombian army the necessary infrastructure to develop its counter-insurgency war. The idea is to create specially-trained army battalions with helicopter gun-ships that can be deployed at very short notice. Plan Colombia disguises the battalions as "anti-drugs," but their true purpose is in the counter-insurgency campaign. Plan Colombia basically justifies further US intervention by pretending it is a "war on drugs," but the truth is that it is an anti-guerrilla war. The policy is designed for the south of the country (large guerrilla presence) while in the north (large paramilitary presence) there is no policy to fight drugs. This policy allows them more flexibility—they are able to support initiatives and operations carried out by the paramilitaries with money earned from the drug trade.

Plan Colombia was thought up in English and written in English. It is impossible that Plan Colombia originated in Colombia or was written in Colombia. The Colombian Congress asked their government for a copy of the plan in Spanish and found that one didn't exist; this was three months after the first draft of the plan was produced in the U.S. Plan Colombia was never discussed in the Colombian Congress or by the Colombian people. It was devised in the U.S. to be applied in Colombia.

There are three versions of Plan Colombia—one in English, another in Spanish that is different from the one in English and another produced especially for Europe that is designed to obtain the money to be invested in social development. The version of Plan Colombia that was written for Europe was designed to make Europe pay for the peace while the U.S. paid for the war.

The aim of Plan Colombia is to supply the army with a capacity for rapid operations—fast movements to surround sites and deny the guerrillas the chance to retreat and regroup. The U.S. wants to strike at the main fronts of the guerrilla movements.

NO TO U.S. INTERVENTION

We believe that the order for U.S. direct military action was given long ago. For many years the U.S. has been intervening in Colombia. There are more than 360 U.S. military experts in Colombia. There are troops on standby in Ecuador, Peru, Brazil and Venezuela. We are not talking about something that is going to happen in the future, we are talking about something that is already taking place. The U.S. is sending an average of three high-ranking military officers to Colombia every week. It seems that they come to supervise the use of the aid that they are giving.

We have no contact with the U.S. government whatsoever. The best contribution that the U.S. can make is not to interfere in our internal conflict. They must allow the Colombian people to resolve their own conflicts without their intervention. However, we have always been open to listening to and talking with any person or government with good will, especially with those interested in supporting the positive development of Colombian society.

THE DRUG TRADE, THE U.S. AND THE GENERALS

We have a strong policy of demarcation with regards to the trafficking of drugs. We have no relationship with the sowing, cultivation, production, trade or export of products related to drugs. We have no connection either with the drugs or the money that it produces. We do not charge traffickers taxes.

To be able to export the large amounts of cocaine that the traffickers are sending to the U.S., they have to rely on the complicity of the authorities, which they gain through bribes. This is clear and has been proven. People in Colombia used to say that the planes that travel to the U.S. are so big that they carry not only the tons of cocaine but also, out front, in the nose of the plane, a check for $20 million. The profits on these loads are between $100 and $120 million, so there is easily enough money to buy the entrance of the drugs into the U.S. market.

It is very well known that some sectors of the armed forces—and numerous politicians—have links with the drug trade. We should check the finances of all the Colombian generals to verify if the salaries that they are earning are high enough to enable them to live in the manner they do. We understand that even the high salaries that some of them have are not sufficient to attain the living standards that they enjoy. We believe there should be close scrutiny of the highest ranks of the military to see where their wealth comes from.

There have always been connections between drug traffickers and the armed forces. It is also well known that the paramilitaries were founded by the drug traffickers and are allowed to operate freely in the north of Colombia. Neither the CIA, the DEA or the Colombian armed forces are fighting the paramilitaries in these areas of high coca production even though everybody knows very well where they are. In these places paramilitary helicopters come to the army garrisons to collect the cocaine to be transported to Antioquiá and then exported. In the areas to the south of Bolivar and Catatumbo the helicopters that come to collect the coca come from the military bases. Therefore you can conclude that they are not just aware of the drug-trafficking business, but are directly involved in it along with their paramilitary friends.

REAL SOLUTIONS TO THE DRUG PROBLEM IN COLOMBIA

The U.S. has never spoken clearly about Colombia's drug problem. They have never had a coherent policy about this problem. What we can say is that in certain regions they have dealt partially with the drug problem while pursuing their own non drug-related interests. In many situations they have used the issue to reach a particular objective, like in Nicaragua with the Iran-Contra affair. But also in the cases of Afghanistan, Burma, Bolivia, Laos and Thailand where they have actively supported drug-trafficking operations.

We believe that U.S. drug policies are repressive and bankrupt. We have different priorities than the U.S. government regarding the world—we believe that there must be democratic and participatory global policies instead of the unilateral policies of imposition that the U.S. is using. Their policy on drugs is based firstly on obstructing the production of cocaine and secondly on deterring the cocaine from arriving in the U.S. Both of these policies are repressive. U.S. attempts at a preventative cure to the problem are always half-hearted. They should try to implement a real policy against the domestic consumption of drugs because if there is more consumption, there is more production.

We don't know what they want with regards to drugs. Do they want to end drug production and consumption? Do they want to divert the drug problem away from the U.S.? We don't know and the world doesn't know either. Everyone remembers that there have been various cases when the U.S. has sided with the drug-traffickers to obtain certain results and objectives.

We believe that a solution to the problem in Colombia must be developed within the framework of a worldwide solution. An international agreement must be developed to resolve this problem and the whole international community must get involved. There must be effective and workable drug rehabilitation policies and steps taken to limit the profitability of the drug business. Modern society is more open to learn and improve in areas relating to health. If there is investment in both education policies and agrarian alternatives we may see a solution emerge. Remember that it is the lack of profits in other commodities which makes peasants plant coca.

Many people support the idea of decriminalization because the outlawing of drugs increases their profitability. All that has to follow, they argue, are policies of rehabilitation, education, prevention and the offering of alternatives to the poor countries where the coca is grown. Whether this is a viable solution to the crisis Colombia and other Latin American countries are suffering is a difficult question. What's certain is that any solution must be a multilateral one, involving the whole international community, because it cannot be achieved by one country alone.

THE PARAMILITARIES

It should be noted that while governments come and go, state institutions and their personnel, like the army, remain in place for years regardless of the government. In Colombia many institutions are historically linked to a policy of protection of the state and in Colombia "protection of the state" means the protection of privileges—protection of the political and economic benefits enjoyed by the elite. Even if we had a government that was opposed to this reality, state institutions like the army would continue in their role as protectors of privilege. So in one way the government cannot really control the army.

Thus the state, as well as the army itself, is used to protect privilege and every case of disagreement with or protest against this situation gets a response of repression, murder and persecution, as state policy. The Colombian state started the disappearances, the torture and the political assassinations; all of this is documented and it is an old practice. What is new is that the paramilitaries are now used to implement this repression and we can see an enormous identity of common interest between state policy and the paramilitary project.

The important thing about the paramilitaries is that they carry out operations to fulfill the objectives of the state—destroying the opposition—while allowing the state to deny responsibility. Basically the state is not involved because the paramilitaries do what the state wants to be done. Paramilitarism exists in Colombia not as a structure but as a modus operandi to carry out undercover operations on behalf of the state. The modus operandi is applied by both the army and the private death squads of Carlos Castaño (national paramilitary commander) and as a result people are afraid to speak out in Colombia and the government chooses to do nothing about it.

The common people in Colombia know that the massacres are committed by the paramilitaries with the help of the armed forces. People understand that the paramilitaries are killing people and that their only way is to slaughter unarmed people because their record in combat with the guerrillas, of guerrillas captured, of weapons recovered, etc. doesn't exist. Their record only talks about massacres and torture and that is all.

The ELN have undertaken massive and risky operations in many parts of Colombia but we have never acted with the deliberate intention to kill unarmed people. There have been casualties but it is never the same as with the paramilitaries. All they talk about is murder, disappearances, cleansing, massacres and all they do is attack civilians.

In all of the areas where we operate where there is also a paramilitary presence that we directly combat. They come to these areas and kill the people who don't agree with the government. They come with the clear intention of attacking people who are not part of the armed conflict. We help the population to organize and defend themselves because they have the legitimate right to take up arms to defend themselves.

The problem is that the massacres take place in areas where the Colombian army operate and have a strong presence. Massacres don't take place in areas that the guerrillas control—they are done in the areas where the armed forces, and to a lesser extent the police, can protect the perpetrators.

We know that the CIA has a long history of destabilizing countries and that in the past they have had links with extreme right-wing death squads throughout Latin America. We also know that the U.S. is not interested in allowing any county to search for its own destiny beyond what it perceives to be its best interests. And it is interesting that it is the very same people who work for Colombia's destiny and not in the U.S. interest who are targeted by the paramilitaries—people like trade unionists, human rights workers, investigative journalists and progressive teachers and academics.

In the case of Colombia there is a long history of U.S. interference. They have many military experts in Colombia and have invested heavily in intelligence infrastructure. Also the DEA has been posing an additional problem because it is so hard to tell whether they are against or in favor of the drug-traffickers and paramilitaries. We know that they have infiltrated many agents within the cartels but as with the CIA agents, sometimes the cover becomes so deep that they forget whose side they are on.

The main paramilitary and drug-trafficker in all of Colombia is Carlos Castaño, but nothing happens to him, nobody fights him. In addition, he is the only drug-trafficker who supports the supposedly "anti-narcotics" Plan Colombia.

Insofar as they are part of the establishment they are part of society because they participate in the exclusion mechanisms applied by the government—massacres, killings and persecutions of all government opponents. Even if they do not say so, they are from the government, they do what the government does—they exclude, persecute, harass and kill the people. All of this corresponds with state policy and even though they deny the links the paramilitaries certainly don't say they are against the government or the state.

THE NATIONAL CONVENTION

We have been talking with various sectors of the Colombian population for two years now—industrialists, political organizations and trade unions. We have also discussed the National Convention with intellectuals, academics, universities, state sector representatives, regional authorities, parliamentary bodies, students and church groups.

There is a lot of interest in the National Convention because it comes from the idea that the solution to the conflict must be a collective one. That we must unite our efforts to create a national consensus in favour of change. This can then be transformed into a political and social force capable of transforming society. What we must agree on is what sort of country we want. There are many people who agree with this so our proposal for a wide democratic form of participation involving all sectors of society has been well-received.

Above all we need international accompaniment that will serve to produce confidence and security in the process. Accompaniment will facilitate initiatives that allow all of society to move towards democracy, human rights and participation in the search for solutions. In this sense we believe that international participation is important. International delegates and their experiences can also help to strengthen the search for a democratic solution and the well being of the country.

The expectations of the ELN and other national forces is that the National Convention can help to create a consensus, a national identity, a country able to identify itself, a country that can say "these are the changes that Colombia needs." A transition toward a democratic society with social justice, well being, without impunity, without human rights violations, where people can move torward the search for different systems of government, where other social forces can participate in the exercise of government, not just the political parties, but the academic sectors, intellectuals, the cultural and art communities, the social organizations and the unions. A pluralist government, not just controlled by the unilateralists of politics, but with the participation of all sectors within society.

The economy Colombia has now can be called irresponsible. We believe that the economy must humanize not dehumanise the population. We want an economy interested in the well-being and promotion of human beings, the respect of their dignity. Only a human economy can make a viable democratic society; the contrary means conflict. This is what we want from the National Convention; a consensus creation, a new economy and an identification of the initial methods and bases from which a transitional society is going to be constructed.

STATE TERROR IN COLOMBIA

LUIS GUILLERMO PÉREZ CASAS AND
THE LAWYERS COLLECTIVE CORPORATION

The Collective Corporation is an NGO human-rights organization that has been together 21 years working to defend victims of human-rights violations. We struggle against the silence, forgetting, impunity and fear. Our goal is to contribute to forging a consciousness of civil resistance against the oppression and exclusion the Colombian people have faced for such a long time.

We are associated with all the human-rights organizations in Colombia and we also work with the Movement for Peace in Colombia.

The assassinations committed by the paramilitaries in Colombia are close to 78 percent of all the crimes against humanity committed in the country, either through selective judicial executions or by way of massacres. It has not been possible to establish statistics in the southern state of Putumayo because of the situation of massive violations of human rights that has arisen there in the last few years. There have been excessive, massive attacks against the population of Putumayo. At the end of 1999 alone, in the city of Puerto Asis, 150-200 people were massacred in one week alone. Actually, selective judicial executions persist in Putumayo at the same time that massacres take place in the rural areas. This explains why the international community is so concerned about what goes on in this zone.

Extrajudicial executions take place every day in Colombia. Political violence in Colombia kills 14 people every day. One person disappears every day for political reasons. These are just the ones that human-rights organizations can record. Of them, 25 percent die in confrontations between the state and the guerrillas. The rest are victims of the paramilitaries. There are massacres every day.

These are just the acts we can record, we are very far from able to record the barbarity that is going on throughout the cities and countryside.

The paramilitaries are part of a counter-insurgency strategy that the armed forces have used for many decades. Today they are fundamentally strengthened by the same forces that have controlled the Colombian state. The paramilitaries are backed by the landowners' associations that finance them.

The paramilitaries appear to be a strategy of the armed forces to fight the insurgency. But it goes way beyond that.

It's not just about defeating the guerrillas but rather about establishing a system of domination and exclusion that will permit transnational investment projects in many zones of the country, along with advancing the politics of neoliberalism.

That's why the paramilitary strategy is conducive to selective elimination of many trade union leaders, for example those who oppose the privatization of public enterprises or reduction of labor guarantees for workers. They are frequently victims of the paramilitary attacks. In 2001 alone we have documented that at least 117 trade unionists were assassinated.

The ranks of the paramilitaries are composed of many officers and former officers of the armed forces, as well as police who were retired precisely for having committed human-rights violations. The paramilitaries have a certain recruiting program that forces the peasants and the populace of certain cities to join them. They tell the people, "Either you work with us or you leave or you die." The people end up working with them because they know the paramilitaries have the backing of the authorities, the military and police, and it is a way to stay alive. The peasants are the paramilitaries' fundamental victims.

The strength of the guerrilla movement is in the countryside. At first, the paramilitaries would pick as their victims peasant leaders or those they thought might sympathize with the rebel forces.

Now the paramilitaries have developed a strategy of mass terror. In certain regions where the guerrillas had a presence, they indiscriminately massacred 30, 40, 60, or 70 people, forcing displacement of the remaining peasants. The tactic is to terrorize the peasants into rejecting the rebels for fear that the rebels cannot protect them against the paramilitary massacres. This is how the paramilitaries seek to force the people to submit to their strategy.

Besides union leaders and peasants, other victims of the paramilitaries include university professors who are for human rights or peace or democracy, popular leaders, the Indigenous and Afro-Colombians. Anyone who defends human rights, anyone who resists is a potential victim.

There are massacres every week.

Recently, in late 2001 in the northern coast of the country, more than 40 fishers were killed in Nueva Venecia. They supposedly had collaborated with the National Liberation Army (ELN). It is clear that in this region, the paramilitaries act in complete collusion with the government military and police authorities.

Another recent example was the massacres carried out in Cauca, where for the first time a governor of Indigenous background had been elected. The paramilitaries wanted to destroy this social movement. They have been carrying out massacres week after week in the area of Santander and municipalities around Popoyán.

High-ranking officials in the military have been responsible for carrying out these paramilitary massacres. For example, officers and members of the Second Brigade worked with paramilitaries led by Carlos Castaño in the Mapiripán massacre in 1997. U.S. Green Berets also played a role in that massacre.

The U.S. Green Berets had been there in the months before the massacre, training members of the Second Brigade. This is an example of the presence of U.S. military and advisory troops contributing to the violation of human rights in our country.

The Colombian government maintains that it is caught between two extremes. The reality is very different.

We don't know of a single debate in the Council of the Republic against paramilitarism or of a case when the attorney general has called on the people to mobilize against the massacres. On the contrary, all we see is complicity. Paramilitarism is viewed as normal.

We demand that if the government wants to show a real will to peace, it dismantle the paramilitary groups and stop the military and police atrocities across the country.

We receive threats against us all the time. We know that every day we are endangering our lives. The way to face these threats is by first overcoming fear. We feel fear when we go out into the streets and know we can be murdered or if we travel to the countryside and we have to face the military or the paramilitaries. You imagine that at any time you can be a victim of those assassinations. But we have to face fear and overcome it. We keep in mind a saying, "It's not that we don't feel fear; as human beings obviously we are affected by fear. But the point is not to be paralyzed or defeated or intimidated by fear." And that's the way to create bravery and civil resistance against this barbarity that is rooted in our country.

In the second place, we count on international solidarity and pressure. If it weren't for that solidarity we would all be killed by now. In the last three years, 52 human-rights workers have been killed and many others detained. I am talking about those who still are detained, disappeared, and possibly killed but we have not found their bodies yet.

In many places, when the rebels have attacked government military camps, we have heard charges of how the government troops helped paramilitaries, rescuing the paramilitary leaders by helicopter. We have received many accounts of how the military protects the paramilitaries from Putumayo, Bolívar, Córdoba and other provinces. People describe how the military forces threaten the peasant population, telling them that the terror will come later for their relatives.

In Colombia, all the labor unions are united in the common struggle of fighting against Plan Colombia and its effects. The main unions have said they are not going to accept a single dollar for personal protection approved by the U.S. for Colombia.

Supposedly $4 million of Plan Colombia is to protect human-rights workers.

We have said we will not accept one single dollar that will produce more human-rights violations. We reject those resources.

The military strategy is also destroying the possibility of a negotiated solution to the armed conflict. In 2001, the ELN proposed holding a National

Convention in the south of Bolívar province. This region is very important in terms of natural resources as well as geographic location near the Colombian coast. There are mineral and gold resources, oil resources and one of the country's most important refineries. Groups tied to the paramilitaries mobilized politically against the proposal. The military strategy, carried out where the ELN has a particular influence, has been to look beyond the massacres to develop a social construction. The paramilitaries used the peasants to mobilize against the zone of encounter, creating their own "non-governmental organizations" that are in reality a front for the state and the media. There is a paramilitary pistol to these peasants' heads.

Finally, we call for uniting against Plan Colombia. The plan has been sold to the world and especially to the people of the United States as a plan to fight against drugs. But that is not true. Fundamentally, it is a plan established by Pres. Bill Clinton against the insurgency and to establish a free-trade zone in the entire continent. Its real aim is to destroy armed insurrections like the FARC-EP, which is why it started in the south of the country. The paramilitaries have said as much openly and they admit that they finance themselves with the profits of the narco-trafficking.

That's why we call on all in the United States to collaborate with us against the application of Plan Colombia in our country. We need your solidarity to bring hope and save lives. We have to look for peace, but a peace that reconciles Colombians.

PEACE WITH SOCIAL JUSTICE

THE FARC-EP's POLITICAL PROPOSAL

RAÚL REYES

Raúl Reyes led the Revolutionary Armed Forces of Colombia-People's Army (FARC-EP) delegation during the talks with the Colombian government from 1999-2002. He is a member of the FARC-EP Secretariat. The article below was submitted in August 2002 especially for publication in this book.

Mr. Andrés Pastrana carried out his election campaign promising peace for Colombians during his government. For this purpose, he committed himself to lead the talks personally with the FARC-EP guerrilla movement, and offered sufficient guarantees to begin the talks amid the war. The FARC-EP made public requests in advance of whoever ended up being elected president. We requested that troops, along with certain elements of the public forces, be withdrawn from five municipalities in order to set up talks amid the war—as did the governments of César Gaviria, Ernesto Samper—and Pastrana did after his election.

Likewise, the FARC-EP asked for the dismantling of the Colombian state's paramilitary groups, with the aim of decriminalizing social protest and pressuring the government to assume responsibility for wiping out the paramilitary bands or groups of mercenary soldiers or police working in the service of the governing caste. Mr. Pastrana, despite the promise he made to the leader of the FARC-EP to use the instruments of the state against the government paramilitary policy, in the end did not do so. On the contrary, the criminality of the army and police, in the name of their death squads known as paramilitaries, increased.

Mr. Pastrana's not carrying out this request of the FARC-EP weakened the process of talks until he himself decided to cancel them for good, frustrating once again those who voted for the pursuit of peace through the route of talks and political negotiation.

Every moment of Colombia's political life confirms for the immense majority of Colombians the imperative necessity of looking for political ways out of the grave situation of political, social and economic confrontation that much more than 30 million of our compatriots suffer, especially the peasants and the humble people from the towns and cities affected by low salaries; growing unemployment in the towns, cities and countryside; high taxes; serious deficiencies in education; health services; housing; potable water; electricity and roads. The fact that all these needs are not solved by the state makes the possibility of reconciling the Colombian family very remote in the short term, because that is the peace with social justice that is desired by the majority. The two dialog processes, with the Betancourt government from 1982-86 and with the Pastrana government from 1997-2002, with the FARC-EP leave absolutely clear the viability of insisting on a political solution to the political, economic, social and armed conflict for the realization of a definitive and lasting peace.

In the course of the process of talks begun with the outgoing Pastrana government, the government and the FARC-EP approved the Common Agenda for a New Colombia. This agenda covered 12 themes in three major groups: first, the social and economic structure of the country; second, human rights and international humanitarian law and international relations; and third, democracy and the political structure of the state. The FARC-EP, with the aim of giving some continuity and development to this agenda, proposed to the new government to withdraw its troops and other elements of the public forces from the departments of Caquetá and Putumayo in southern Colombia. This proposal was made to the government of Mr. Uribe because the FARC-EP's political proposal has been, is, and will continue to be the search for peace with social justice.

ÁLVARO URIBE VÉLEZ'S ELECTION

Mr. Uribe carried out his election campaign calling for more repressive measures against the guerrilla insurgency. He arrived at the presidency with this platform, aided by the most reactionary oligarchy of the Liberal and Conservative parties, along with the big landowners and landlords, the paramilitaries, the drug traffickers, the big ranchers, industrialists and merchants, the country's main economic groups with their media, the upper ranks of the armed forces and police and sectors of the Colombian Catholic church.

The new government headed by Uribe has prioritized total war without talks, convinced that he has enough capacity to wipe out or defeat Colombia's revolutionary, popular and guerrilla movement by military means through the use of the state's war powers. The new tactic of the caste in power, representing the oligarchy, is total war without talks in order to impose its policies of greater exploitation, poverty, misery and repression by the state and its government against the working people and their popular mass organizations.

This is a government that will bring the country toward the greatest political, economic, social and armed confrontation in its history, with unpredictable outcomes.

IMPACT OF PLAN COLOMBIA ON ALL OF LATIN AMERICA

The misnamed Plan Colombia is a strategy of the United States state and government to expand even more its geopolitical presence in the southern region of the continent, with its well-known policy of intervening in the internal affairs of dependent countries like Colombia. In this case, U.S. policy has in its favor the unconditional support of Uribe's government and the caste that is currently governing the country; they are all waiting for millions of dollars in aid from the United States to finance their strategy of total war and to divert substantial resources from this aid to their own accounts.

In other words, one can say that the U.S. by virtue of Plan Colombia will exercise greater control and domination over the Amazon countries with the clear objective of appropriating the immense natural resources of this region. The Colombian ruling class, in aiding the policies of Mr. Bush, will also receive their dollars, applause and slaps on the back for their hypocritical surrendering of the sovereignty and sacredness of a whole people.

That is the way it is. The carrying out and execution of Plan Colombia is and will be a dangerous factor in disturbing and destabilizing the internal life of the people of Latin America.

The political climate created in Washington by the so-called "war on terrorism" managed to confuse the Colombian governing political class even more. They mistakenly thought that the problems of hunger, unemployment, endemic and epidemic diseases, of the great deficiencies in education, housing, high taxes and the lack of public services, corruption, impunity, and the very physical existence of the revolutionary and popular organizations led by the guerrilla movement would disappear for fear of being included in the hated terrorist lists of the governments of the capitalist system. The governments deliberately forgot that they are the ones representing the states, the ones responsible for guaranteeing the defense of the human rights of their people. When they cease to carry out that obligation, they are facilitating the popular mass struggles, including the armed uprisings of the people, for their demands.

The Colombian people, with their guerrilla organization the FARC-EP, will continue forward in their political struggle until they achieve peace with social justice, with definitive independence and a dignified life for the dispossessed. Nothing and no one will stand in their way. The FARC-EP learned from the struggles of other peoples, as well as their own struggles, that nothing can be expected from the class enemy in power but death, destruction, lies and slander.

MESSAGE TO PROGRESSIVE AND ANTI-WAR FORCES IN THE U.S.

I would like to say to the progressive friends, the popular sectors, and to the organizations that struggle against war in the United States that you have in the FARC-EP a natural ally in your objectives of political harmony on the basis of free self-determination of peoples.

The women and men, the banners, the programs, and the political convictions of the FARC-EP are at the service of the objectives of peace with social justice for all Colombians. The FARC-EP is obliged by the state and its governments to use the arms of the people to defend themselves and to conquer in the political struggle the privileges of a definite and lasting peace.

You should know that your struggles encourage us favorably to continue the promise we have with our people to struggle until the conquest of political power, to govern and to begin the construction of the new society, without exploiters or exploited.

COLOMBIA ANSWERS

Below is a statement by 60 Colombian social, human rights, non-govern-mental and peace organizations declared in June 2000.

We declare our decision to support the need for international aid to contribute to resolving the armed conflict by way of political negotiation, to democratize Colombian society and the economy, to develop real and integral solutions to drug trafficking, to design a new and agreed model of development, to strengthen new democratic institutions and to rebuild the nation.

We reject Plan Colombia because it uses an authoritarian concept of national security exclusively based on a strategy against narcotics. It will lead to the escalation of the social and armed conflict. It fails to provide real solutions to drug trafficking. It endangers the peace process. It attacks the Indigenous populations by destroying their culture and their way of life and it will seriously affect the Amazon eco-system. It will worsen the humanitarian and human-rights crisis, increase forced displacement and aggravate the social and political crisis.

We demand that the Colombian government and request that the international community rethink the underlying concept of national security in Plan Colombia, conceiving national security as that which enhances human, civil, political, economic, social and cultural rights, that provides a sense of belonging to citizens. These are the foundations of national sovereignty.

We request that the international community consider its support to Colombia using universal humanitarian principles: the right to life, human rights, social development and the protection of the environment. These have all been eroded by the Colombian conflict.

We propose a real process of consensus-building between the various social actors in Colombian society and the international community, in which civil society is a significant interlocutor and which enables us to find solutions to our conflicts and to build a stable and lasting peace.

As social organizations and as members of Colombian society we are willing to initiate a process of dialog in order to discuss the analysis, design strategies, define methods of implementation and monitoring of a plan with these objectives.

Sincerely,

Asamblea Permanente de la Sociedad Civil por la Paz; Asamblea Nacional de Jóvenes por la Paz; Red de Iniciativas contra la Guerra y por la Paz-

REDEPAZ; Organización Nacional Indígena de Colombia; Plataforma Colombiana de Derechos Humanos, Democracia y Desarrollo; Red Nacional de Mujeres Regional Bogotá; Ruta Pacífica de las Mujeres; Mandato Ciudadano por la Paz, la Vida y la Libertad; Partido Comunista Colombiano; Asociación Nacional de Usuarios Campesinos-ANUC-UR; Central Unitaria de Trabajadores CUT; Federación Sindical Agraria FENSUAGRO; Frente Social y Político Amplio; Red de Universidades por la Paz y la Convivencia; Instituto de Estudios para la Paz INDEPAZ; Asociación Nacional de Estudiantes Universitarios ACEU; Asociación Nacional de Estudiantes de Secundaria ANDES; Unión Sindical Obrera; Asamblea por la Paz de la USO; Asociación de Trabajo Interdisciplinario-ATI; Colectivo de Abogados José Alvear Restrepo; Corporación para el desarrollo Social Alternativo MINGA; Comité de Solidaridad con los Presos Políticos; Corporación Región; Benposta, Nación de Muchach@s; Centro de Investigación y Educación Popular CINEP; Comisión Colombiana de Juristas; Fundación Cultura Democrática; Juventud Comunista JUCO; Casa de La Mujer; Consultoría de Derechos Humanos y el Desplazamiento; ASMEDAS; Grupo de Apoyo a Organizaciones de Desplazados; Instituto Latinoamericano de Servicios Legales Alternativas, ILSA; Proceso de Comunidades Negras; Vamos Mujer; Viva La Ciudadanía; Asociación Nacional de Ayuda Solidaria ANDAS; Corporación de Promoción Popular; Corporación de Luchadores de la Paz y la Democracia; FUNCOP; CENSAD AGUA VIVA; Coordinación Nacional de Desplazados; Corriente de Renovación Socialista; Comisión Intergregacional JUSTICIA Y PAZ; Unión de Ciudadanas de Colombia; FAUSALUD; Comité Local de Derechos Humanos; Corporación Nuevo Arco Iris; Corporación Centro de Promoción y Cultura; Red Nacional de Salud; Unión Patriótica; Fundación para la Educación y el Desarrollo FEDES; FIDHAP; Movimiento Cimarrón; Confederación General de Trabajadores Democráticas CGTD; ULTRADEC; Colectivo de Abogados Guillermo Marín; Corporación Madre Tierra; Fundación Ecológica Bacatá

COLOMBIA AT THE CROSSROADS

COORDINATING GROUP OF COCA AND POPPY GROWERS (COCCA)

Excerpted from a statement presented at the Transatlantic Social Forum, Madrid, May 13-18, 2002.

INTERVENTION

There are interconnected, complementary plans to convert the areas and territories of Latin American into markets for products coming from the United States. These include Plan Colombia, now called the Andean Regional Initiative, directed straight from the U.S. and the Free Trade Area of the Americas. They come at the cost of destroying national productive apparatuses, quashing democratic structural change in our countries, and eliminating the popular and revolutionary forces that oppose this intervention.

In the face of this, the peoples of Latin America must organize, strengthen their ties for Latin American unity and step up resistance against the new imperialist deployment.

As the worldwide ultra-right positions itself, it in turn becomes a reference point for the ultra-right in Colombia. Destructive interventionist winds—for example, the campaign to portray popular and revolutionary forces as international political criminals—are blowing harder. This is all possible because of the Colombian oligarchy's lackey attitude.

These new conditions give rise to the arrogance that drives the right to overturn the conquests and rights of workers and the people, to impose greater repression against organizations and social protest, to move toward breaking off talks with the insurgent movement. It is all to try to maintain the decrepit scheme of political, economic and social domination whose clearest expression is the neoliberal model.

We need to be conscious that breaking off talks would not only escalate the war and intensify the forced displacements and other crimes against humanity. It would also exacerbate state terrorism—the fascist project of the ultra-right tied with paramilitarism and with transnational groups linked to both war and megaprojects exploiting national resources and labor.

While it is true that the ultra-right is trying to consolidate, it is no less true that there are democratic and revolutionary sectors in Colombia that are disposed to challenge this possibility. The document of the Committee of Notables from the broken-down peace process between the FARC-EP and the government makes serious strides along the path of dialog.

The Colombian political regime is sharpening its authoritarian, intolerant character, inclined toward force as the only way out of Colombia's problems. It is increasingly concentrating power in the executive branch while persecuting and blackmailing the opposition and marginalizing or isolating those who do not go along with the state's policies. In this way the regime is trying to hide the grave social crisis facing the vast majority of Colombians. This crisis includes high unemployment rates, abysmally low worker wages, the farming crisis, reversion to big landholdings through violent expropriation of land, further marginalization of the peasants, precarious conditions of life and work and growing poverty.

Law 684 on Security and National Defense (temporarily struck down by a decision of the constitutional court), corresponding to an updated version of the sadly celebrated security statute, restricts individual guarantees, gives extraordinary powers to the military command—questioned internationally for complicity with paramilitarism—and tries to legitimize this paramilitarism instead of fighting it as a brutal expression of state terrorism. An "antiterrorist" statute like this one proposed by the government is a weapon against the people and against political liberties.

THE POLITICAL WAY OUT

The political way out of the internal conflict and crisis in Colombia requires substantial changes in the political regime. These changes would permit construction of an economic model with social justice that redistributes wealth and generates employment with respect for workers' rights, and that offers healthcare, education and recreation, widening the right to social security for the peasants. A new economic model cannot pass over the agrarian question—understood as true and lasting agrarian reform that benefits salaried peasants and small and medium property holders as a function of the productive development of the economy— or the social and cultural promotion of the working people.

Big capital relies on the struggles of diverse sectors of the population remaining fractured and dispersed. Unity and popular convergence are therefore necessary, tying together social and political currents, expressions, forces that are prepared to play a role in the short, medium and long term. With this unity, the fundamental axes of action to solve the political, social and armed conflicts are: restoring national sovereignty, democratizing institutions and constructing an alternative democratic economic model.

CONCLUSIONS

• The current version of the Colombian political, social and armed conflict has lasted for over five decades, based fundamentally on failure to resolve the agrarian question. The small-scale landholding peasantry has been violently expropriated throughout the years by the landlord and big landholding class linked to the traditional oligarchic elites in power. Enormous peasant masses have been brought through forced displacement to the urban centers as well as into the jungles, opening the agricultural frontier in new colonization zones in the east, west, the Magdalena Medio region and considerably to the south of the country. Another sector of the politicized peasantry, organized on the basis of mass peasant self-defense against the aggressions of the state, became the guerrillas of today.

• Social conflict, regional inequalities, marginalization and exclusion will sharpen in the Colombian cities and rural territories with the implementation of the neoliberal economic model that prioritizes imports, interest payments, speculation and absentee landlordism. The import of 8 million tons of food a year makes the peasant economy unviable. As recent history shows, the development of neoliberal capitalism in the countryside does not alleviate the situation of the peasantry; bringing capitalist methods is accompanied by the massive dislodging of the peasants from the land.

• We are also experiencing a period of bankruptcies of small and medium private businesses, including large state enterprises that are beginning to be privatized by the multinationals at the expense of the public ones. Accumulation is concentrated much more. Limited systems of social redistribution are collapsing while the losses of the market model are being assumed collectively at the heart of the society.

• The bankruptcy of the peasant economy leads the peasantry to search for alternatives for subsistence in the new regions of colonization, where the level of state social investment is almost nil (a product of the demands of the financial usurers of global capital). These are inhospitable regions in the Amazon and Colombian Orinoquía regions, the Pacific jungles, the eastern mountain range, and Magdalena Medio, with soils not suited for agriculture and totally cut off from the country, with precarious systems of health, education, housing and public services. In this openly anti-peasant and antisocial context, the only viable alternative for the peasants has been growing coca and poppy.

• Meanwhile, the new heights reached by the Colombian guerrilla movement's political and military campaign—explained in large part by the country's worsening economic and sociopolitical conditions and the consequent polarization of society—have put the economic and political interests of the United States in the region at risk. In order to reposition its strategic interests, the U.S. is planning a new regional intervention under the sophism of a "war on drugs." They are designing Plan Colombia, completely narcotizing the Colombian social conflict and ignoring its structural foundations.

• The vicious cycle of fumigations is presented as the "war on drugs" (yet for each acre sprayed, three more are planted), while it sponsors militarization and allows the strategies of dirty war to be used against the peasantry and the social organizations, as is the case with paramilitarism.

• With this measure and with the implementation of Plan Colombia, a proposed model for development is being strengthened. It is based on a reverse agrarian reform and favoring megaprojects in infrastructure, extractive economy and agroindustry. To consolidate this exclusionary model of development, territories are secured, and this entails violent expropriation of land and systematic commission of sick crimes under the shelter of institutionalized impunity.

• The total militarizing and paramilitarizing of public life (the security law and statute) allows for social protest to be penalized and social organizations and movements that stand for equality and emancipation to be persecuted.

• Peasant coca crops (less than three hectares per family) are an alternative for survival and resistance in the colonization zones into which the peasants have been forcibly displaced, where the only presence of the state has historically been repressive and military. These crops are conjunctural. Making a problem out of them does not in any way explain the conflict, which clearly has structural causes. The "war on drugs," with which the United States justifies its intervention in the region, is only a mask that hides the multinationals' and the Colombian establishment's real interest in the region: extracting profit.

To achieve structural changes in the country it is necessary to move forward in social organization and popular unity, elevating the Colombian people's political consciousness so they can see beyond the immediate and economist struggles. Otherwise, left at that level, they are subject to manipulation by the system's ideological apparatus, principally the big media, that generate new forms of subordination and alienation of the masses.

Two Women Commandantes

Women in the FARC-EP

Arturo Alape

They are guerrilla commanders.

Rubiela's face reveals deep traces of the Indigenous. She is dynamic, very strong. Sonia looks fragile, and her face is hard and stern. She immediately expressed distance, distrust. Later on she became less complicated and loosened her words, at the end she smiled.

We talked of the critical moments of life's decisions—the ones that define everything and turn accumulated life experience around. I asked them why they joined the guerrilla.

Rubiela had never seen the guerrilla. She explained: "One day I saw a group of guerrilleros; they told us not to be afraid, that they were just regular people, very simple people. What attracted me the most about them was that they knew really good revolutionary songs. So I said: 'I'm going to join the guerrilla.' That was about 14 years ago. I'm from Caquetá. My parents are from Palmira, Valle."

Sonia had heard of or seen the guerrilla on TV, they awoke a certain interest in her. She lost herself in her memories: "I went to meetings they had, and then I studied why there was a need to join the guerrilla, because of how women are exploited in Colombia, the need for rights we women have coming to us."

Rubiela joined the guerrilla when she was 17 years old. She confessed that at that age she had never been out of her house. She was quiet, "without much free-dom.. in the guerrilla you start to change your behavior, so it's not hard to adapt. ... At the beginning you miss your family, you think about it constantly. Then you start to create the idea that no one has made you come and you made your own decision and so you have to adapt. It's not a trick, no one tricked you in to com-ing, it was you, so you come and keep up the struggle."

For Sonia, joining the guerrilla was an abrupt change. "It's very different as a civilian when you are free: you go wherever you want, you come back when you want, you ask your parents for permission. Here everything is different, even going to the bathroom or any other place—you have to ask permission for every-thing. There is an internal order that must be followed and it's for everyone, you start to butt heads, you know? Because you can't go wherever you want when you want and come back when you want—no, you have limited time and you have to follow the rules. From the time you join they explain these norms to you and if you promise to follow the norms and statutes that guide it, then you have to do it."

Sonia explained that through studying and the knowledge she is acquiring in the guerrilla, "consciousness is increased and you start to have your own confidence in the fact that you can follow the rules. But it always takes time. Another thing: You also have to leave your family, everything you have, so it's hard to get used to that. After that you acquire certain knowledge, so family is secondary in the guerrilla, you know what I mean? Family becomes secondary and the movement is primary."

I asked her to explain this radical change with the family. She said: "Because here you have to carry out your tasks, first you have to fulfill the missions they assign to you, then come your family commitments. You can't say, every now and then, well, give me a pass so I can go home and see my mamá, you can't. When conditions allow or require it, you request permission, and if you have earned it for good behavior, then they grant it."

Sonia has been in the guerrilla for 11 years, "going on 12," she clarified.

I asked: "Sonia, as a woman what was your experience when you joined the guerrilla, in the midst of a world that, I suppose, is also very machista, with so many guerrilleros. What change is there?"

"It's just that you encounter something different. What you say about machismo doesn't exist here in the guerrilla, we are all equal, men and women have the same rights and we all treat each other like brothers and sisters in arms."

She explained machismo in civilian life: "You have to take orders and do what they tell you to do, if you get married then you have to stay home, the man runs the house. You understand? Here no. Here we all work for everyone."

I insisted that in the guerrilla they also take orders. She replied, "We do take some orders, but for our ideas and the cause we have committed ourselves to, for the fight we are waging."

Do you feel like a fulfilled woman in the guerrilla? "I do because you have what you need, they give you what you want, you have your rights. If you want to have a compañero, you get one, then in that sense you feel fulfilled. Plus, you don't have to take orders from your compañero. In the guerrilla love is secondary, the struggle is primary; first you have your orders to obey, the material you have to study and studying itself, to train yourself and be able to aspire to something."

So you think that the woman in the guerrilla is a very free being? Rubiela answered: "She is free in the sense that Sonia explained—if we get a compañero we are not going to be subject to him or to what he wants, like maybe he'd want us to wash his clothes. We might do it, but only if we want, it's not an obligation."

In the guerrilla Sonia is "free to study, to educate myself in the field that I want, politically and militarily. We are free within the disciplinary structure of the guerrilla."

Sonia explained that she is educated in the politico-military area.

When you are the leader what is your role? What do you do as a leader? "Well, when you are the leader you are an official of service. You have to organize anything that has to do with the unit's daily routine. And if you are a squadron commander, you are in charge of the squadron. What do the people need? What has to be done?"

Would you like to be a woman who climbs the military ladder? Rubiela explained: "When I joined there was still machismo; they didn't want a woman to lead them because they were men. Things are changing now for women."

I asked Sonia: What has your experience been? What have you learned? What do you like about the guerrilla outside of all the seriousness? They both laughed. Sonia released some of the tension she felt at first: "In the guerrilla it's important for us to learn. There is an article in the regulations that says that guerrilleros need to be well-rounded people. Well-rounded means knowing a little about everything, about all the arts needed in the guerrilla. So I have been in the infirmary and did well, I had a class in explosives and have set three or four mines, not more, and the same goes for other activities. I like the military part of it too, and I have participated in actions and done well."

Sonia is part of the high command of Front 14. I asked her about her concept of a leader. She went into detail: "The concept of commanding troops has to include authority, the gift of leadership so you can guide your people. You have to know how to lead—you have to know who you are leading, and how to lead them, because the orders you give them must be well-received, the ones who are going to obey them must receive them with satisfaction. You have to know the troop's mood. We don't all have the same mood, or the same character, some like to be led one way, some like to be spoken to harshly. A commander must prepare herself, she has to keep herself updated on all areas—on the national political situation, and the international situation, so she can orient the troop. Because a commander who has no knowledge then has no authority for leadership, nor can she control her troop."

I asked Sonia to explain how she manages this leadership authority during military action. An impassioned spark flickered in her eyes: "On the front lines with your unit, making a front, organizing it—deciding what flank you have to cover, how you should organize your troops, how you are going to advance on the enemy, how you are going to take a particular post, or that particular flank you have to cover. This is how you get this leadership authority. If a commander sends her troops into action and she stays behind, then she loses leadership authority and has nothing to yell at the troops about."

Sonia talked about her leadership experience during the exercises in El Billar:

"We didn't have any military intelligence, we only knew the enemy was in a certain place. I started to move my people, to circle the area the army was in. Our troops advanced until we surrounded the army. There were about 250, in the end we didn't even know. We annihilated the Third Mobile Unit. Very few got away. It was a day- and night-time action, it lasted 17 hours. It started at 4 p.m. and ended the next day around 2 p.m."

Rubiela talked about the fear you face in a military action. "You always feel fear, because they didn't make pants for fear. But you are not alone, you are with your other compañeros and they encourage you a lot."

I asked Sonia about death. "I don't really have an opinion," she said. "It would be hard to have an opinion about this because you don't know how death is going to take you." And when death comes to someone else because of you, what do you think? "I think it would be a terrible failure if a compañero died because of someone else." And what if it's the enemy? "If we lower our guard, they'll kill us, you know what I mean? If they aren't careful, we kill them. Even though we know we are fighting against our own people. That's why we prefer them to surrender instead of killing them."

In the end both confided what they would do if the war is resolved peacefully. Rubiela would like to continue her military career. Sonia would like to return to civilian life and become a politician to govern a municipality or a department.

They hug as they leave, then turn around and are lost in their lean-tos.

III.
U.S.
INTERVENTION:
THE
REGIONAL
PICTURE

CULTURE, SOVEREIGNTY AND INTERVENTION

FIDEL CASTRO RUZ

Excerpts from a speech given on June 11, 1999 by Commander in Chief Fidel Castro Ruz, First Secretary of the Communist Party of Cuba Central Committee and President of the Council of State and Council of Ministers, at the closing ceremony of the first International Congress on Culture and Development.

Esteemed ministers and culture leaders in the countries of Latin America or Ibero-America,

Distinguished guests, dear delegates to the first International Congress on Culture and Development,

We feel that united we would be worth the sum of many and very rich cultures. In this token, when we think about our Americas, as (José) Martí called it, the Americas down from the Río Bravo (Río Grande), although it should have been from the Canadian border because that portion also belonged to our Americas until an insatiable expansionist neighbor seized the whole territory of the west of what is today the United States of America. It is that integration which I have in mind, but including the Caribbean nations.

The sum of all our cultures would make up one enormous culture and be a multiplication of our cultures. Integration should not adversely affect, but rather enrich, the culture of every one of our countries.

In this context, when we talk about unity we still do so in a narrow framework. But I like to go beyond that. I believe in the unity of all the countries in the world, in the unity of all the peoples in the world and in a free unity, a truly free unity. I am not thinking of a fusion but of a free unity of all cultures in a truly just world, in a truly democratic world, in a world where it would be possible to apply the kind of globalization that Karl Marx talked about in his time.

I will rely on concrete facts and I am not talking theory or philosophy but things that we can all see, what even a near-sighted person can see: namely, that there can be no culture without sovereignty. (Minister of Culture) Abel (Prieto) outlined how a handful of brilliant personalities succeeded in saving the national culture from American neocolonialism and hegemonism in Cuba.

Another country has more merit than we do: Puerto Rico, which has been a Yankee colony for 100 years now but where neither their language nor their culture have been destroyed. It is admirable!

Of course, imperialism has today much more powerful means to destroy cultures, to impose other cultures and homogenize cultures—much more powerful means. Perhaps, at this moment, it can be more influential in 10 years than it was in the past 100 years. However, the example I gave you sheds some light on the peoples' capacity to resist and on the value of culture. The Puerto Ricans were deprived of all sovereignty, and despite everything, they have resisted.

Although it is possible to find examples to show that there can be culture, or that a certain degree of culture can be preserved without sovereignty, what is inconceivable or unimaginable in today's world and toward the future is the existence of sovereignty without culture.

We are already looking at an imperialism that is using all its might and force to sweep away anything that stands in its way and culture is one of those things very much in its way. They are the owners of the vast majority of the communication networks, that is, 60 percent of the world communication networks and of the most powerful and unrivaled television channels. And they have the almost absolute monopoly of the films shown in the world.

When we speak about culture we do not forget the political culture. It is one of the sectors whose development is badly needed and which is very much lacking in the world. It is impossible to believe or imagine that an average person in the United States has a higher political culture than a Cuban or a European. I admit that Europeans have a higher political culture than Americans but, in general, Europeans do not have a higher political culture than Cubans. That is for sure. You could even have a contest to compare the European average political knowledge and the Cuban average, a contest between people who unfortunately live alienated by millions of things and people who do not live like that.

In our Latin American countries, sometimes necessity and poverty help in the development of a political culture higher than in those very rich countries that do not suffer the calamities that we do. Of course, awful things happen in Latin America that have not been seen for quite some time in Europe where the unemployed enjoy benefits that, according to some, allow them to vacation abroad for 15 days and more a year.

Where none of that exists, people suffer much more. We have more fertile ground to become politically cultured. In our case, we also have the experience accumulated by the country in very difficult battles against imperial aggression and in very great difficulties. And difficulties make good fighters.

I am explaining all this because they can help understand these phenomena of sovereignty, this battle. Because there are so many lies, so much demagogy, so much confusion and so many methods devised to disseminate them that an enormous effort should be made at constant clarification. If some things are not understood, the rest cannot be understood.

LATIN AMERICAN AND CARIBBEAN UNITY

When we are all integrated in a Latin America and Caribbean union, our concept of sovereignty will be different. We will have to give up a lot of those principles to obey the laws and the administration or the decisions of a supranational state. Moreover, a Marxist can never be a narrow national chauvinist. Marxists can be patriots, which is different, and love their homeland, which is different, too.

A long time before today, there were men who dreamed, like [Simón] Bolívar almost 200 years ago, of a united Latin America. There were men like Martí who, more than 100 years ago dreamed of a united Latin America. At that time, when Bolívar proclaimed his dreams, Latin America was not made up of free independent countries, not yet.

In fact, the first independent country following the United States of America was Haiti, a country that provided material assistance to Bolívar in his struggle for Latin American independence and which also contributed, with its ideas and exchanges, to consolidate Bolívar's consciousness about the impossibility to defer the slaves' emancipation which was not attained after the first triumphant independence movement in Venezuela.

As you know, in the United States there was a struggle for independence and a declaration of principles in 1776. But it was only after almost 90 years and a bloody war that the emancipation of slaves was formally declared. Of course, the slaves' situation was often worse off afterwards since they were no longer any master's property, they were no longer their owners' assets so, if they died, the former masters did not lose a dime.

In Latin America, slavery as a system disappeared at a much earlier stage than in the United States. There were men who dreamed about those things. There were men who, for the creation of a great, united and strong republic dreamed that each of our current countries, without renouncing their national sentiments, would lay down their prerogatives or aspirations to the separate national independence of each of them.

PRETEXT FOR INTERVENTION

The United States, captain and leader of the doctrines fostered by NATO, wants to sweep away the foundations of national sovereignty. It simply wants to take possession of the markets and natural resources of the Third World countries including those that were part of the former Soviet Union, like Azerbaijan, Uzbekistan, Turkmenistan and others. It is already almost the master of the great oil reserves of the Caspian Sea. It wants to play the role of a new Roman worldwide super-empire, which, of course, will last much shorter than the Roman Empire—and it will meet with universal resistance.

The empire's pretext for intervention today is humanitarian reasons! Human rights is one of the reasons they give for which it is necessary to liquidate sovereignty and internal conflicts that must be resolved with "smart" bombs and missiles.

Whose proposal is this? Looking back, recalling what happened in our hemisphere in the past few decades, who fathered all the coups d'état? Who trained the torturers in the most sophisticated techniques? Who was responsible for there being relatively small countries where more than 100,000 persons were vanished and a total of about 150,000 were killed? Or the fact that, in other nations, tens of thousands of men and women had a similar fate? I am talking here only about people who were vanished after horrible torture. Who trained the sinister culprits? Who armed them? Who supported them? How can they now claim that national sovereignty must be removed in the name of human rights?

Likewise, there has been no repressive government in the world that the United States would not support. How could the apartheid regime have seven nuclear weapons? They had seven when we were there, on the Namibian border, and the United States intelligence service, which knows everything, did not know about it! Did it not know? And how did those weapons get there? This is one question that could be asked and one of the things that will be known in full detail one day when some documents are declassified, because the day will come when absolutely everything will be known.

Who supported the acts of aggression against the Arab countries? The United States did. I am in absolutely no way an anti-Semite, far from it. But we have been very critical of the wars against the Arab countries, the massive evictions, the diaspora of Palestinians and other Arabs. Who supported those wars? And there are many other overt or covert wars and other similar incidents that I am not going to mention, which have been done and continue to be done by those who want to sweep away sovereignty or the principles of sovereignty in the name of humanitarian reasons. Of course, that is only one of the pretexts but not the only one, as we see in Africa.

The Africans themselves are rightly concerned about tackling the problems of peace in their continent. They are trying to unite. They have a strong sense of unity. They also have their regional groupings and are trying to settle their conflicts. But who occupied and exploited Africa for centuries? Who kept it in poverty and underdevelopment? Who drew those border lines that cut through ethnic groups now separated by them?

The colonial powers created all that. They are responsible for centuries of exploitation, backwardness and poverty. Are we going to resort to a racist interpretation of the reasons for the poverty of those African peoples when it is a known fact that, in that continent, various civilizations had attained remarkable progress at a time when in Berlin, Paris and many other places of civilized Europe there were only wandering tribes? A thousand years before, there already existed a civilization in Egypt, Ethiopia and other parts of Africa.

Now they want to invade countries where poppies are planted, and not by the country but by a number of hungry and sometimes desperate people. Impoverished nations, aware of the huge market for drugs in the United States— one which was not created by a Latin American country or any other nation in the world—plant poppies or coca for the colossal consumption of the industrialized and rich countries.

The question could be asked of how much drugs per capita are consumed in the United States and in Europe. Possibly much more than in Brazil or Argentina, Uruguay or Paraguay, Central America or Mexico, or even in Colombia itself. The market is up north. It was a disgrace for our countries, those where the crop arose, that there was such a high demand in the United States.

The so-called global threats are also considered enough reason to fully justify an intervention. We will quote four of those threats. The first three are drugs, terrorism and the possession of weapons of mass destruction. Of course, this has nothing to do with them. They can have all the weapons of mass destruction they want, thousands of nuclear weapons, as it is the case of the United States. They can also have rockets that, with great accuracy, they can position anywhere in the world and a whole arsenal of laboratories devoted to producing biological weapons—they have used biological weapons against us—and any other kind of weapons. They have reached agreements among themselves to eliminate chemical and biological weapons. But, at the same time, they develop other even more deadly weapons.

According to the doctrine described, a Third World country could have a nuclear weapon and for that reason become the target of a sudden air strike and invasion. And what about all those who possess nuclear weapons? It is a matter of wars, either pre-emptive or punitive, to preserve the monopoly of nuclear weapons and other kinds of weapons of mass destruction that are very far from being humanitarian.

The fourth reason is the massive violation of human rights.

Up to now, the great promoter, the great patron, the great fatherly educator and supporter of those who committed massive violations of human rights has been the United States. Massive destruction of the infrastructure and economy of a country, as it has just happened in Serbia; genocide using bombs to deprive millions of people of crucial services and their means of life, genocidal wars like the one launched against Vietnam. They were the culprits.

I am not talking of the time when more than half of Mexico was conquered. I am not talking of Hiroshima and Nagasaki, a terrorist experiment into the effects of nuclear weapons on cities where hundreds of thousands of people lived. I am talking about things that have happened since World War II. Who were their allies? Why did the Franco government in Spain remain in power for almost 30 years after the end of a world war against fascism that lasted six vicious years and cost no less than 50 million lives? Because he had the support of the United States, which wanted to have military bases there. Who supported utterly repressive governments in countries like Korea? They did. Who really supported the massive carnage of ethnic groups like Chinese, for example, or of communists or left-wing people in Indonesia? They did. Who supported the horrendous apartheid regime? They did.

Do you realize what I mean? It is the development of a whole philosophy aimed at sweeping away the United Nations Charter and the principles of national sovereignty. The doctrine can be divided into three categories of intervention: humanitarian interventions due to internal conflicts; interventions due to global threats, which we have already described; and interventions due to external conflicts, to which are added the very confusing Yankee concept of "diplomacy supported by force." This means, for example, that if Colombia cannot solve its internal conflict—a difficult battle, of course—if it cannot achieve peace, for which many are working, including Cuba, this could become a reason for intervention. At the same rate, if it does not succeed in eradicating drug cultivation it could be the target of an armed intervention.

COLOMBIA AND THE DRUG TRADE

I have tried to collect precise information on what is happening with drugs in Colombia, how encompassing the phenomenon is and how many hectares of coca are planted. Some have told me that there are about 80,000 hectares of coca, just coca. It has been growing. And some have talked to me about up to a million people working in the cultivation of coca and the harvesting of leaves.

I asked about coffee and they told me that there are problems because the salary of a coffee harvester can come to 10 or 12 U.S. dollars while those who harvest the coca leaves or clean the plantations, weed the crop and do other similar activities, earn five or six times higher wages.

What I do not know yet is whether they fertilize it, although that is seemingly a natural process. Perhaps, with a certain regime of rain and climate, the coca plant fertilizes itself. Maybe it is like the marabú. The marabú is a very harmful plant for agriculture here, terribly aggressive and thorny. It reproduces and spreads easily. It cannot be used to feed the animals but it is a leguminous plant, so it does not need to be fertilized. It feeds itself from nitrogen through the nodular bacteria in its roots. Apparently, something similar happens with the coca.

Can you imagine what the situation must be like in a country where a million people in the rural areas can earn 50, 60, 70 U.S. dollars in the coca fields while the same working day in other crops would bring them 10 U.S. dollars at most? And at harvest time—and coca can be harvested three times a year—it is only a matter of pulling off leaves.

Trying to learn about this I have almost become an expert by now, just by asking questions. I say, "Tell me, explain to me, are they all small plantations?" They tell me, "No, there are large estates of hundreds of hectares and plantations of as much as thousands of hectares." I ask, "How much does someone earn, for example, with a hectare of coca?" "That one receives the least," they say. The others receive more: the ones who turn it into the basic paste, the other ones who refine it and, fundamentally, those who market it. Before that phase, many airlines, transport companies and firms providing other services obtain high incomes. When such a cancer is introduced in a society it becomes a real tragedy, in every sense, because the danger that internal consumption may spread is multiplied.

Taking back the problem of Colombia, somebody told me, "One hectare of coca can provide an income of up to 4,000 U.S. dollars." I said, "And if it were planted with corn, in that tropical and rainy plain?" You all know that the Colombian plains are not a corn-growing area. The corn-growing area is a bit further north, at the same height as the central plains in the United States and also at the height of Europe, although corn originated in this hemisphere, in Mexico, Central and South America. Therefore, I assure you that planting corn there without fertilizers or anything would hardly give the peasant one ton per hectare. A ton of corn on the international market is worth more or less between 100 and 150 U.S. dollars. In Argentina and other places, the export price has decreased to 90 U.S. dollars. We have to import them so, we know the cost of each of these grains.

I have not talked about wheat, which cannot be planted there. Corn, for example, can be planted for self-consumption or to market it. How much is the producer paid for his ton of corn that the middleman then sells in the market? On the other hand, if custom barriers are also removed then the grains produced abroad would enter freely. That is what the United States wants from its trade agreements with Latin America.

In that case, the Colombian would eat U.S. corn because it is produced cheaper than Colombian corn. They obtain six, seven or more tons and cultivation there is very mechanized. They produce it cheaper than the French. The French should be careful about U.S. corn because they will put it in France at a lower price than it costs to produce a ton of corn there. That is why agricultural issues become the great obstacle for the free-trade agreements.

The Yankees are reckoning: "I will give you some industrial advantages as soon as possible. I will give you X number of years for you to start reducing the tariffs on the grains that I will export until the day that entry is unrestricted." We know very well what is going to happen: these countries will end up with no corn farming, then corn will be very expensive and to the extent that the price rises there will not be any other corn but American corn.

But how much would our farmer earn after changing a hectare of coca for one of corn? Instead of $4,000, he would earn whatever he is paid for his corn by a middleman or by a chain of middlemen. It might be $60 or $100. So, where are the possibilities for alternative crops?

THE COST OF U.S. INVASION IN COLOMBIA

They have already created a drug culture. They have alienated millions of people with their voracious market and their money laundering. It has been the United States banks that have laundered the vast majority of the funds coming from drugs. They are not just a market but practically the financiers, the drug money launders. Moreover, they do not want to spend money to really eradicate the growing of coca or poppies, although they invest billions in repressive procedures.

I think that, theoretically, there might be a solution—but it would cost billions of U.S. dollars, even if those resources were rationally invested. What are they going to do with those who live massively on drug growing. Are they going to be exterminated? They could also go there themselves and invade that country on account of "a global threat" even if the drug problem cannot be controlled with simple repressive measures. Of course, invading it would be madness because the heat in the forests of the Colombian plains would finish off their soldiers who are used to drinking Coca-Cola on combat missions, cold water at every hour, ice cream of the best quality. Actually, Vietnam is a well-known case in point. The mosquitoes and the heat would almost suffice to finish them off.

They could cause a real disaster if they intervened there to eradicate drugs. Certainly, that would not be the kind of war to use B-2 bombers because the coca crops cannot be fought with laser-guided bombs, smart missiles or planes. There, they would surely have to go in with ground forces, either to wipe out an irregular force in the jungle or to eradicate crops. On the other hand, since they describe guerrilla warfare as terrorism, insurgency and a great risk—practically a global threat—there we have a country with two possible pretexts for intervention. I am talking of two categories: internal conflicts and drugs. Two causes for intervention according to the theories they are trying to impose.

Would an invasion or the bombing of Colombia solve the internal conflict? I wonder if NATO could solve that problem now that it is establishing the right of action beyond its borders. In principle, they agreed on that during the 50th anniversary celebration. Along such lines you can imagine so many cases. Is there anybody who believes that could be the solution?

I know, through opinion polls, that in their desperation at the violence and the problems in the country, not a few people in Colombia itself—actually a number of people worth taking into consideration—have expressed support for the idea that, if there is no other solution to the violence, it be resolved through the intervention of an outside force.

Of course, the fighting and patriotic tradition of the Colombian people should not be overlooked. I am sure that such an act of madness against a country like Colombia, in the style of what they did in Serbia, would be a disaster, absolute madness. But, no one knows, really, since international law, the principles of respect for sovereignty and the United Nations Charter no longer provide a reliable coverage. There are formulas that, in my view, are so complex and difficult that I would tend to call them utopian because there is not one war there but three or four. There are significant guerrilla forces with political motivations but divided into two organizations fighting on their own. There are extremely repressive paramilitary forces at the service of the landowners and there are the forces of the drug growers, people armed to shoot down the crop-spraying helicopters, for example.

Colombia's situation is really complex. I have mentioned it in the context of the theories that I have described and the consequences that they might have.

We should all help! It should never be said that the diplomatic and peaceful ways have been exhausted, the discussions should never stop. A process has already begun. Venezuela wants to cooperate. We cooperate to the extent of our possibilities and so do other countries. Colombia's domestic problems have no solution other than a political and peaceful settlement. This is crystal clear to me. Let us help the Latin Americans find these solutions!

A LATIN AMERICAN SOLUTION

If one day we had a federation of Latin American states, if there were unity, we would give up many of the attributes of our sovereignty. Then, domestic order would become the prerogative of a supranational state that is ours and does not belong to a foreign superpower that has nothing to do with us or to a powerful Europe.

We want to get involved in friendly relations with Europe, also in trade, science and technological development, but it also has absolutely nothing to do with the domestic problems of our countries. We would surely be capable of solving our domestic problems ourselves politically, without bombings, destruction and bloodshed. We do not need anyone to do it for us.

They are always inciting and scheming against Cuba, trying to stir up conflicts inside our country. They go to great lengths to create any kind of internal conflict that would justify monstrous crimes like they have just committed against the Serbs.

Those irresponsible people who in our country put themselves at the service of the United States and receive a salary from the U.S. Interests Section are really toying with sacred things. They are toying with the lives of our people and they should be aware of that. The empire, knowing that Cuba would not give in, longs to accumulate enough forces with its blockade, its propaganda and its money to create internal conflicts. We are not talking of family remittances, we are talking of the United States government money. It has been publicly recognized there as well as in its own laws or amendments.

THE CUBAN EXAMPLE

What can they say about us on humanitarian issues? That we have not a single illiterate person, that we have not a single child without a school, not a single person without medical care. That there are no beggars here, although there are sometimes irresponsible families who send out their children on errands. That is associated with tourism and it affects, if not our identity, at least our honor. There is nobody abandoned in the streets. What can they say? That we have a massive number of excellent doctors as I have been telling you about.

A country like Cuba that has gone through a hard experience—without fuel, steel, lumber, anything and has survived without a dime from any international agency—knows that with its huge resources that country would not need any credits. As simple as that. I shall say no more. Just that if we had those resources we would be growing at a two-digit rate. Without anything and despite everything, including the blockade, we are growing and this year we shall grow from 3 to 4 percent, approximately.

We do not have the immense Siberian forests, oil and gas fields. We do not have a significant steel industry and machinery either. If we only had raw materials and today's experience, because we must add that we have learned to be more efficient and make a better use of our resources, the Cuban economy might grow perhaps 12 or 14 percent.

I can certainly speak of another global threat, namely, ideas. Clear ideas, all that you have analyzed and adopted. We should all help globalize ideas, help them expand. We should all work the miracle of sending them everywhere, as I said the first day. Those are indeed global threats: speaking, reasoning, thinking, explaining, showing. If in your opinion I have been too extensive, in my opinion I have not.

It has been a pleasant experience to discuss all this with you, and I have told you a number of things, many of which I have exposed for the first time. I have done it with great pleasure, with great satisfaction. It is the least I can do for the honor of your visit, because you have come without any fears and under certain circumstances you need to be brave to come and visit us.

VENEZUELA:
OUR STRENGTH IS THE PEOPLE

DR. ARISTÓBULO ISTÚRIZ

In the war of ideas, nothing proves a political thesis more convincingly than living events. The April 2002 coup attempt in Venezuela clarified, for all willing to see, that the U.S. business-political establishment has erected a huge edifice of lies to conceal its real relationship with Latin America. It claims high-minded ideals to justify the Pentagon's costly intervention in the civil war in Colombia, right next door to Venezuela. But these claims were proven utterly false when Washington embraced the coup leaders in Caracas.

The original myth employed to justify sending U.S. troops and hundreds of millions of dollars in military aid to the Colombian government was the "war on drugs." After many embarrassments, including the arrest and conviction for drug-money laundering of the U.S. colonel in charge of the whole operation, that rationale was discredited.

It is now the openly admitted position of the U.S. government that the troops are there to win the civil war against the revolutionary guerrillas of the FARC-EP and the ELN. This is supposedly based on U.S. support for a democratic political process, including free and fair elections. The Bush administration, it should be noted, seems immune to any self-examination on this subject, considering the election fraud in Florida that secured the presidency.

With its embrace of the "golpistas" in Venezuela, the Bush administration showed what it really thinks of elections when the masses are able to use them to vote in a candidate committed to social justice. Hugo Chávez has been elected president twice, in 1998 and again in 2000, with the overwhelming support of the people and in defiance of the open hostility of Venezuela's wealthy and their U.S. allies. When he proposed creating a National Constituent Assembly to rewrite the Constitution, 88 percent of the voters supported the idea in a special referendum on April 25, 1999. Some 1,170 candidates ran for seats in that assembly. Over 90 percent of those elected were "chavistas." If any national leader has proven through the electoral process that the people are with him, it is Hugo Chávez.

On May 10, 2002, Venezuela's minister of education, Dr. Aristóbulo Istúriz, gave an intimate, eyewitness account of the coup attempt in his country to progressive labor unionists in New York gathered at the offices of AFSCME District Council 1707.

We are faced with external factors in Venezuela. There's always been this debate in the United States over what to do about the situation down there. But we see that we're up against a situation where there's the imposition of the Free Trade Area of the Americas, for example, that is in opposition to the resurgence within Latin America. Also connected with the FTAA we see the imposition of Plan Colombia, which is the military arm of the FTAA.

But what they (in the United States) see is a situation where they have a change and transformation in Venezuela, a change and transformation coming in Brazil, with the elections and Lula (Luiz Inacio "Lula" da Silva, leader of the

Workers Party of Brazil). He's at the head of all the polls right now, and so what is being envisioned is a Latin America with Lula, with Chávez, a Latin America whose political complexion is in the process of changing.

We not only had these external factors that we were confronting and dealing with, but there were all the internal factors going on with the development of the government headed by Hugo Chávez. We had to elaborate and develop a model that was different, we had to transform the state in such a way that it would give a voice to the people themselves.

I myself was vice president of the Constituent Assembly at that time (when it was writing a new constitution) and we were confronted with the task of not just providing a political democracy where people can vote on candidates. What we had to do was establish a social democracy where there can be real participation.

The process of democratization involved different factors to create a state of justice that hadn't existed before. We tried to reform several different aspects. One was the law regulating hydrocarbons, land and fishing rights. It established that the petroleum industry had to stay within the hands of the nation itself, confronting the globalization of the petroleum industry.

In terms of protecting fishing rights, we had to confront these international concerns that are dragging their nets along the coasts of the nations of the world. The third issue was the large estates—the latifundio—to reform and democratize the land so it stays in the hands of those people who are actually working on it.

These factors have come together in an interesting dynamic. Within Venezuela there is no freedom of expression through the means of communication. There is a monopoly of the means of communication and it is very clearly against the government. They don't give expression to our thoughts and what we believe in.

Chávez was forced to confront the traditional and historical control exercised by Televisa, the company which was supposedly a national company but was always in the hands of the elite in Venezuela and always directly tied in and intimately linked with the financial sectors. Chávez was very clear. He knew he had to confront this elite and make sure that the industry itself comes within the service of the people. It meant touching a lot of nerves and stepping on big toes.

This helped bring about what came to be known as the battalion of generals. They were a battalion of generals, but they didn't have the soldiers beneath them.

These generals were very intent on creating an image, not just nationally but for international consumption, that the coup in progress in Venezuela had massive, tremendous popular support. Organizations like Fedecámaras, the chamber of commerce, and members of the elite invested tremendous amounts of money to make sure the mobilization projected that image.

There was a demonstration at that time of people who were supposedly defending PDVSA, the Venezuelan state petroleum company. They changed the route and started marching toward Miraflores, the presidential palace. When that happened a call was made to make sure that didn't in fact come about. So the people stood in front of Miraflores to prevent the other demonstration from coming there.

Sharpshooters started firing at the people defending the presidential palace. They killed somebody inside the palace. The National Guard captured three of the sharpshooters (the coup regime later released them).

Nine compañeros had fallen on our demonstration, but the people stayed there. At that time, some of our people went to look for Chávez to find out where he was. Some took up arms against the shooters. The press did not record the actions of the sharpshooters, just the actions of our side. What they projected to the world media was that the chavistas were opening fire against this other demonstration. But why did they change the route and start moving toward Miraflores? They knew that 100,000 people were already there taking care of the palace.

This was the provocation the generals were asking for. They wanted a death so they could be "provoked" into action. I myself was inside the palace with the president and the cabinet. We left many times to talk to the people.

A portion of the generals betrayed the president. In the afternoon they asked Chávez to resign. But the middle ranks of the armed forces and the troops were with the president.

When we tried to go out to talk to the people, they brought down our means of communication. So we were isolated there at Miraflores and were able to talk only to those people in the immediate vicinity. The television channels reported nothing from us, neither did the radio stations.

They gave Chávez a short time to resign. We studied the alternatives. We had three. One was that the president, the cabinet, could go to Maracaibo where there was an old unit of Chávez paratroops. They were very loyal. In the nearby cities were other units loyal to the president.

Another choice was to stay in the palace and resist along with the people outside. The third alternative was to accept the idea that the president was a prisoner. We told them that we wouldn't give up the president, that we were in accord with the idea of resistance, but we weren't going to be in agreement with the massacre of the 100,000 people who were standing outside. The president asked that we be left alone to figure it out. I was a little concerned because I had a pistol at my side and I remembered [Chilean President Salvador] Allende. We told Chávez, we're not going to leave you.

The president said that if we opted to go to Maracaibo, then in escaping they could capture us; if we went by air, they could shoot us down. We wanted to resist, but within the palace was the whole leadership of the popular movement and we couldn't leave the people without leadership.

We noted that this was a coup of the generals, not of the soldiers at the base.

We had to avoid the spilling of blood at this time. Chávez proposed that we stay there and if they kidnapped him, that would be an example for the world to see, that the ones who are violating the constitution and democracy are precisely them.

While we were there we received a telephone call from one of the generals that we had 10 minutes left before they would start bombing the presidential palace. That was about 3:30 in the morning. The president said, let's put an end to this, you take me prisoner and explain this before the people and the world.

We accompanied the president to where the generals were and he was taken to Fort Tuna. The ministers were basically told by the generals that we should go home and prepare to surrender tomorrow. The ministers left. I drove around with the labor minister and the ambassador from Cuba trying to get a feel of what the streets of Caracas were like.

Within the city there was this idea circulating around that Chávez had resigned, so at 5:30 in the morning we began calling friendly journalists and met with them. We said we wanted to get out the word and needed help. We said it wasn't true that Chávez had resigned. In fact, it was a coup d'etat.

In all the media, they were putting forward that there was no coup d'etat, that Chávez had resigned, and they had this document they showed, supposedly his statement that he had resigned. But it didn't have his signature. They also said that he had told his vice president and ministers to get out. All the big newspapers had headlines saying that Chávez had resigned.

We tried to have a press conference. Chavistas were banned by all the TV, radio and newspapers. Police were going to all the ministries and to our houses. They named names on television as if we were all criminals. They held raids on our houses, but we didn't show up. Raids on the houses of ministers were televised, along with certain groups of people going to the houses, spitting and screaming.

They had these images of going into these houses of deputies and governors, physically attacking them. I was at home but they never got to me. They went to my mother's house. One of the reasons they couldn't find me is that I don't live in the sectors where some other folks live. I live in a very popular community. About 300 people congregated on the sidewalk outside my house.

I invited the journalists in. We began to work with the international press, sending out emails, faxes, we began communicating with everyone. I made contact with the Interamerican Commission on Human Rights and directly with Mr. [Santiago] Canton by way of our ambassador in Washington, talking for 15 minutes about what was going on. I spoke directly to Cuba, I spoke to CNN Atlanta because they were carrying nothing about what was actually going on. I directly communicated with TV from Spain, Italy, Germany, many parts of the world, and it was precisely the international press that saved us because on the national level we got absolutely nothing. Part of the raids they were conducting were against the popular, alternative TV and radio stations, they raided them and broke up and destroyed a lot of the apparatus.

This was during the first six hours of the coup. The first six hours of a government that lasted for one day.

Six hours of a government that was fascist. Venezuela had never seen such a dictatorship, such a fascist regime. When we compare those six hours with the three years when Chávez was in power, there is absolutely no comparison on the level of human rights between what (coup leader Pedro) Carmona did in that very short period of time and the tremendous advances Chávez made during his period in office.

In that six hours they were killing, they were persecuting, they were attacking the people. In the afternoon Carmona went to Miraflores and he brought together all the oligarchy who were in control of the economy, but, interestingly, he left the mafia leaders who control the unions outside, basically because they looked too much like us.

When they came to Miraflores they brought together the heads of the banks, the heads of the means of communication, to carry out their plan to eliminate the National Assembly, eliminate the Constitution, eliminate the governors, eliminate the mayors. In the presidential palace they took down the picture of Simón Bolívar and threw it into the garbage.

Then the tide started to change, because there were other radio transmissions like Fe y Alegría, there were certain reports from Cuba and on CNN, there was also the declaration of the attorney general that this had been an unconstitutional act. So people started in the afternoon to get the idea that something was really wrong, they began to hit the streets, they came out with their pots and their pans in a really massive way.

The people were turning on and off their lights, were blocking the streets, were making their way to the fort where Chávez was being held. Fort Tuna was the nerve center of that sector of the armed forces. The masses of people began to concentrate and demand the liberation of President Chávez. Interestingly at this very time when you had this tremendous concentration of people in front of the fort, on TV they were showing comedies, music, nothing at all about what was going on.

All the social networks on a national level were starting to communicate with one another. In all the cities and towns across the country people started leaving their houses and concentrated in front of the forts where the armed forces were located.

They were demanding that all the military leaders define their positions. In Maracaibo, Valencia, all over they were in front of the barracks. In all these areas the troops themselves would come out and raise the banner of Venezuela in solidarity with the people. The coup already had plans envisioned to swear in the new government and ministers the next day. But the people were communicating by way of telephone, cell phone and email, and everyone was out in the streets.

Because the concentration was getting so intense they took Chávez out of Fort Tuna and moved him eventually to an island.

The people took over Channel 8. Community TV stations started trying to get on the air. They directed people to surround Miraflores. I don't know how so many people got there so fast.

Women, youths, old people, unarmed, they all took hold of the fence and demanded Chávez. The soldiers were happy to see the people. An honor guard came out of the palace. A captain told a colonel that if you don't do something for Chávez, we will. The colonel started crying and agreed.

The coup leaders went literally running out of the palace, including Carmona. Around 12:30 p.m. Saturday the ministers returned to Miraflores, saying: "This is our time. If they are going to kill us, it will be with the people." We were cheered by the huge crowd.

We knew the government had left, but we didn't know where the military stood. I went to the door and said let me in. Only ministers can get in, they said, so I went in. Then I went back out to talk to the people by megaphone. When the soldiers saw me, they started shooting up in the air and cheered. The soldiers then carried me on their shoulders to Fort Tuna. We passed some guys under arrest— the coup ministers.

All the barracks started declaring themselves for Chávez. Meanwhile, around 7:00 p.m. the media are still saying that Carmona is the president and everything is normal.

But they still had the real president, and they wanted to take him out of the country. It was a delicate time for the chavistas. We had to guarantee his safety. We told them, "Don't do anything to the president or else the country will erupt."

They threatened to exile him, and proposed we accept "Chavismo without Chávez." We said: "We have no power to negotiate. You can only negotiate with Chávez. We demand he be returned to Miraflores right now."

Our strength was the people, but the others were holding Chávez prisoner. Finally the paratroopers had to go in and rescue him, and he was back around 3 a.m.

The coup had lasted 48 hours. We saw the face of fascism for those hours. The people were able to compare chavismo with fascism. In those 48 hours the opportunists were all unmasked. All those who thought of Friday as the end of Chávez forgot there would be a Saturday.

Chávez had been betrayed by some of the generals who we thought were loyal. But seven elections had been held in the three years of Chávez, and that helped to organize the people.

ECUADOR: MILITARY AND REGIONAL IMPACT OF PLAN COLOMBIA

LUCIO E. GUTIÉRREZ

The following is a transcript of a talk given by Lucio Gutiérrez, now president of Ecuador, at the July 2001 Conference in Solidarity and for Peace in Colombia and Latin America, held in El Salvador. Gutiérrez delivered the address on behalf of the January 21 Patriotic Society.

Allow me to thank the committee of solidarity with the struggles in Colombia, organizers of this great event for peace in Colombia and in Latin America, for inviting me. Also, let me congratulate you for the tremendous success that this event has had, I believe that in the end we all come out ahead. The challenge is to bring about peace with dignity and social justice, respecting the sovereignty of a Colombia on the road towards building a worthier future, one that is more just, more humane, and truly democratic for all members of its society.

I will address myself to the military aspects of Plan Colombia, to consider what awaits Latin America if we do not stop it and neutralize it. I will draw three or four specific conclusions, so in the workshops we can work out together the regional effects of Plan Colombia.

BACKGROUND TO THE ECUADORIAN INVOLVEMENT

The government of the United States, forced by the agreements it signed with Panama and under the international pressure, had no alternative than to leave the Panama Canal and the military bases it had there. It immediately initiated diplomatic contacts to find other countries in which to install military bases. It had no difficulty when it turned to the servile government of Jamil Mahuad in Ecuador. Under the pretext of collaborating to fight drug trafficking, this government turned over the base at Manta, Ecuador, signing, on November 12, 1999, an agreement entirely harmful to the interests of the Ecuadorian people. Not only because Ecuador gave up everything in exchange for nothing, or because it is a total violation of our sovereignty, but also because it dragged us into—even worse than simply involving us—Plan Colombia—which is an unnecessary war on our sister republic of Colombia. It is very true that the United States can operate from the high seas, as they have done in the Middle East, from the Persian Gulf. But not only was this far more costly, but the results of direct control would be less effective, as they would be using the base at Manta, if we allow that.

The United States have not only militarized Colombia and Manta, Ecuador, but also have installed military bases in Aruba and Curacao; Comalapa, El Salvador; Liberia, Costa Rica; Vieques, Puerto Rico; and at the Peruvian bases at Nanai in Loreto (near the Colombian border) and in the Upper Huallaga Valley.

WHY PLAN COLOMBIA?

During the closing years of the Twentieth century, the constant victories of the FARC-EP forced the military and police forces to acknowledge to congress that if a new strategy for the fight against this organization were not put into effect, the war would be lost. All the actors involved in the crisis began to realize that what was really at stake in the region was a struggle for power, not only the political power of Colombia, but there was also developing the embryo of a transnational power in South America. Once again the winds of freedom and of regional integration first introduced by Bolívar, San Martín, Morazán, Zapata, Eloy Alfaro and other patriots, were blowing through the Andes and once again, it would be necessary to bring this to an end. This is the true strategic objective of Plan Colombia.

What is happening is that the Colombian revolutionary process is not the classic guerrilla war, but a civil war, with the growing support of the national population, and the sympathy of the progressive and democratic countries and international organization. The FARC-EP has demonstrated, even to the skeptics, that they are a revolutionary political and military organization, with a plan for social and economic justice, equality, and well-being of the entire Colombian population.

There are two points of views concerning the situation in Colombia, depending on the position and the interests of who is doing the analyzing:

- The most conservative power sectors inside and outside the United States simplify the struggle to that of a battle against drug trafficking, a position placed on the international agenda by Ronald Reagan, when that administration took the position that a greater quantity of drugs were coming onto the domestic market than it could bear, and thus it became a criminal phenomenon that had to be fought. That was it in a nutshell.
- Progressive sectors in the United States and the great majority of Latin-American leaders tend to view the problem in the form of the classic civil war of the region, solved during the decade of the sixties and seventies with peace processes and international assistance.

These are visions that continue to believe that what is happening in Colombia is a political and military crisis that has taken longer than expected to be resolved. This seeing only part of the picture with certain aspects emphasized avoids looking at the problem as a whole as it is actually playing out.

In summary, both ways of viewing the crisis fail to take into account that in that country a new model of state is being born, under the sign of a struggle against the capitalist global neoliberalism led by the United States. In Colombia, not only is the security and stability of the region for the next decade at stake, but also taking place is a battle of a kind never before seen with a transnational power that, by the very nature of its dynamic, could call into question the decision-making ability of the national states of the region, their social legitimacy and even the very existence of the incipient democratic societies of South America, that could be overwhelmed by the new global power, if they do not act together decisively to face this threat.

BRIEF DESCRIPTION OF PLAN COLOMBIA

Plan Colombia is an initiative of the government of Andrés Pastrana to confront the problems afflicting Colombia due to internal and external difficulties generated by the process of globalization and the internationalization of the economy, by the problems inherited from its own history and from the proliferation of the drug trafficking. It is also the result of the need to reassert and consolidate power, as the people have lost confidence in the credibility of their military and police forces and in their judicial system, due to the high level of corruption generated by the vast economic power of the drug trafficking networks.

The axes on which Plan Colombia is based are the following:

- Negotiation with the insurgent groups, which is the core of Pastrana's strategy, for the urgent resolution of the armed conflict that has gone on for more than 40 years;
- The defense of and strengthening of democratic institutions, to successfully stave off the international pressures and doubts that are a product of this process;
- To assume the leadership in the struggle against drug trafficking by seeking an alliance between the narcotics producing nations and the consumer nations, avoiding mutual retaliations and recriminations and thus internationalizing the supposed fight against the drug trafficking;
- The strengthening of the military and police force, their agility and capacity to respond as well as their commitment to respect human rights, with the aim of restoring the confidence and safety of Colombian citizens;
- To guarantee to Colombians an environment in which they can exercise their rights and fundamental freedoms, as well as the education and development

of the adequate and timely fulfillment of their duties with the state and to society;
- Reform and modernization of other institutions and structures, so the political process might function as an effective instrument for economic progress and social justice;
- To guarantee in a period no greater than five years universal access to education, healthcare, to strengthen the local administration and to promote the participation of Colombians in the fight against corruption, kidnapping, violence, and the displacement of people from the communities in the conflict zones;
- The shoring up of Colombia economically and the creation of jobs, a goal which the government has pledged itself to fulfill in accepting international support and the access to international markets with highly competitive export products.

That is how they are disguising Plan Colombia and marketing it as necessary and an expression of goodwill.

THE STRATEGIES OF PLAN COLOMBIA

The plan oddly labeled as one for peace, prosperity and strengthening of the state, is simply a plan for war, that will bring destruction, death, oppression, subjugation and greater poverty to the nations of the region.

The government is supposedly determined to fight against drug trafficking in the areas of transport, production, consumption and whatever other elements support such activity, and thus threaten democratic institutions and the integrity of the nation. The purpose of this strategy is to strengthen the fight against drug trafficking through the coordination of all the elements of the police and military forces against traffickers. In this way they deceive, while at the same time satisfy the consciences of the countries that support this genocide. The U.S. says that the goal is to eliminate the production of drugs, but they have no intention of doing that, because from the economic point of view as well as from the perspective of intervention, that would not be in their interest. They would lose a magnificent pretext for intervening in Latin America. The real goal is to destroy the revolutionary organizations. The line along which this strategy is based is the following:

As we have seen, this is total war coming our way, wearing a mask of ethical precepts and moral concepts and social colorations, that are by themselves hard to refute, but will lead to a violent, bloody and fratricidal regional war, more merciless—to the horror of humanity—than that developed in Vietnam under similar pretexts as those now being used to put Plan Colombia into effect.

REGIONAL CONSEQUENCES OF PLAN COLOMBIA

This conflict is already regional: Ecuador, Peru and Venezuela are suffering the consequences, which will have an irremediable impact on the peace of the continent and the world. On the border between Colombia and Ecuador, an act of truly environmental terrorism is unfolding with aerial fumigation depositing a toxic herbicidal fungus. Thousands of people have come down with stomach illnesses or skin conditions; displacement, violence and delinquency are out of control, normal business tourism at the border has been reduced to zero; kidnappings, rapes and killings, as well as the attacks against the trans-Ecuadorian oil pipeline, are already bleeding us and—pay attention—the real war has not yet even started.

Plan Colombia is definitely not an action against drug trafficking. That is a social and economic problem. And because the drug trafficking cannot be solved with a military action, it is a grave and bloody error. Plan Colombia is a military operation against the revolutionary movements in Colombia and a covertly neoliberal action aimed at neutralizing the new social actors in Latin America, like the peasants, Indigenous, intellectuals, and nationalist and patriotic military that are bringing their new ideas to solve economic, social and political problems from a position other than that of the free-marketeers.

With Plan Colombia the United States hopes to gain an advantageous geopolitical and geo-economic position in relation to the European Union, China and Japan, maintaining its complete military, economic and political hegemony over the region and Latin America as a whole. When that is accomplished, they believe, they will be able to impose their will and their narrow interests—the Free Trade Area of the Americas (FTAA), the control of the Amazon Rainforest, biodiversity, the drinking water, the oil, the oxygen and the resources over which the wars of the future will be fought.

Some of the problems that the regional Armed Forces have to overcome are that they will have to face a war for which they are not psychologically prepared. It is not the same thing to fight an international war to defend the sovereignty of your land, as it is to fight in a war knowing that you are defending the interests of transnational corporations, knowing you are squandering resources on armaments and war materiel that are desperately needed to solve grave problems of your peoples—education, health, jobs, basic services, etc. The possibility of the region turning into another Vietnam haunts them constantly; they feel it but cannot express themselves because they have that exhausted sense that their opinion doesn't count.

From this tribunal for peace, I cry out to the Armed Forces, at least those from Latin America, to go back to their place of birth, to their heritage and legacy of our great liberators, to the fathers and mothers of our homeland, that is to say, to the defense of the sovereignty that rests in our peoples, that may they never again be manipulated by the free-market owned oligarchies that sell out the integrity, the life, the dignity and the independence of our nations.

And I am not talking about utopias. I am talking about realities, things that are possible to bring about. We did it January 21, 2000 in Ecuador, when a corrupt government and free-market oligarchy ordered repression, to fire guns at people calling for justice, begging for bread, that they be allowed to get their money arbitrarily frozen in the banks. They were protesting because they did not want their most valuable state-owned enterprises to be privatized for the benefit of the same thief as always. They were protesting, because they wanted to put an end to the savagery of the banks, they wanted to rescue the dignity, the sovereignty and the identity of the Ecuadorian people.

The military, instead of repressing and shooting the people as we were ordered, joined together in a legitimate cry for justice. We said, "Enough to a corrupt government, hostage to the oligarchy and the bankocracy!" And together with the brave Indigenous and mestizo people, we stripped away their mandate and authority. So here we are—we lost our jobs, they threw us out of the army, but we gained spiritual strength.

Life is so short, so ephemeral that we must not die without doing something to end this unjust and lacerating history. And thus I firmly invite you to join me in committing ourselves on our honor to continue the struggle to leave as a legacy to the future generations, a worthier, more just planet, with greater solidarity, greater humanity and with genuine democracy.

When people abandon their pre-conceived notions and they allow the development of humanity, if we have a relative degree of freedom it is because there were men and women with a vision of the future and with an inextinguishable spirit of struggle, who faced down a powerful opponent, but they were victorious, and broke the chains of slavery. We hope to follow their marvelous examples, as we hope to justify our existence, to leave a profound mark during our fleeting lives. To do this we must go beyond our own limits. Let us be greater than the adversaries. We must convince them of their errors, which they must then rectify.

There is the key of the success, breaking out of the normal, to break free of mediocrity. Let us dream, plan and let us start moving. Let us conquer the world, not necessarily with violence; let us reach the mind of the people, with ideas. This is a more effective way, a more profound and permanent way to seal our triumph.

Let us repeat with the revolutionary Ecuadorian president, General Eloy Alfaro, "There can be no redemption without sacrifice."

Long live freedom, equality and social justice!

VIEQUES: U.S. EAVESDROPPING ON LATIN AMERICA

ISMAEL GUADALUPE

One of the lesser-known aspects of the struggle to oust the U.S. Navy from Vieques, Puerto Rico, is the opposition to the military radar called Relocation Over The Horizon Radar (ROTHR).

Ismael Guadalupe, ex-political prisoner from the Puerto Rican island of Vieques and a leader of the Committee for the Rescue and Development of Vieques, spoke at forums in 2001 in New York and Philadelphia about this issue. Both meetings took up the issue of Vieques within the context of the Latin American anti-imperialist struggle, considering that the U.S. uses Vieques as a bombing range for its military hardware, as well as for its military/war practices.

The following are excerpts from Guadalupe's talk about the dangers of the military radar project.

In 1994, one year after the formation of our Committee for the Rescue and Development of Vieques, we found out that the U.S. Department of Defense had plans to build a radar installation in the western part of Vieques. They proclaimed that it was an effort in the U.S. "war on drugs."

We immediately realized that it was a U.S. Navy military project and started agitating against it. It was strange that overnight the Defense Department and the Navy were to engage in an issue more proper for the Drug Enforcement Agency.

Within these debates the scientific community started to say that it was proven that the electromagnetic waves that would radiate from this radar were hazardous to health and would not do anything against drug trafficking.

Even the U.S. General Accounting Office and the Office of the Budget have said that this radar is not effective against drugs. Drug trafficking increased after the construction of the radar in Virginia.

This radar consists of a transmitter in the western part of Vieques and 372 pairs of receptor antennas on the southern coast of the big island, Puerto Rico. The transmitter in Vieques is located in the area that according to President Clinton's directive of January 2000 was to be returned to that municipality as of Dec. 31, 2000. However, the 100 hectares where the radar was built are not included in this plan.

In addition, the Navy will restrict the use of an additional 850 hectares to prevent any obstruction to the reception. This means that the surrounding land cannot be used for planting or tending animals that exceed one meter, cannot have electric wiring, air traffic, houses nor road traffic.

The radar in Vieques is now fully operating. It is connected to two similar ones in Virginia and Texas. Through the network of these three radars, the U.S. can keep an eye on all of Central America, the Caribbean and northern South America. When we look at the scope of these radars, they cover different areas, two of them overlapping in some parts. However, there is one part where the coverage of the three radars converge, and that is in Colombia!

In 1962 the U.S. invaded Cuba, in 1965 Santo Domingo, in 1983 Grenada against the New Jewel government of Maurice Bishop. All these invasions have been practiced in Vieques. Our land has been used to violate the sovereignty of other countries and we have no doubt that this radar is going to be used for the same purpose.

We have to get the U.S. Navy out of Vieques now, not only for our benefit, but for the benefit of all the people in Latin America, the Caribbean and the world. We cannot forget that 80 percent of the U.S. planes that participated in the war against Yugoslavia trained in Vieques.

THE FOURTH REVOLUTIONARY WAVE

NARCISO ISA CONDE

*The following speech was delivered by Narciso Isa Conde, a Dominican activist
and poet, as the closing statement of the First International Conference in Solidarity
and for Peace in Colombia and Latin America held in July 2001, in El Salvador.*

It is an honor to say these words after such fruitful, wonderful days of discussion. But it is also a challenge. Those present here are a very diverse group of
people, different in many aspects. Together we have representatives of a variety
of organizations: social, popular, community, political, cultural, solidarity movements, for human rights; there are also intellectual personalities and artists who
add a special and beautiful touch to this conference.

This is a sample, although small, of humanity's dignity and respect. Old and
new combatants, people of all ages, many, many women comrades—which is
very hopeful, for they have carried on their backs a great load, the many forms of
oppression they have been subjected to. Here we have the manifestation that
women's participation is increasing.

As a Cuban comrade said, the youths have come together with more mature
generations. The fervor of youth is combined with women's work and the experience of many fighters.

That is why this conference has been so fruitful. Certainly, as [Handel]
Schafik [of El Salvador's Farabundo Marti National Liberation] said, we are all
a torrent, we are all walking on the same path. A path that is widening in this period, in this stage, after heroic resistance. Because we are physical, ideological and
cultural survivors of a difficult phase of the transforming movements. The path
widens and I am certain that it will turn into a great avalanche. There are splen-
did signals that this will happen.

All this has happened within the framework of the Salvadoran comrades'
generosity. El Salvador is the "Tom Thumb" of America. That is, one of the greatest examples of heroism in modern history. A generous hospitality and solidarity,
because at this moment they face very hard times resulting from the impact of
earthquakes and the consequent impoverishment. Under these conditions the
FMLN, the Colombia solidarity organizations and the movements for peace in
Colombia took on the challenge of organizing this first conference called to point
the finger at the very center of the imperial strategy. Generous solidarity, for it
had to overcome persistent interventionist obstructions from the United States
through its embassy that tried to prevent this extraordinary event.

We are in a very special period and this has been clear throughout the different presentations given during this conference. It is an acute moment of neoliberal offensive, of manipulated globalization and specifically, of U.S. imperialist strategy of recolonization aimed at destroying our nations and brutally impoverishing our peoples—for the sole purpose of accumulating enormous wealth in a small sector of humanity.

But we also have to say, as our people say: The donkey thinks one thing and the person who harnesses it, another. We are carrying out this conference at a time when the neoliberal offensive is being discredited, when the imperialist strategy is getting a response from those it targets. Because Plan Colombia, its extension as the Andean Initiative, Plan Puebla-Panama, the effort to accelerate the dollarization, are all efforts to smash symbols of sovereignty. The efforts to culminate the privatization processes, privatizing the services of water, electricity, ports, airports, highways, scientific reserves and immense natural resources, in turn, elicit powerful popular responses.

These plans already have a strong counterpart. It is not that there was no resistance during the last few years. Resistance never ended. But now it is stronger.

This is the time of the resistance's qualitative leap. We are at the threshold of a new continental revolutionary wave centered in the northern part of South America, with ripples toward Central America, the Caribbean and southern South America. For that reason when the time comes for the empire to define or renew its strategy's military component, (because this continent has always been infested with U.S. military bases, personnel and interventions), when it draws on its Plan Colombia, it also draws an angle toward the Caribbean with bases in Aruba and Curacao, an angle toward Central America with the base right here in El Salvador, an angle toward the south with a base in Manta, Ecuador and all the components in the interior of Colombia that are part of the Plan.

This is added to the network of bases in the Caribbean installed in Puerto Rico that have encountered the resistance of the Puerto Rican people. The struggle of the Puerto Rican people to get the U.S. naval base out of Vieques has a high qualitative value. Because it is not only that this is an island with 9,000 residents. It is that military troops there train and try new weapons that are used in the Middle East, even in Iraq, and of course in Latin America and the Caribbean. That is why I would like to stress that we have also denounced the U.S. negotiations in the Dominican Republic to try to occupy first the Saona Island located in the east of our island and afterward the key Alto Velo located on the southwestern coast.

However, I should point out, it will be extremely difficult to attain this goal. They always look for other places when they get displaced. We have a great challenge when it comes to defying the military component of this strategy of domination, a very dangerous and destructive U.S. strategy. But regarding this dangerous strategy today, it is not an accident that inscribed in its chapter will be an heroic response, as José Carlos Mariátegui said. Because this is what the Bolivarian Revolution is, a heroic creation. It is also the Zapatista uprising and its impact on every Mexican structure. It is the popular Indigenous uprisings in Ecuador, Bolivia and Peru. It is the piqueteros struggle with their blockades in Argentina; the electoral gains in Uruguay, El Salvador, Nicaragua, Brazil. It is the landless, the homeless, the increasing uprisings in Jamaica and the increasing protests in the Dominican Republic.

All this shows that the continent is full of protest movements and transforming processes. It is this growing movement that the U.S. military strategy targets. And, of course, this strategy is part of the Free Trade Area of the Americas (FTAA) as a project of economic recolonization, part of the dollarization and the culmination of the privatizing process.

Let us talk of a fourth wave, because the first had its center in the Caribbean, the Cuban Revolution, so transcendental in this period, the process of socialist transformation in Cuba. It was unthinkable to many that this process could survive and thrive under such enormous difficulties. (The fact that it did) is indeed a signal that it is possible to resist and succeed. For it is precisely these difficult circumstances that show who really are great revolutionaries.

The second wave took place in the South: Allende, the Montoneros, the struggles in Brazil. The third was in Central America, where the struggle has resurfaced with old and new players, with an impressive diversity, with the reappearance of progressive military currents in Venezuela and Ecuador. The spirits of Torrijos, Velasco Alvarado and Caamaño, who led the April Revolution in our country the Dominican Republic in 1965, are latent in many countries. This indicates that the domination strategy, enormously destructive and exclusive, is giving way to a player who is multicolor, diverse, difficult to articulate but is going forward, step by step, showing great signs of existence. And beyond our continental borders, there are the great anti-globalization networks: Davos, Prague, Seattle, and most recently, Genoa. These are signs that rebelliousness and protests are growing. This new internationalism is being articulated, more than proletarian, it is popular. It is integrating more diverse sectors of those who have been oppressed, super-exploited, those who have been socially and politically excluded.

That is why in this fourth wave, the geographical and social space is wider. With careful optimism we can say that we see the light at the end of the tunnel. We can feel the beginning of a force that could be converted into a great continental and worldwide force. We are at the dawn of this process. The challenge is built progressively through different and multiple struggles. In these meetings, those like the Social Forum and the São Paulo Forum, that will eventually have to adjust. It is also built through multiple seminars, and in coordinated mobilizations both inside and outside the continent.

There are definitely reasons to be optimistic. We can see a better horizon. I am convinced that we have moved in that direction in these three days. This should be a reason for collective pride. A little grain of sand in the forward move, persistently, in a great and long task. Certainly utopias, like feasible dreams, show up on the horizon. If we move toward it, it reappears. They wanted to steal our dreams, our hopes. But in these times, dreams take form and become embodied. This was possible because we resisted, because there was no place in the popular, social and revolutionary movement for regrets, for renegade positions and betrayal that today put to shame many of those who believed the story about the end of history.

Prehistory is just ending. From now on, history begins. And history begins because we summon, loyal to the Aymará and Haitian traditions, the ceremony of the Spirits. As the legend goes, in difficult times, the Aymará Indian and the Haitian Blacks played their drums and summoned their great dead with the drum beat to join the living in the struggle against the oppressors. I sincerely say that I have felt the presence here of Bolívar, Che, Martí, San Martín, los Camilos, Caamaño, and all the other heroes and heroines of our continent. They give us the strength to go on, they give us the strength to say: They live, the struggle continues.

THE GEOPOLITICS OF PLAN COLOMBIA

JAMES PETRAS

When this article appeared in the Monthly Review in May 2001, James Petras could not have known how events would unfold in the ensuing months. However, his analysis proved so relevant that many of his predictions have come to pass.

Plan Colombia, to be understood properly, should be located in a historical perspective both in relation to Colombia and the recent conflicts in Central America. Plan Colombia is both "new" policy and a continuation of past U.S. involvement. Beginning in the early 1960s, under President Kennedy, Washington launched its counterinsurgency program, forming special forces, designed to attack "internal enemies." The targets were Colombian self-defense communities, particularly in Marquetalia. Subsequently, the Pentagon continued its counterinsurgency presence in Colombia. Thus, Plan Colombia is President Clinton's extension and deepening of President Kennedy's internal war. The differences between the earlier version of the internal war doctrine and its current reincarnation are found in the ideological justifications for U.S. intervention, the scale and scope of U.S. involvement and the regional context of the intervention. Under Kennedy, counterinsurgency was based on the threat of international communism, today the justification is based on the drug threat. In both instances there is total denial of the historical-sociological basis of the conflict.

The second major difference between Clinton's Plan Colombia and Kennedy's counterinsurgency program is the scale and scope of intervention. Plan Colombia is a long-term billion-dollar program involving large-scale modern arms shipments. Kennedy's counterinsurgency agenda was much smaller. The difference in the scale of military operation is not because of any strategic or political difference; the cause is found in the different political context in Colombia and the world. In the 1960s the guerrillas were a small isolated group, today they are a formidable army operating on a national scale. Kennedy was concentrating militarily on Indo-China, today Washington has a relatively free hand. Plan Colombia is thus both a continuation and an escalation of U.S. politico-military policy—based on similar strategic goals, adapted to new global realities.

Another historical factor that needs to be taken into account in discussing Plan Colombia is the recent growth of regional conflicts, namely the U.S. intervention in Central America. Plan Colombia is heavily influenced by Washington's successful reassertion of hegemony in Central America following the so-called "peace accords." Washington's success was based on the use of state terror, mass displacement of population, large-scale and long-term military spending, military advisors, and the offer of a political settlement involving the reincorporation of the guerrilla commanders into electoral politics. Washington's Plan Colombia is based on its success in Central America and its belief that it can replicate the same outcome in Colombia. Washington believes it can repeat the "terror for peace" formula of Central America via Plan Colombia in the Andean country.

What follows is an analysis of the geopolitical interests and ideological concerns that guide Plan Colombia, the consequences of U.S. military escalation and a critique of Washington's misdiagnosis of the "Colombian question." The essay will conclude with a discussion of some of the adverse unanticipated consequences that Washington may incur in pursuing its military policy in Colombia.

PLAN COLOMBIA AND THE RADICAL TRIANGLE

Its critics describe Plan Colombia as a U.S. authored and promoted policy directed toward militarily eliminating the guerrilla forces in Colombia and repressing the rural peasant communities that support them. U.S. policymakers describe Plan Colombia as an effort to eradicate drug production and trade by attacking the sources of production that are located in areas of guerrilla influence or control. Since the guerrillas are associated with the coca producing regions, this line of argument proceeds, Washington has directed its military advisory teams and military aid to destroying what they dub the "narco-guerrillas." More recently, particularly with the political and military successes of the two major guerrilla movements—the Revolutionary Armed Forces of Colombia-People's Army (FARC-EP) and the National Liberation Army (ELN)—Washington has increasingly acknowledged the fact that its war is directed against what is now dubbed the guerrilla insurgency. While the economic stakes are substantial in Colombia, for both Washington and the ruling oligarchy in Bogotá, the larger and more important issue is the rapid and massive build-up. U.S. military involvement in Colombia is geopolitical. Strategists in Washington are concerned with several key geopolitical issues that could adversely affect U.S. imperial power in the region and beyond.

The Colombian insurgency question is thus part of a geopolitical matrix that is in the process of challenging and modifying U.S. hegemony in northern South America and in the Panama Canal Zone. Secondly, oil production, supply, and prices are linked to the challenge in the region and beyond (in OPEC, Mexico, etc.). Thirdly, the core conflicts with the empire are found in Colombia, Venezuela, and Ecuador (the radical triangle) but there is growing leftist and nationalist discontent in key adjoining countries, particularly in Brazil and Peru.

Fourthly, the example of successful resistance in the radical triangle countries is already resonating with countries further south—Paraguay and Bolivia, on the basis of the successful political struggles by the peasant-Indian movements in the Ecuadorian highlands and the "bolivarian appeals" of Venezuela's President Hugo Chávez, along with the ever-present national-populist consciousness in Argentina. Fifthly, the strength of the radical triangle, particularly the oil diplomacy and independent policy of President Chávez, has shattered the U.S. strategy of isolating the Cuban revolution and has further integrated Cuba into the regional economy. Beyond that, President Chávez' favorable oil deals (trade at subsidized prices) have strengthened the resolve of the Caribbean and Central American regimes to resist Washington's efforts to turn the Caribbean into an exclusive U.S. lake. While the guerrillas and popular movements represent a serious political and social challenge to U.S. supremacy in the region, Venezuela represents a diplomatic and political economic challenge in the Caribbean basin and beyond, via its leadership in OPEC and its non-aligned foreign policy. In more general terms, the radical triangle can contribute to undermining the mystique surrounding the invincibility of U.S. hegemony and the notion of the inevitability of free market ideology.

In more specific terms the conflict between the radical triangle and U.S. imperial power focuses attention on the fact that much of what is described as "globalism" rests on the foundations of the social relations of production and the balance of class forces in the nation-state. The recognition of this fact has particular relevance to the U.S.-FARC-EP conflict in Colombia. The assumption here is that without solid social, political and military foundations within the nation-state, the imperial enterprise and its accompanying global networks are imperiled. Thus there is a need to look rather closely at the nature of its proxy war in Colombia in which Washington, through its client regime, attempts to destroy the guerrillas and decimate and demoralize their supporters in order to restore the local foundations of imperial power.

THE GEOGRAPHY OF THE CHALLENGE TO WASHINGTON

In the 1960s and 1970s the challenge to U.S. imperial power was located in the Southern Cone of Latin America—namely Chile, Argentina, Uruguay, and Bolivia. Washington responded by backing military coups and state terror in overthrowing governments and terrorizing the popular opposition into submission. During the 1980s, Central America became the centerpiece of revolutionary challenge to U.S. imperial power. The revolution in Nicaragua and the popular guerrilla movements in El Salvador and Guatemala posed a serious challenge to U.S. client regimes and geopolitical-economic interests. Washington militarized the region by pouring in billions of dollars of arms, and financing a mercenary army in Nicaragua, and state terrorist military activity in El Salvador and Guatemala. The war of attrition waged by Washington eventually imposed a series of peace accords that restored U.S. client regimes and U.S. hegemony at the cost of over 200,000 deaths in Guatemala; 75,000 in El Salvador and at least 50,000 in Nicaragua. In the late 1990s and into the new millennium, the geography of resistance to the U.S. empire has shifted to northern South America—namely Colombia, the Eastern highlands of Ecuador and Venezuela. In Colombia, the combined guerrilla forces control or influence a wide swathe of territory south of Bogotá, toward the Ecuadorian border, northwest toward Panama and in several pockets to the east and west of the capital, in addition to urban militia units. Parallel to the guerrilla movement, large-scale peasant mobilizations and trade union-convoked general strikes have increasingly shaken the Pastrana regime. In Venezuela, the Chávez leadership has won several elections, reformed state institutions (Congress, the constitution and the judiciary) and taken an independent position in foreign policy, leading OPEC to higher oil prices, developing ties with Iraq and extending diplomatic and commercial links with Cuba. The Confederation of Indigenous Nationalities of Ecuador (CONAIE), a powerful Indian-peasant movement linked with lower military officials and trade unionists, toppled the Mahuad regime in January 2000. While the military intervened to topple the popular junta, CONAIE and its allies were able to sweep the subsequent legislative elections in the Ecuadorian sierra. As a result, the Pentagon's military strategy of encircling the Colombian guerrillas by building a military base at Manta, Ecuador, has come under serious attack.

The armed and civilian movements in all three countries, along with the Chávez regime, have called into question Washington's interventionism and its promotion of the neoliberal economic agenda. The resistance in these three countries takes place in a region that is oil rich: Venezuela is a major U.S. supplier, Colombia is a producer state and has substantial untapped reserves, as is the case on a lesser scale, for Ecuador. Thus the oil issue is a two-edged sword: a stimulus for an aggressively interventionist U.S. policy (like Plan Colombia, and the intervention against the Ecuadorian popular junta) and a lever of power in challenging U.S. domination, as Chávez has demonstrated.

However, Plan Colombia cannot be extrapolated from the geoeconomic matrix of the oil rich triangle of northern South America, a strategic resource to fuel the empire as well as an economic resource allowing nationalists to challenge any boycott and to finance potential allies. Plan Colombia is also a wider strategy to contain and undermine the appeal of the Colombian revolutionary advance in other Latin American countries. The existence of the FARC-EP, CONAIE, and the Chávez regime in adjacent territories is mutually supportive. While Venezuela's nationalist-populist project has its roots in the popular revulsion to corruption, the decay of its political institutions and the destitution of the majority of its people, the fact of a powerful social-revolutionary movement at its doorstep strengthens Venezuela's borders from any U.S. inspired destabilization policy. Likewise, the Chávez regime's refusal to allow U.S. reconnaissance planes overflights in Venezuelan airspace to search and target guerrilla forces, lessens the military pressure on the guerrillas. The fact that in Ecuador a large-scale peasant-Indian movement opposes U.S. militarization of the Ecuadorian-Colombian border weakens the imperial war effort. The Ecuadorian regime's embrace of the dollarization of its economy and the construction of a U.S. military base has de-legitimized the regime in the midst of growing impoverishment and heightened sociopolitical tensions.

The radical triangle and the conflict with the U.S. empire can spill over into neighboring countries. Peru, a staunch U.S. client formerly run by CIA-sponsored secret police chief Vladimir Montesinos, is in a period of instability as popular mass movements compete with neoliberal politicians for power and influence. In Brazil, the reformist left Workers Party won a series of important municipal elections including the mayoralty in São Paulo, while President Cardoso's party continues its downward spiral. More importantly, the Landless Workers Movement (MST) continues to organize and occupy large estates and resist state repression in a tense and conflictual countryside. Further south, major peasant and urban mobilizations have, with increasing frequency, paralyzed the economies of Bolivia and Paraguay, while in Argentina, the provinces are in continual rebellion, cutting highways and attacking municipal political institutions. It is in this context of growing continental mobilization that Plan Colombia has to be seen as an attempt to behead the most advanced radicalized and well-organized opposition to U.S. hemispheric hegemony.

To date, the upsurge of the multi-faceted opposition in the radical triangle has checkmated or reversed U.S. policies at the edge of imperial concerns. Washington's historical policy of isolating the Cuban Revolution from Latin America and the Caribbean has been effectively shattered. Chávez' visit and the oil agreement consolidates Cuba's energy sources. The Ibero-American Conference in Panama in November 2000, calling for an end to the Helms-Burton Act, totally isolated U.S. diplomats. Washington's carefully calibrated steps to weaken the Chávez' regime have been repulsed. OPEC elected a Venezuelan, Alí Rodríguez, to head the organization. The Caribbean countries eagerly sought out and signed beneficial oil agreements with Venezuela. The conflict in the Mid-East has strengthened Chávez' hand in dealing with the U.S.: witness his public attack on Plan Colombia and the favorable diplomatic responses from Brazil, Mexico and other key countries.

The strategy of Washington follows a "domino approach": Plan Colombia means first, to defeat the guerrillas, then surround and pressure Venezuela and Ecuador before moving toward escalating internal destabilization. The strategic goal is to reconsolidate power in northern South America, secure unrestricted access to oil and enforce the "no alternatives to globalization" ideology for the rest of Latin America.

MAINTAINING THE MYSTIQUE

Plan Colombia is about maintaining the mystique of the invincibility of the empire and the irreversibility of neoliberal policies. The power elite in Washington knows that the beliefs held by oppressed peoples and their leaders are as effective in retaining U.S. power as the actual exercise of force. As long as Latin American regimes and their opposition continue to believe that there is no alternative to U.S. hegemony they will conform to the major demands emanating from Washington and its representatives in the international financial institutions. The belief that U.S. power is untouchable and that its dictates are beyond the reach of the nation-state (which the rhetoric of globalization reinforces) has been a prime factor in reinforcing U.S. material rule (i.e. economic exploitation, military base construction, etc.).

Once U.S. dominance is tested and successfully resisted by popular struggle in one region, the mystique is eroded as people, and even regimes elsewhere, begin to question the U.S. defined parameters of political action. A new impetus is thus given to opposition forces in challenging the neoliberal rules and regulations facilitating the pillage of their economies. Where such destabilization occurs, capital, threatened with a revival of nationalist and socialist reforms and redistributive structural adjustments, will flow out. The reversion to more restricted markets and the constraints of risk and declining profit margins within the U.S. empire will threaten the position of the dollar. A flight from the dollar will in turn make it difficult for the U.S. economy to finance its huge current account imbalances.

The fear of this chain reaction is at the root of Washington's hostility to any challenge anywhere that could set in motion large scale and extended political opposition. Colombia is a case in point. In itself the economic and political stakes of the U.S. within Colombia are not overly substantial. Yet the possibility of a successful emancipatory struggle led by the FARC-EP, ELN and their popular allies could undermine the mystique, and set in motion movements in other countries and perhaps put some backbone in some Latin American leaders. Plan Colombia is about preventing Colombia from becoming an example that demonstrates that alternatives are possible and that Washington is vincible.

More significantly, a Cuba-Venezuela-Colombia alliance would provide a powerful political and economic bloc: Cuban social and security know-how, Venezuela's energy clout, and Colombian oil, labor power, agriculture and industry. The complementary political-economies could become an alternative pole to the U.S.-centered empire. Plan Colombia is organized to destroy the potential centerpiece of that political alliance: the Colombian insurgency.

VACUOUS PHRASES AND CONCRETE REALITIES

Plan Colombia has the virtue of being a straightforwardly military operation directed by the U.S. to destroy its class adversary in order to consolidate its empire in Latin America. The anti-drug rhetoric is more for domestic consumption than any operational guide to action. The guerrilla leaders and their movements understand this and act accordingly, mobilizing their social basis of support, securing their military supplies and fashioning an appropriate anti-imperial strategy. Faced with this stark political-military polarity, clearly defined by each adversary, many academic and putatively progressive intellectuals retreat to apolitical abstractions divorced from the real power configurations and class struggle into obscurantist and reified concepts. They speak of the "world capitalist system," "accumulation on a world scale," "historic defeats," "the age of extremes"—vacuous phrases written large and repeated as a mantra which explains nothing and obscures the specific class and political basis of the growing anti-imperialist movements and class struggle. Given the strategic importance of the Colombian outcome in the eyes of Washington and the potential this struggle has as the cutting edge for the breakup of U.S. hegemony in Latin America, it is obvious that accumulation of U.S. capital depends critically on the results of political struggles within nation-states. Moreover, recognizing the centrality of oil as the primary source of energy for the United States, a politico-military victory for the United States in Colombia would isolate Chávez and facilitate efforts to undermine his regime. While the FARC-EP/ELN exists as the radical "greater evil" (in the eyes of Washington), U.S. policy planners have to move cautiously against Chávez' foreign policy for fear he will radicalize domestic policy in line with the Colombian left. For all his nationalist foreign policy pronouncements, Chávez has followed a fairly orthodox fiscal policy, respected and even invited new foreign investors, and has scrupulously met Venezuela's external (and internal) debt payments. Thus Washington has followed complex policies toward its adversaries in the triangle, maintaining cool but correct relations with the Chávez regime, while sharply escalating its support of the war against the FARC-EP/ELN.

WASHINGTON'S MULTI-TRACK POLICY

Washington is pursuing a multi-track policy in relation to the different kinds of opposition that it faces in the region. In relation to Colombia where a U.S. client controls the state apparatus and the guerrilla formations represent a systemic challenge, the State Department has declared all-out war, the centralization and expansion of the war machine and the marginalization of autonomous popular organizations in civil society. While the demilitarized zone where peace negotiations take place is tolerated, Washington is intent on tightening the military encirclement of the region, taking control along the border (particularly the Ecuadorian-Colombian frontier) and preparing for an eventual all-out military assault on guerrilla leadership within the demilitarized zone. U.S. military strategy has increasingly focused on the expansion and operational efficacy of the paramilitary forces. For over a decade the CIA aided in the formation of paramilitary groups ostensibly to combat the drug cartel. Over the past three years, Washington has escalated clandestine support to the paramilitary forces via its military aid to the Colombian Armed Forces and tolerated their drug activities. The paramilitary terrorists play an essential role in Plan Colombia: aggressively "social cleansing" entire regions of peasant activists suspected of guerrilla sympathies. The paramilitary force, estimated to be 10,000 strong, is Washington's "card" for scuttling the peace negotiations and turning the Colombian conflict into a total war. Washington's tactic is to push for the presence of the paramilitary forces in the peace negotiations and then allow Pastrana to mediate as a centrist between the two extremes, imposing a settlement that sustains the socio-economic status quo. Most likely this will cause a breakdown in the negotiations and total war.

Washington combines a two-track policy with the paramilitary forces: "paper criticism" in annual State Department reports, and large-scale material support via U.S. military aid to the Colombian military. While the U.S. follows an almost exclusively military track with Colombia (accompanied by minor financial incentives to coopt NGOs to work on alternative crops), in Venezuela, Washington seeks to avoid precipitating a major confrontation prematurely. The State Department realizes that the balance of forces within Venezuela is unfavorable to any direct military political action. Chávez has reformed the judiciary, won Congressional elections, appointed constitutional-minded senior officers and secured solid majority support among the populace. Washington's allies among the business elite, in the traditional parties and the state apparatus are not in a position at this time to provide effective channels for a Washington funded and directed destabilization effort. The strategy for now is to wage a propaganda war based on creating favorable conditions for future full-scale destabilization and a civilian-military coup.

U.S. tactics in Venezuela are thus the reverse of its policies toward the Colombian regime. In opposition to Chávez, Washington speaks against the authoritarian dangers of his centralization of power—the State Department promotes greater autonomy for its clients' elites in civil society. Washington's goal is to fragment power and provide a platform on which to reorganize the discredited traditional parties. While in Colombia the United States supports the IMF-Pastrana austerity programs, in Venezuela Washington focuses on mass poverty and unemployment, hoping to stimulate popular disaffection.

In Ecuador, as in Colombia, Washington strongly backs the centralist leadership of the executive power, the repression of the social movements and the marginalization of the opposition representation in Congress. The dollarization of the economy and the concession of a U.S. military base are the clearest indications of Ecuador's conversion to U.S.-client status. Hence, the U.S. multi-track policy of military confrontation (Plan Colombia) via the state apparatus and paramilitary forces in Colombia, diplomatic and political pressure via elites in civil society in Venezuela and political-economic co-optation of the Ecuadorian executive define the complex pattern of intervention.

It is far too early to make a definitive judgment about this multitrack policy. In its early stages, Plan Colombia has led to a more aggressive use of paramilitary forces and greater civilian casualties, but no effective "roll-back" of the guerrillas. On the negative side, the further deterioration of the economy has increased urban disaffection and weakened Pastrana's political position as evidenced by the sharp losses in the municipal elections late in 2000. In Venezuela, the Chávez regime is consolidating institutional power, building support in the trade unions via new free elections while retaining mass support. In Ecuador, the social movements and the Indian-peasant coalition retains the power to mobilize support, even as Washington's allies have at least temporarily succeeded in pushing through military agreements and the overt subordination of the Ecuadorian economy to the U.S. Treasury (via dollarization).

CONSEQUENCES OF U.S. MILITARY ESCALATION

Plan Colombia, a typical low intensity war (where large-scale U.S. financing and arms and low level ground troop commitment are combined), has already had a high intensity impact (on peasants and workers) which is internationalizing the conflict. Despite predictable denials, U.S. military and intelligence agencies have been active in directing Colombian paramilitary forces to decimate civilian—largely peasant—supporters of the FARC-EP/ELN in the villages. Dozens of suspected peasants, community activists, schoolteachers and others have been assassinated, in order to terrorize the rest of the population. Frequent paramilitary sweeps in regions occupied by the U.S.-advised Colombian military have led to the displacement of over a million peasants. Paramilitary terror is part of the repertoire of U.S. counterinsurgency tactics designed to empty the countryside and deny the guerrillas logistical support, food and new recruits.

As Plan Colombia escalates the violence, thousands of peasants are fleeing across the borders into Venezuela, Ecuador, Panama and Brazil. Inevitably cross border attacks by the paramilitaries on refugees has widened the military conflict. Families and relatives of guerrilla activists put to flight retain their ties and contacts. The frontier and borders have become war zones in which squatter refugees living in squalor are partisans in the conflict and are targets of the Colombian military. Rather than containing the civil conflict, Plan Colombia is extending and internationalizing the war, exacerbating instability in the adjoining regions of neighboring countries.

Plan Colombia clearly escalates the degree and visibility of U.S. involvement in Colombia. With an estimated 300 U.S. military advisors, and additional sub-contracted mercenaries flying helicopters, U.S. involvement has moved down the chain from planning, design, and direction of the war to the operational-tactical level. Moreover, U.S. policymakers have used their financial levers to reward pliant and cooperative Colombian military officials and to punish or humiliate those who do not sufficiently respond to U.S. commands or advice. The perception (and reality) among Colombians is that Plan Colombia is transforming a civil war into a national war.

There is absolutely no doubt that the Colombian elite and sectors of the upper middle class are in favor of even greater and more direct U.S. military intervention. Among the peasants however, the greater U.S. presence means greater use of chemical defoliants, increasingly aggressive and destructive military forays to eradicate coca and food plants and to eliminate persons that stand in the way. Plan Colombia is transforming a civil war into a national liberation struggle. This nationalist dimension could provide added urban support to the guerrilla struggle from students, professionals and trade unionists, while pushing apolitical farmers into the guerrilla camp on the grounds of household survival.

Plan Colombia's prime emphasis on a military approach to popular insurgency is militarizing Colombian society—increasing the overseas outflow of professionals and others fleeing the growing intimidation of the unleashed military/paramilitary forces in the cities. Putting Colombia on a war footing intimidates the average Colombian, but it also alienates lower-middle class Colombians, subject to arbitrary searches and interrogation. The loss of the limited urban space where Colombians carry on civil discourse will increase underground activity for some while forcing further withdrawal from public life for others. Trade union and civic demands are deemed "subversive to the war effort" by the government, civil oppositions are "fifth columnists acting on behalf of the guerrillas." The result is an increase in the already record high number of trade unionists and journalists assassinated. Intimidation of some will be accompanied by the radical rejection of the state by others.

Plan Colombia draws $3.5 billion dollars from the Colombian treasury—at a time when the government is imposing austerity measures and cuts in social expenditures that adversely affect wage and salaried groups. By increasing Colombia's military spending, Plan Colombia increases the public's opposition to the state, which in turn increases the demand by the military and U.S. policymakers to increase the repressive apparatus. Neoliberal policies and the militarization of the conflict require a bigger centralized state and a shrinking and constricted civil society—at least among the popular classes of civil society. The reinforcement of the state and its commitment to fight a two front war—a war in the countryside with arms, and with neoliberal austerity policies in the cities—not only deepens the polarization between the regime and the civilian populace, but it increasingly isolates the regime and makes it more dependent on Washington and the burgeoning military and paramilitary organizations in the cities as well as in the countryside. Plan Colombia has many unintended consequences that, far from containing the conflict and building up support for the state, extend and deepen the conflict and isolate the regime. Essentially this is because Washington and its Colombian clients, blinded by the single-minded pursuit of imperial power, have a false reading of the revolutionary challenge.

WASHINGTON'S DIAGNOSIS: FOIBLES AND FACTS

Essentially Washington's Plan Colombia operates from three mistaken assumptions: 1) a false analogy extrapolated from its victories in Central America; 2) a series of false equations about the nature of the Colombian guerrillas and their source of strength and 3) a misplaced emphasis or exaggerated focus on the drug basis of guerrilla political power.

The FARC-EP/ELN challenge to power cannot be compared to the Central American guerrilla struggles in the 1980s. First of all, there is the time factor—the Colombian guerrillas have a longer trajectory, accumulating a vast storehouse of practical experience, particularly about the pitfalls of peace accords that fail to transform the state and make structural reform the center of a settlement. Secondly, the guerrilla leadership of the FARC-EP is made up mostly of peasant leaders or individuals who have developed deep ties to the countryside, unlike the Central American commanders who were mostly middle class professionals eager to return to city life and an electoral political career. Thirdly, the geography is different. Not only is Colombia far larger, the topography favors guerrilla warfare.

Moreover the guerrilla political-terrain relationship in Colombia is more favorable. The guerrillas by social origin and experience are much more familiar with the terrain of warfare. Fourthly, the FARC-EP leadership has put socio-economic reforms in the center of their political negotiations—unlike the Central Americans who prioritized the reinsertion of the ex-commanders into the electoral process. Fifthly, the Colombian guerrillas are totally self-financing and are not subject to the pressures and deals of outside supporters—as was the case in Central America. Sixthly, the FARC-EP has passed through a peace accord—between 1984 and 1990 in which thousands of its supporters and sympathizers were assassinated and no progress was made in reforming the socio-economic system. Finally, the guerrillas have observed the results of the Central American accords and are not impressed by the results: the ascendancy of neoliberalism, the impunity of the military's human rights violators and the enrichment of many of the ex-guerrilla commanders, some of whom have joined the chorus supporting U.S. intervention in Colombia.

Given these differences, Washington's two-track policy of talking peace and financing alternative crops while escalating the war and promoting crop eradication, is doomed to failure. The carrot of a peace settlement for the commanders, and the war of attrition against the base, will not drive the FARC-EP to settle for a peace accord in which electoral insertion, military institutional continuity and rampaging neoliberalism remain in place. The second fallacious assumption of U.S. policymakers is the simplistic analysis they make of the sources of FARC-EP power. Washington's strategic thinkers equate the FARC-EP with the drug trade, building its strength and recruiting fighters with the millions of dollars they accrue and to the "terror tactics" they practice to intimidate the populace and gain control of swathes of the countryside. The simple equations are: FARC-EP = drugs; drugs = dollars; dollars = recruits; recruits = terror; terror = growth of territorial control.

This superficial approach lacks any historical, social and regional dimension, thus completely missing the social dynamics of the FARC-EP's growing influence. First, it overlooks the historical process of the FARC-EP formation and growth in particular regions and classes. The FARC-EP has become a formidable guerrilla formation through the accumulation of forces over time, not in a linear fashion, but with setbacks and advances. Family ties, living and working experiences in regions abandoned or harassed by the state have played a big role in recruitment and movement-building over a 35-year period. Via trial and error, reflection and study, the FARC-EP has been able to accumulate a vast store of practical understanding of the psychology and material bases of guerrilla warfare and mass recruitment. Throughout its history of championing land reform and peasant rights the FARC-EP has with considerable success been able to create

peasant cadres who link villagers and leaders and communicate in both directions. These historical links and experiences, far more than the drug trade tax, are
instrumental in the growth of the FARC-EP. In fact, the role of the FARC-EP
sales tax is shaped by its historical-political evolution and not vice versa. The
decision to tax drug traffickers and reinvest the funds back into the movement—
isolated examples of personal enrichment to the contrary notwithstanding—
reveals the political character of the movement. In areas of FARC-EP control,
drugs are not sold or consumed. The FARC-EP protects the peasant producers,
while the U.S. political and military allies and banks commercialize drugs and
launder the profits.

Socially, the FARC-EP is inserted in the class structure via interlocking with
villagers and defending peasant interests. The FARC-EP recruits from the peasants and the urban poor with whom it works, and with which in many cases it has
family ties. To the extent that military/paramilitary depredations uproot villagers,
they make young peasants available and willing recruits for the guerrilla armies'.
The same goes with coca crop eradication programs: destroying the peasants'
livelihood creates propitious conditions for the guerrillas' call to arms. The guerrilla strength in the provinces is derived not only from the exploitative and abu-
sive rule of the economic elites but from the concentration of state spending and
consumption in Bogotá (and to a lesser extent the other major cities). The historical urban-rural polarization has contributed to the formation of rural armies, by
regional politicians as well as the guerrillas. But the arbitrary and violent intervention in the countryside by the military at the service of the Bogotá political
elite and the resident landlords increases the distance between the political class
and the peasants, many of whom feel closer to the guerrillas. Finally U.S. policymakers over-emphasize the centrality of drug income in the guerrilla war. No
one would deny that the drug tax is an important factor, a necessary source of revenue for financing arms and food purchases. But it is hardly sufficient.

What the ideologists of Plan Colombia ignore or underestimate is the importance of FARC-EP's struggles on behalf of basic peasant interests (land, credit,
roads, etc.), their political education and ideological appeals, the social services
and law and order that they provide. In most of their dealings with the rural population, the FARC-EP represents order, rectitude and social justice. While drug
taxes buy arms, it is this ensemble of social, political, and ideological activities
that resonates with the peasantry and attracts the peasants to the call to arms.
Drug taxes and arms do not buy class loyalties and village allegiances. Otherwise
the military and paramilitary forces would be an unbeatable force! The strength
of the FARC-EP is based on the interplay of ideological appeals and the reso-
nance of its analysis and political practices with the everyday reality of peasant

life. To undermine the FARC-EP, Washington would have to change the socio-economic reality that Plan Colombia is designed to defend.

RESULTS AND PERSPECTIVES OF A 'MISDIAGNOSIS'

Washington's Plan Colombia is a typical example of an imperial power pouring arms and money to prop up a loyal client (the Pastrana regime) that increasingly relies on coercion (the military and paramilitary forces) and political-economic allies who appropriate land and dispossess peasant families. The military relies on conscripts with no stake in the military outcome and trains military professionals who have no rapport with the people (but loyalty to the hierarchy) and are unfamiliar with the terrain of struggle. The military officials are trained in high-technology weaponry and are mainly concerned with professional promotion. In general the U.S. directed militarization program has not raised the low morale among the conscripts or even the lower ranks of the officers. The military tactics target civilian groups from which many of the conscripts are recruited. The large-scale destruction of crops and villages has little attraction for normal recruits—that is why the military relies on the hired assassins in the paramilitary groups to carry out the "dirty war." Plan Colombia provokes fear and flight among the peasants and perhaps the paramilitary formations recruit a few of the uprooted young. However, it is doubtful for reasons of history, biography, and social-economic background that the paramilitary forces can match the FARC-EP/ELN in securing new recruits.

The continuing and deepening war and the increasing isolation of the regime is leading to greater U.S. military engagement. Already U.S. military advisors are teaching and directing high-tech warfare, and providing operational leadership in close proximity to the battlefield. Washington is pushing for and extending operational bases to new regions and these garrison bases will become targets of the guerrilla forces. If the Colombian forces are not up to the task of defending the forward bases from which U.S. advisors operate, will that be used as a pretext to send more U.S. troops to protect the bases? This would be the beginning link in a chain leading to greater U.S. ground troop engagement. While serious questions may be raised about the degree and depth of future U.S. military involvement, there is no question that Plan Colombia means deepening the war and that will surely lead to a further undermining of the Colombian economy. The treasury will be drained to finance the war; the increased air and land war will provoke a massive increase in refugees and destabilize regional (and ultimately national) economies. Refugee camps have frequently become hotbeds for radical politics—the politics of the uprooted.

Drug, contraband, and other criminal activity will flourish, straining the capacity of border policing by neighboring countries. History teaches us that the United States will not be able to localize the effects of its war. What goes around has a way of coming around.

THE BLOWBACK CONSEQUENCES

Blowback refers to the unanticipated adverse effects of U.S. involvement in overseas wars. For example, the U.S. training of Cuban exiles and Afghan Islamic fanatics to fight communism led to highly organized drug gangs who supplied U.S. and European markets and later engaged in terrorist activities, in some cases attacking U.S. targets. The big narco-traffickers in Colombia are not the people described by Washington's anti-drug boss and propagated by Plan Colombia's ideological defenders. The so-called "narco-guerrillas" and peasant coca growers receive less than 10% of the earnings because they only produce and tax the raw materials. The big profits are in the processing and commercialization in the export market and in the laundering of drug profits. The real powers and beneficiaries of the narcotics traffic are all strategic U.S. allies in the counter-revolutionary war.

If we look at the drug routes across Central America and the Caribbean, they pass through important client regimes obviously with official backing. The same is true in South Asia and the Middle East. Drug production, processing and transport follow a route via past or present U.S. clients. Turkey is the centerpiece of the whole European drug trade with the active protection of the Turkish military and intelligence agencies. They have deep ties, not only with the drug trade in Afghanistan, Burma and some ex-Soviet Republics, but also with Bosnian, and especially Albanian gangsters whose activities are facilitated by the strong U.S. military and political backing of Albania/Kosovo and Bosnia. With official backing, these gangsters have combined drugs, white slavery and gunrunning.

In some cases, Washington's strategic allies and anti-communist clients have turned against it, in many instances following arms training and supply by the CIA. For example, former CIA clients have organized terrorist cells that have even bombed targets like New York's World Trade Center. Colombia presents a similar blowback potential. The traffickers who buy the coca leaves, process the paste, and turn out the final product (powder) are either working with, or are themselves, members of paramilitary groups, high military officials, landowners, and not a few bankers and other respectable capitalists—who launder drug money as investments in real estate, construction, etc. Profits from overseas operations are laundered in leading U.S. and European banks as any number of past and present investigations have revealed. Key U.S. political allies in Colombia and influential economic elites in U.S. banking are the major players in the narcotics trade, undermining the fundamental ideological prop of Washington's Plan Colombia and revealing its true, imperial underpinning.

Drug traffickers backed by the United States today are thus active in promoting the drug abuse and crime that continues to plague U.S. cities—especially among minority youth. The violence associated with the drug trade also creates extortionists known to shake down U.S. and European overseas business. By engaging in violent confrontations the narco-paramilitary officials further destabilize the investment climate perpetuating insecurity and inhibiting longterm investments.

As the breach between the U.S. anti-drug ideology and its actual links to the narco-military/paramilitary becomes clearer, this will likely provoke dissent within the United States. There is no prospect of a large-scale opposition movement in the United States at present. Still, in Colombia, Venezuela, Ecuador, and the rest of Latin America—exposed to the full brunt of the war to save the empire—the advance of the revolutionary struggle in Colombia has revealed contradictions that cut right through their societies and extend beyond, into the world economic order, with portentous implications both for their future and U.S. imperial rule.

IV.

THE

WORLD

RESPONDS

TO

PLAN

COLOMBIA

First International Solidarity Conference Resolution

Over 400 people from 35 countries, representing about 50 organizations, made the First International Conference in Solidarity and for Peace in Colombia and Latin America a resounding success. The conference took place on July 20-22, 2001 in El Salvador.

Most of Central and South America were represented, as well as countries in the Caribbean, Europe and North America. The overwhelmingly youthful crowd cheered, waved flags, chanted and applauded the many international speakers who spoke out against Washington's Plan Colombia, for peace with social justice and in defense of the revolutionary movement in that country. Below is the gathering's final resolution.

We underline that this first conference has been an outstanding expression of international unity and solidarity of the Americas and the world in the face of the continual imperialist aggressions against the peoples that are fighting against neoliberalism for liberation, social justice, participatory democracy and for the sovereignty of the peoples.

Plan Colombia is a project of interventionist war by the United States against the peoples of Latin America and the Caribbean, for the purpose of crushing the diverse and growing expressions of struggle, rebellion, popular and patriotic victories and impeding the appearance and consolidation of participatory democracies contrary to the hegemonic plans of that imperial power and its aim of imposing the so-called Free Trade Area of the Americas (FTAA).

Closely tied to Plan Colombia and the FTAA are the ominous processes of dollarization, concretely manifest in El Salvador and Ecuador and the installation of various American military bases, concrete cases being in Aruba, Curacao, Comalapa, El Salvador and Manta, Ecuador.

The turning back of these imperialistic and recolonizing initiatives is an unavoidable duty. It is as unavoidable as is the rejection of the onerous payments of the external debt.

With all this, and the culmination of the privatizations extended to ports, airports, water, electricity, science reserves, forests, coasts, etc., the United States is trying to make the recolonization of the continent irreversible.

The pretext with which the justification of this new military escalation in the continent of America is being attempted is the so-called "war on the narcotics traffic." In this framework, the United States not only includes the guerrilla movements, the Revolutionary Armed Forces of Colombia-People's Army (FARC-EP) and the National Liberation Army (ELN), but also the other forms of struggle and popular and democratic expression that openly confront imperialism.

This plan under way forms part of a global strategy of economic, political and military recolonization by U.S. imperialism, for the purpose of dominating the peoples and nations of our sub-continent in an absolute and permanent manner.

It will also have ominous consequences for our countries since it aims to impede processes toward real democracies; that is, participatory democracies with social justice and national sovereignty. As well, it is blocking the reconstruction of their economies devastated as much by the economic crisis as by natural disasters, diverting efforts and resources to feed an absurd war that gravely compromises the security and sovereignty of our nations and is creating great centers of military tensions. These generate an uncontainable arms race from which the big arms-producing and -trafficking enterprises are making profits.

Plan Colombia and its chemical warfare component would destroy the Amazonian forest, resulting in the disappearance of the planet's main lungs and the world's largest reserve of fresh water.

The aerial spraying and the official violence practiced by the interventionist, local and paramilitary forces, which are one and the same, are aggravating the problem. For these reasons, we condemn Plan Colombia/the Andean Initiative. We demand that it be annulled for the sake of continuing the pursuit of a political solution to the social and armed conflict Colombia is experiencing, by means of the paths of dialog at the Table of Dialogs.

The struggle against the plague of the narcotics traffic must be fundamentally directed to prevent the growth of demand in the countries of principal consumption, to punish and expropriate the big chiefs of the international mafias who move around freely with their capital in the world of finance and investment, to control the flow of the chemicals required by this sinister industry, to direct more resources to the medical recovery of the sick; to substitute illicit crops with manual, voluntary eradication arranged with the poor peasants and workers who carry on this activity as a means of subsistence. It requires policies that guarantee to raise the standard of living of the rural inhabitants.

In this way it would be totally unnecessary to use military means to confront a problem with profound social and economic roots.

To persist with Plan Colombia is equal to escalating the war and involving more of the continent's governments in support of this destructive policy that immediately targets the heroic Colombian insurgency and opposes the Bolivarian revolution headed by President Hugo Chávez and the significant growth of the popular and patriotic struggles in other countries of the continent.

All of this falls within the United States' plan to exercise perpetual and universal domination over the planet. In today's reality, this constitutes a dangerous threat against humanity and is generating a crisis of civilization and of survival for the immense majority of the Earth's inhabitants.

Nevertheless, since the causes that determined the great revolutionary changes in world history have not disappeared and instead have sharpened, the resistance and struggles of the peoples at this beginning of the 21st century confirm the relevance of revolutionary ideals and the necessity of an alternative world to the system in force, one that guarantees development, justice, human dignity, democratic participation and peace for the peoples.

And therefore, we, the organizations, entities, persons and movements participating in this gathering, declare before the Americas and the world our resolute solidarity with revolutionary Cuba and with the struggle against the criminal blockade imposed on it by the United States; our solidarity with Bolivarian Venezuela; with the Zapatista rebellion and the democratic forces of Mexico; with the heroic insurgency and all the progressive sectors of Colombia; with the Puerto Rican patriots who are fighting to remove the yankee troops from Vieques and achieve the independence of Puerto Rico; with the struggle of the aboriginal peoples for their inalienable rights; with the beautiful rebellion of women and of all the sectors subject to discrimination; with the fighting social and political movements in Brazil, Bolivia, Ecuador, Paraguay, Argentina, the Dominican Republic, Jamaica and other countries; with the patriotic and popular struggles of the left and progressive political forces of the continent; with the anti-globalization and anti-neoliberal movements impacting on Europe and the U.S. and with the efforts of the political parties and movements working for change that are achieving new advances and electoral victories.

At the same time, we condemn the shameless interference of the government of the United States of America in the Nicaraguan electoral process in favor of the Liberal Party, and likewise we reject, similar although more discrete, interventions put in motion in other countries where the left and progressive forces are advancing toward new electoral triumphs. Consequently, we demand that the United States cease its policy of blackmail in the face of the possible Sandinista victory in Nicaragua and we demand the sovereign right of the peoples of the continent to elect their governments freely, without pressure and interference.

We demand liberty for all political prisoners, beginning with Mumia Abu-Jamal and the five Cuban patriots in the United States, the Argentines of the Tablada, headed by Roberto Felicetti and the already sentenced Emilio Ali and the 2,500 social fighters who have been tried and are threatened with aberrant sentences. We demand liberty for the Peruvian, Puerto Rican and Colombian political prisoners.

Our solidarizing will today stand with all the just causes in the world, among which the heroic struggle of the Palestinian people against Israeli imperialist genocide has unique stature. At the same time, we reject all the imperialist aggressions and blockades such as the ones the United States persistently exercises against Libya, Iran and Iraq.

Likewise, we stand in solidarity with the struggles of the peoples of Africa, Asia and Oceania.

We take up as a whole the legacy of the Liberator, Simón Bolívar, and of the heroes and heroines of our first independence and we commit to make their aims and dreams reality.

We express our sincere gratitude for the hospitality and affection displayed by the Salvadoran people and organizations that sustained this event. We salute their effort for the success of this First International Gathering of Solidarity and for Peace in Colombia and Latin America, carried out in difficult conditions in view of the destructive results of the recent earthquakes which significantly affected the economy and conditions of life, and in the face of the persistent obstacles created by the embassy of the United States in its stubborn desire to impede this fruitful gathering. All this increases the value of this gesture of internationalist solidarity generously unfolded by the Salvadoran brothers and sisters. We express our sincere recognition to all those who have made this success possible.

RESOLUTION ON PLAN COLOMBIA AND SUPPORT FOR THE PEACE PROCESS

EUROPEAN PARLIAMENT

February 1, 2001

The European Parliament, having regard to its previous resolutions on Colombia, having regard to the conclusions of the General Affairs Council of October 9, 2000, having regard to the statement by the EU Presidency of October 25, 2000,

A. Whereas, in spite of concerted efforts at dialog with the guerrillas and the peace talks under way, the parties have not yet succeeded in bringing an end to a conflict which has lasted for over three decades,

B. Recalling the undertaking given by the Clinton administration and President Pastrana in September 1999 on the joint implementation of a "plan for peace, prosperity and the strengthening of the state," otherwise known as Plan Colombia,

C. Whereas, Plan Colombia is not the product of a process of dialog amongst the various partners in society and whereas acceptance of the strategy for peace by all of the country's institutions would be a most welcome development which should involve not only action to combat drug production and trafficking but also a strategy for social and economic recovery, the strengthening of institutions and social development, all of which need to be supported,

D. Whereas, one of the objectives of Plan Colombia lies in stamping out drug trafficking and the spread of illegal crops by means of a strategy which favours aerial crop spraying and the use of biological agents, methods which are leading to the forced displacement of families and communities and are seriously affecting Colombia's rich biodiversity,

E. Having regard to the declaration by the Support Group for the Peace Process in Colombia (Madrid, July 7, 2000), in which the participants expressed their full political support for the peace process under way, and the declaration by the EU delegation calling for greater efforts by the Colombian government with a view to breaking up paramilitary groups,

F. Having regard to the statement by the General Affairs Council of October 9, 2000, in which the European Union reaffirmed its support for the ongoing peace efforts and its willingness to play an active role in the negotiating process, which should involve consulting civil society and obtaining the agreement of all parties with a view to achieving peace which is founded on respect for human rights, humanitarian law and fundamental freedoms,

G. Whereas, the problem of drug trafficking and related offenses calls for a global approach based on the principles of shared responsibility and internationalal cooperation between drug-producing and drug-consuming countries, with a particular view to further action to stamp out the laundering of money derived from drug trafficking,

H. Having regard to the dialog established at the meeting held in Costa Rica in mid-October and the growth in dialog between civil society and armed groups; having regard to the meeting of the Support Group for the Peace Process in Colombia (Bogotá, October 24-25, 2000) attended by representatives of the Commission and the EU Presidency,

I. Whereas, acts of violence and terrorism, assassinations, kidnappings and massacres, aimed at the civilian population in particular, have increased while the peace talks have been taking place and considering the impunity enjoyed by the perpetrators of such crimes and, in particular, by those who order the crimes to be carried out,

J. Having regard to the recent visit by Mrs. Mary Robinson to Colombia and the attention which she drew to the inadequacy of the measures taken against paramilitary groups and to impunity in general; whereas not only tens of thousands of Colombians but also Europeans have been the victims of crimes which have gone unpunished, such as the Spanish volunteer Iñigo Eguiluz, the Belgian Daniel Gillard, the Italian Giacomo Turra, the Swiss Hildegard Feldmann and many others;

1. Reiterates its firm support for the peace process initiated by President Pastrana and urges the parties to pursue their efforts in this regard, in spite of the difficulties involved; calls on the FARC-EP to return to the table and to continue the peace negotiations;

2. Takes the view that, in addition to their military dimension, the prevailing situation and conflict in Colombia have a social and political dimension whose roots lie in economic, political, cultural and social exclusion;

3. Believes that stepping up military involvement in the fight against drugs involves the risk of sparking off an escalation of the conflict in the region, and that military solutions cannot bring about lasting peace;

4. Warns that Plan Colombia contains aspects that run counter to the cooperation strategies and projects to which the EU has already committed itself and jeopardizes its cooperation programmes; expresses particular concern at the current situation in the Putumayo region;

5. Considers that the European Union must support the aspects of the peace process which involve the strengthening of institutions, alternative development, humanitarian aid and social development, since these are the ones which are most in accordance with its cooperation strategy;

6. Believes that the social movement, which has been severely affected by repression, NGOs and local communities must play an active role in the ongoing peace process; welcomes the fact that their role has been affirmed (in particular at the meeting in Costa Rica) and believes that it must be coordinated with the efforts being made at the negotiating table;

7. Believes that lasting peace cannot be achieved in Colombia without deep-seated changes to the means by which wealth is distributed, since many of the problems confronting the country stem from the fact that peasant farmers do not own land;

8. Highlights the importance of encouraging genuine agrarian reform, using notably land confiscated from drug barons, which presents peasant farmers with economic alternatives; therefore urges the Colombian government to implement ambitious reform policies designed to curb the increasing concentration of land and improve social conditions;

9. Stresses that European Union action should pursue its own, non-military strategy combining neutrality, transparency, the participation of civil society and undertakings from the parties involved in the negotiations;

10. Welcomes the conclusions of the October 9, 2000 Council meeting, which contain announcements concerning the implementation of a "substantial European programme of socio-economic and institutional support for the peace process in Colombia, aimed at promoting and protecting respect for human rights, humanitarian law and fundamental freedoms, improving the living conditions of the local populations, encouraging the cultivation of alternative crops and the protection of biodiversity and supporting the introduction of structural reforms in all fields which fuel armed conflict;"

11. Expresses its outrage at the large-scale massacres of country dwellers which have recently been carried out by paramilitary groups in the regions of Magdalena, Magdalena Medio, Cauca and Putumayo, and the threats which have been made to country dwellers in the Tumaco region and elsewhere; takes the view that securing significant results in the fight against impunity and against armed groups which violate human rights and contravene international humanitarian law is essential to the credibility of the rule of law; urges the Colombian government to continue its fight against paramilitary groups and its efforts to strengthen the foundations of the rule of law, and to implement immediately and in their entirety the United Nations recommendations on human rights;

12. Considers that the European Union must play a more determined role in the political protection and the funding of organisations (in particular

organisations for the families of victims) which campaign to have crimes against humanity investigated, to preserve the memory of the victims of such crimes and to ensure that the perpetrators thereof do not go unpunished;

13. Welcomes the proposal by Commissioners Patten and Nielson to grant substantial support for the peace efforts in Colombia amounting to EUR 105 million for the period 2000-2006; stresses that, so as to give credibility to the Union's action, initial measures contributing to the peace process should be introduced without delay and be aimed at promoting respect for human rights, humanitarian law and fundamental freedoms, improving the living conditions of the local populations, using civil society organisations and social movements as channels and bearing in mind the forced displacement of a section of the rural population, of which women and children form the vast majority;

14. Welcomes the decision by the Council of Ministers to undertake a six-monthly appraisal of the state of the peace process, the progress in implementing programmes and compliance with the respective undertakings and obligations of the Colombian government and the groups involved in the negotiations to strengthen peace, and asks the Council and Commission to inform Parliament at the same time;

15. Is convinced that, in the fight against illegal crops, negotiated and agreed solutions, agrarian reform and alternative crops, together with criminal proceedings against traffickers and money launderers, should take precedence over crop-spraying campaigns; believes in this regard that the Union must take the necessary steps to secure an end to the large-scale use of chemical herbicides and prevent the introduction of biological agents such as fusarium oxysporum, given the dangers of their use to human health and the environment alike;

16. Highlights the importance of strengthening regional cooperation and dialog on the basis of the principle of international coresponsibility, given that past experience in the fight against illegal crops has shown that tackling this problem in one country alone merely serves to transfer it to neighbouring countries;

17. Stresses the need to step up inter-regional cooperation to curb and stamp out drug trafficking and combat money laundering; in this respect, the European Union ought to support Colombia's request to sign the Strasbourg Convention;

18. Calls on the Venezuelan government to cooperate with the Colombian government in jointly establishing mechanisms which will make it

possible to resolve the border problems relating to the fight against drug production and trafficking;

19. Urges the Colombian government to follow the approach used in the talks with the FARC-EP in establishing dialog with the other guerrilla groups with a view to promoting the principles of neutrality and transparency and thus earning the support of the various armed groups for planned programmes and projects;

20. Urges all the armed groups to support a humanitarian agreement under which they would cease kidnapping, release their hostages, refrain from committing terrorist acts, from recruiting under-age supporters and from carrying out attacks on the civilian population, and conclude a serious cease-fire agreement;

21. Reiterates its support for the Office of the UN High Commissioner for Human Rights and its efforts to secure a humanitarian agreement in Colombia;

22. Instructs its President to forward this resolution to the Council, the Commission, the governments of Colombia, Venezuela and of the mediating countries.

100 LATIN AMERICANS OPPOSE PLAN COLOMBIA

April 16, 2001

To President George W. Bush, United States of America,

As your Administration considers the future direction of U.S. policy towards the Andes, we ask you to suspend and reformulate U.S. support for the implementation of Plan Colombia, placing a greater emphasis on supporting the peace process.

We, the undersigned Latin Americans, know there are no easy answers or quick fixes to Colombia's tragic dilemma of warfare and drug-related violence. And we believe the United States has a legitimate interest in reducing the damage done by illegal drug use. But we are gravely concerned that current policy will cause more harm than good in Colombia and in the region at large, while having little or no effect on the drug problems of the consumer countries.

Plan Colombia's predominantly military emphasis will intensify the internal conflict and undermine the ongoing peace process, which offers the only hope of a lasting solution to the conflict. The expected environmental damage, increase in forced displacement and worsening of the humanitarian crisis will affect the entire Andean region. Yet history shows that forced crop eradication campaigns in Latin America have consistently failed to stop the flow of drugs north. After more than a decade of such efforts, there has been no significant decrease in total drug production and trafficking. New sources of supply have inevitably arisen to satisfy undiminished global demand.

We join the European Union in calling for a consultative process to develop realistic proposals to address the root causes of the violence. Instead of expanding misguided, ineffective and harmful policies, the international community should offer its resources for health, education and economic development programs, and support efforts to negotiate a peaceful settlement of the longest running conflict in the hemisphere.

As Latin Americans, we are witnesses to the terrible consequences our society suffers every day because of drug trafficking. Now more than ever, we are convinced that there is no choice but to work together, both within our countries and across borders, to reduce these harms and accept our "shared responsibility." Colombia and the Andean region need and deserve the support and solidarity of the international community to confront major challenges. We therefore hope that the Summit of the Americas provides you and the other participating heads of state with the opportunity to explore more peaceful and effective approaches to our common drug problems.

Sincerely,

ARGENTINA
Graciela Fernández Meijide, Former Senator, Former Minister of State; Adolfo Pérez Esquivel, Nobel Laureate, President, Peace and Justice Service Foundation; Juan Gabriel Tokatlian, Professor of International Relations, University of San Andrés; Horacio Verbitsky, Journalist, President, Center for Legal and Social Studies; Juan Carlos Volnovich, Doctor

BOLIVIA
Carlos Aguirre Bastos, National Academy of Sciences; Antonio Araníbar Quiroga, Former Minister of Foreign Relations; Edgar Camacho Omiste, Former Minister of Foreign Relations; Roger Cortéz Hurtado, University Professor; Alfonso Ferrufino Valderrama, Former Vice-President of the Chamber of Deputies; Julio Garret Aillón, Former Vice-President of Bolivia; Juan del Granado Cossio, Mayor of La Paz; Horst Grebe López, Former Minister of Labor; Lydia Gueiler Tejada, Former President of Bolivia; Carlos Quiroga Blanco, President, Commission for International Policy, Chamber of Deputies

BRAZIL
Pedro Casaldaliga Pla, Catholic Bishop, São Felix do Araguaia; Cardinal Paulo Evaristo Arns, Archbishop Emeritus of São Paulo; Paulo Roberto Martins Maldos, Advisor to the Council for Indigenous Missionary; Mauro Morelli, Bishop of the Diocese of Duque de Caxias, Rio de Janeiro; Maria Thereza Rocha de Assis Moura, Lawyer

COLOMBIA
Apecides Alvis, President, Confederation of Colombian Workers; Armando Balbuena, President, National Indigenous Peoples' Organization of Colombia; Ana Teresa Bernal, National Coordinator of Redepaz; Jaime Bernal Cuellar, Former Attorney General of the Nation; Wilson Borja, President, National State Workers' Federation; Antonio Caballero, Writer and Journalist; José Fernando Castro, Former Human Rights Ombudsman; Piedad Córdoba, Senator; Gloria Cuartas Montoya, Former Mayor of Apartado; Parmenio Cuellar Bastidas, Governor of Nariño; Bruno Díaz, Bogotá City Council; Eduardo Díaz Uribe, Former Minister of State; Juan Carlos Flórez, Bogotá City Council; Daniel García-Peña, Former High Commisioner for Peace; Luis Eduardo Garzón, President of the Central Workers' Union (CUT); Carlos Gaviria, Former

Magistrate of the Constitutional Court; Ignacio Gómez, Journalist; Monsignor Leonardo Gómez Serna, Bishop of Socorro and San Gil; Camilo González, Former Minister of Health; Guillermo González, Journalist; Iván G. Guerrero Guevara, Governor of Putumayo; Claudia Gurisatti, Journalist; Hernando Hernández, President of the Trade Union of Workers (USO); Guillermo Jaramillo, Governor of Tolima; Nestor León Ramírez, Former Mayor of San Vicente del Caguán, Caquetá; María Emma Mejía, Former Minister of Foreign Relations; Alfredo Molano, Writer and Journalist; Antonio Morales, Journalist; Luis Gilberto Murillo Urrutia, Former Governor of Chocó; Antonio Navarro, Member of Congress; Rafael Orduz M., Senator; Juan Manuel Ospina, Senator; William Ospina, Writer; Rodrigo Pardo, Former Minister of Foreign Relations; Gustavo Francisco Petro Virego, Member of Congress; Roberto Posada, Journalist; Jaime Prieto Amaya, Bishop; Carlos Rosero, National Leader of Afro-Colombian Communities; Gonzalo Sánchez G., Professor Emeritus, National University of Colombia; Horacio Serpa, Presidential Candidate; Floro D. Tunubala, Governor of Cauca; Alejo Vargas, Professor, National University of Colombia; Carlos Alfonso Velásquez R., Retired Colonel, University Professor; Carlos Vicente de Roux, Former Presidential Advisor for Human Rights; Gloria Zea, Director of Museum of Modern Art; Jaime Zuluaga, Professor, National University of Colombia

CHILE

Sergio Bitar, Senator; Ariel Dorfman, Writer; Paulo Egenau, Clinical Psychologist; Pablo Lagos Puccio, Lawyer; Ibán de Rementeria, Former UN Official, International Consultant on Drug Control Policy

ECUADOR

Israel Batista, Secretary General, Latin American Council of Churches-CLAI; Monsignor Gonzalo López Marañón, Bishop of Sucumbios; César Montúfar, Professor, Director of International Studies, Simón Bolívar Andean University; Monsignor Luis Alberto Luna Tobar, Prelate of the Catholic Ecuadorian Church; Nina Pacari, Member of Congress; Julio Prado Vallejo, Former Chancellor; Julio Cesar Trujillo, Constitutional Academic, Ecuador

GUATEMALA

Helen Beatríz Mack Chang, President, Myrna Mack Foundation; Xabier Gorostiaga, S.J., Professor, Rafael Landivar University; Rigoberta Menchú Tum, Nobel Laureate, UNESCO Goodwill Ambassador

HAITI

Claudette Werleigh, Former Prime Minister

HONDURAS

Leo Valladares Lanza, President, Ibero-American Federation of Ombudsman

MEXICO

Sergio Aguayo, Professor, Mexican Academy of Human Rights; Miguel Concha Malo, Prior Dominican Provincial; Carlos Fuentes, Writer; Vilma Fuentes, Writer; Oscar González, President, Mexican Academy of Human Rights; Miguel Angel Granados Chapa, Journalist; Ignacio Hernández, Poet; Ofelia Medina, Actress; Jesús Ortega, Senator; Samuel Ruiz García, former Bishop of San Cristobal de las Casas; Rodolfo Stavenhagen, National Social Sciences Award; Felipe de Jesús Vicencio, Senator; Luis Villoro, Philosopher

NICARAGUA

Miguel D'Escoto, M.M., Maryknoll Missionary

PANAMA

Miguel Antonia Bernal V., Professor Emeritus of Constitutional Rights and International Public Law, University of Panama President of the Panama Institution of Constitutional Rights and of the Institute for Political and International Studies; Samuel Delgado Diamante, Former Governor of Colon

PERU

Alberto Adrianzén, Presidential Advisor; Rolando Ames Codram, Professor of Political Science, Catholic University of Peru; Alberto Arciniegas, Former President, Supreme Council of Military Justice; Javier Diez Canseco, Member of Congress; Julio Cotler Dolberg, Researcher, Associate of the Institute of Peruvian Studies; Juan José Gorritti Valle, Secretary General of the Peruvian Confederation of Workers; Alfonso Grados Bertorini, Former Minister; Agustín Haya, Former Member of Congress; Gloria Helfer, Former Minister of Education; Sofía Macher, Executive Secretary, National Coordinating Committee for Human Rights; Jorge Santistevan de Noriega, Former Human Rights Ombudsman; Francisco Soberón, Vice President, Internacional Federation of Human Rights; Henry Pease García, Second Vice-President of Congress

URUGUAY

Eduardo Galeano, Writer

VENEZUELA

Simón Alberto Consalvi, Former Minister of Foreign Relations, Venezuela; Carlos Ayala, Former President, Interamerican Commission on Human Rights, Venezuela; Julio Borges, Representative to the National Assembly for Justice First, Venezuela; Pedro Nikken, Former President, Inter-American Court for Human Rights, Venezuela; Rodrigo Penso Crazut, President of the Andean Consultative Labor Council, Venezuela; Luis Ugalde, S.J., Rector of the Catholic University "Andrés Bello," Venezuela

SÁO PAULO FORUM MEETS IN HAVANA

BERTA JOUBERT-CECI

José Ramón Balaguer, chief of International Relations of the Cuban Communist Party, opened the 2001 São Paulo Forum by placing the gathering in the context of the Sept. 11 attack, a topic that would be central to the discussions in the days that followed.

> Today we can say that the terrorist attacks of Sept. 11 in the U.S. show, in a tragic, insensate, and unjustifiable manner, the validity of the conclusion reached by the São Paulo Forum all these years," said Balaguer. "This conclusion is that a handful of powerful nations cannot monopolize all the wealth, the development, the technology, the culture, the education and the public health and, at the same time, be immune to the political, economic and social polarization consequences that this process provokes at a global scale.

The forum is a group of leftist and progressive organizations and parties of Latin America and the Caribbean formed in 1990 in São Paulo, Brazil. It held its 10th meeting Dec. 4-7, 2001 in Havana, Cuba. About 500 people from member countries as well as invited guests, including several from the United States, attended.

Balaguer summarized the suffering of the people, exacerbated by the U.S. "free trade" campaign:

> Transnational monopolies turn their excess products into the Latin American and Caribbean markets, privatization, labor deregulation, tax-free initiatives, dollarization, increase of regressive taxes paid by the poorest, increase of unemployment, electoral fraud, corruption, violence, increase in crimes, acute polarization and political, financial and social marginalization.

The forum's stated purpose is "unity despite diversity." It has varied political currents—social, Indigenous and political movements from social-democratic forces to socialist and communist parties.

The forum seeks alternatives to neoliberalism and its political, ideological onslaught. Before September, the working groups of the forum had met and formulated a document that would be the conference centerpiece.

The main issue in the document this year was the struggle against the Free Trade Area of the Americas, understood as a process of annexation and recolonization of the region.

Another crucial matter for discussion was external debt. Latin America owes more than $750 billion to imperialist banks and dedicates 56 percent of its income to debt payments. Other issues included the anti-globalization movement, Plan Colombia and the participation of forum members in other international meetings.

In order to facilitate discussion and incorporate the greatest contributions, working groups were divided into regions: the Caribbean, Central America, the Andes and the South. They were responsible for formulating resolutions that would be discussed and approved by the plenary.

PENTAGON WAR CREATES NEW URGENCY

The U.S. war gave a new urgency to the meeting, impacting on resolutions and plans of action. The case of the five Cubans imprisoned in the United States received much solidarity from attendees, who rededicated themselves to breaking the blockade against Cuba. U.S. pressures on Venezuela, Colombia and Vieques, Puerto Rico, were predominant in the discussion.

In Venezuela, the right wing is attempting to sabotage the current progressive constitution that prohibits the use of the country's airspace and land to wage war against neighboring countries like Colombia. The Venezuelan ruling class is waging destabilizing attacks on the government of Pres. Hugo Chávez and is endorsed in this by the Bush administration. The economic interests of these rich and powerful land and media owners are threatened by the social movement that elected Chávez.

Tareq Saab, from the Fifth Republic Movement, gave a passionate speech highlighting the gains attained by the Venezuelan process. He pointed to fair oil prices that allow for integration of Central America and the Caribbean, a sovereign and independent foreign policy, a pact of cooperation with Cuba and other gains.

Saab paraphrased Hugo Chávez, saying, "Ours is a peaceful, democratic revolution, but not unarmed."

Saab appealed to all international organizations to explain the truth about the Bolivarian/Venezuelan Revolution and to form solidarity movements with the people of Venezuela. His proposal to the members and guests of the forum was endorsed by all the Venezuelan delegates and approved with long applause by all present.

DEFEAT PLAN COLOMBIA, U.S. NAVY OUT OF VIEQUES!

Representatives from the Revolutionary Armed Forces of Colombia-People's Army (FARC-EP) also presented an urgent statement. As a result of the U.S. "anti-terrorist" plan, the struggle in Colombia has suffered.

Before September, the FARC-EP was in a process of dialog with the Colombian government for a political solution to the war. After Sept. 11, 2001, increasing difficulties prompted a break-off in the bilateral discussions.

On Oct. 7, 2001, the Colombian government authorized flights over FARC-EP-controlled airspace. This and other hostile measures are acts of war, says the FARC-EP, that prevent it from returning to the negotiating table.

The FARC-EP is under increasing pressure, both nationally and from the United States and Europe. The media, the FARC-EP representatives say, do not call them "narco-traffickers" anymore. Now they are called "terrorists," a dangerous signal coming from the imperialists.

But, the FARC-EP members said: "We are not terrorists. Terrorists are those who commit isolated acts with the purpose of causing panic in the population. We are with our people, we build a clandestine communist party, a clandestine Bolivarian movement. We work with the peasantry and with the people in the cities. ... We believe that the guerrilla is an indispensable motor in Colombia, but we also work to make possible the insurrection in Colombia."

The struggle to get the Navy out of Vieques, Puerto Rico, was prominent for the first time in the São Paulo Forum. Carlos Zenón, a fisher from Vieques, gave an update on the situation in that island-municipality. Several speakers, including Cuban President Fidel Castro, referred to the Vieques struggle. A resolution was passed to send a delegation to the island.

GLOBALIZE THE STRUGGLE AGAINST REACTION

MIGUEL URBANO

The following speech was delivered at the Second International Gathering in Solidarity and for Peace in Colombia and Latin America held in Mexico City, Mexico in March 2002.

Sisters and brothers,

We are gathered here in Mexico City in order to show our solidarity to a people that has been for many years a victim of a policy of oppression and violence by one of the most anachronistic and cruel oligarchies on the American continent.

Unforeseen events have aggravated the situation in Colombia in comparison to the one that presented itself last July, during the first solidarity conference held in San Salvador.

The strategy of militarizing the planet, conceived and carried out by the U.S. system of power, entered a new phase with the war of aggression and genocide against the people of Afghanistan. In order to supposedly fight terrorism, the U.S. government is making state terrorism a fundamental instrument of its foreign policy.

President George W. Bush's inclusion of the Colombian revolutionary movements on the list of organizations defined by him to be terrorists has translated into the intention of intensifying the application of Plan Colombia. This constitutes a powerful incentive to the forces in that country that have opposed from the beginning the creation of the demilitarized zone and have not hesitated in asking for direct military intervention by the United States.

The decision of President Andrés Pastrana to end the peace process has therefore not really been a surprise. His gesture, nevertheless, because of the circumstances that surrounded it, had a very negative impact in the international arena. The Secretary General of the UN was not the only one who lamented the end of the peace negotiations. The countries in the Facilitating Commission that accompanied the talks between the FARC-EP and the government in Los Pozos, also expressed that they had been deceived. Events clearly show who bears responsibility for downsliding.

Two hours after Pastrana's speech, the Colombian army penetrated the demilitarized zone. The air force began massive bombings of the area, and paratroopers landed in San Vicente del Caguán. What is shocking is not only the unilateral character of the president's attitude. In violating the pledge that established a period of 48 hours for the FARC-EP to retreat from the whole cleared area that they legally occupied since the end of 1998, the government proved that it acted with premeditation. Its image outside the country is now one of a vassal administration whose word has no value. While the High Commissioner for Peace Camilo Gómez was talking about peace at the table of dialogs, but only to slow down the discussion of the agenda approved at the beginning of February 2002, the armed forces were preparing down to the tiniest detail the invasion of the demilitarized zone and the air attack on dozens of targets.

It must be emphasized that militarily the operation was a failure. The victims were civilians: three dead, among them a little boy. The indignation of the local population was so great that the president had to go to San Vicente del Caguán in an attempt to explain the inexpicable. The return of the army brought violence and death to a zone in which crime had been practically eliminated with the arrival of the FARC-EP to the city.

Obviously, the finger of Washington is visible. The pressures of the armed forces and the big economic groups, encouraged by Bush's aggressive State of the Union speech, will have been decisive.

But the fact that we are dealing with a puppet president does not diminish Pastrana's responsibilities. His speech breaking off the talks will remain in memory as an example of hypocrisy and political cynicism. In his effort to justify the war, he accuses the FARC-EP of not complying with promises it had taken on. He does not limit himself to ignoring the proposal on substitution of illicit crops presented by the FARC-EP to the executive and to international organizations. He also accuses the FARC-EP—incredible but true—of having built bridges and roads, going beyond the text of the signed agreements.

What are we to think of a president who presents himself in San Vicente del Caguán surrounded by upper-level officials of the U.S. army? What are we to think of a government that promotes paramilitarism, and then defines as a challenge and a crime the building of over 1,000 kilometers of roads in five municipalities where three years ago it was only possible to get to certain towns by airplane or by the large rivers?

In the official perspective, the paving of the majority of roads in San Vicente del Caguán, previously almost unusable, has also been a crime. In the same way, it has been a crime to repair the landing strips in the cleared zone.

"For three years," the FARC-EP responded in a serene communiqué, "we looked for solutions to the grave problems that afflict 30 million Colombians—problems that the government has not responded to by way of dialog and negotiation. It has always claimed not to have heard the complaints. The presence of more than 30,000 compatriots that participated in the public audiences and round tables, presenting at the table proposals for changes to democratize the political and economic life of the country, along with the solicitude of the Secretary General of the United Nations and the president of the Episcopal Conference in Colombia, confirm the need of these transformations to achieve peace with social justice in our country."

At the table of negotiations, the FARC-EP had insistently defended the Platform for a Government of Reconstruction and National Reconciliation. The government remained deaf and has blocked discussion on the social items on the approved agenda.

"It remains clear," the FARC-EP concluded, "that the true objective that motivates the government to make the decision to break off the dialogs is to make the fundamental themes contained in the common agenda disappear from in front of the Colombian people's eyes, themes that trace the road through the table of dialog toward a new Colombia."

The generals in Bogotá are making toasts to victory. How weak is their memory. Imitating their U.S. colleagues in Vietnam and their French colleagues in Algeria, they talk about the last 15 minutes of the FARC-EP. Nevertheless, what awaits them once again is defeat. The great offensive in the ex-demilitarized zone will have the same destiny as the ones before. The FARC-EP have never thought about defending the cities of the region. They withdrew from them to fight in the jungles and mountains, where they are struggling in an epic saga from decades ago.

In June I had the opportunity to spend three weeks in a FARC-EP encampment. I shared life there with those guerrillas that are so slandered by imperialist propaganda. Why are they struggling? To change the monstrous society in which they were born and raised. They are convinced that possible happiness is the goal of human existence. They are young; they like to laugh and to cultivate friendship and love.

But they know that death can come at any moment. It is the price of the choice they have made. The fusion of the feeling with the word, like that which I picked up in my contact with these men and women is materialized in revolutionary collectives like that of the FARC-EP, pledged to transform history using arms as a last resort, but above all by the force of reason.

CRISIS AND RESISTANCE

We face in these beginnings of the 21st century a crisis of civilization, perhaps the greatest in history. The U.S. empire's strategy of planetary domination carries the danger of fascism of a new type. The crimes committed in Afghanistan (I cite as examples the massacre of prisoners in Mazar-e-Sharif and the sacking of Kandahar) were crimes commanded by officials of the U.S. army. I speak with knowledge of the topic, I know Afghanistan well, having visited four times, in order to affirm here that such massacres are only seen before in those carried out by the SS in Hitler's German Third Reich.

In the battle of the peoples against this strategy that threatens humanity as a totality, Latin America plays a fundamental role. Never before today have there been conditions so favorable for a continental globalization of struggle. In Argentina the masses have taken to the streets for months now, condemning neoliberalism and rejecting its recipes in gigantic demonstrations of protest that are scaring the transnationals and Washington. In Bolivarian Venezuela, the democratic and progressive forces are courageously and imaginatively defending a peaceful and original revolutionary process. In Brazil, the Landless Movement MST is making the big landowners and the government that protects them tremble. In Ecuador, Bolivia and Peru, the challenge of the Indigenous masses is assuming proportions that alarm Washington and its local pro-consuls.

Everywhere, consciousness is deepening the resistance against the FTAA. If this project goes forward, Latin America would be totally recolonized, turning back the clock by centuries.

It is in this context that we return to meet in Mexico to reaffirm our solidarity with those, with arms or without, in the FARC-EP, in the ELN, in the ERP, in the unions, in the factories and fields, that are struggling for a New Colombia and against Plan Colombia as a symbol of the imperial ambitions of the United States.

WORKERS UNITED WITH STUDENTS AND CAMPESINOS

NATHALIE ALSOP AND RAMÓN ACEVEDO

On September 16, 2002, only one month after Álvaro Uribe Vélez took office, over 800,000 people protested the Uribe government's policies of war and repression throughout Colombia.

When the national mobilization was mentioned publicly, the minister of defense, Marta Lucía Ramírez, said that the guerrillas were behind the mobilization and threatened numerous repercussions for those who participated. Despite this climate of state intimidation, the Colombian popular movement took to the streets in an impressive demonstration against the Uribe government and United States support for his policies, both financially and politically.

The day after the march the Colombian press and the Uribe government were intent on downplaying the importance of this huge national mobilization. The press described the day as one without much turmoil, even though the state forces attacked numerous marches and arbitrarily detained and beat protesters throughout the nation while paramilitaries threatened campesinos in at least two departments.

But what really happened? A strong popular movement demanding peace with social justice encountered repression imposed by a corrupt government directly supported by the United States government, economically militarily and politically.

The national mobilization was a conglomeration of different sectors of society, primarily workers, campesinos and youth. Each took action with a set of demands that spoke to their particular needs. Workers demanded the elimination of three economic reforms currently in Congress that set the stage for union-breaking, ending pension privileges, increasing the age for receiving pensions and eliminating government jobs. The campesinos demanded a repeal of the agrarian reform, which is not a reform but a continuation of the neoliberal policies that take land from the campesinos. And the youth demanded the right to public education on all levels and the right to political and public participation in the practices of the State.

Even though each had separate demands they supported the demands of the other sectors. Workers, campesinos, youth, and many others marched united under three main themes: against Uribe's plans of war and repression, which creates the conditions for fascism; for a politically negotiated solution to the armed conflict, not an expansion of war and against all forms of U.S. intervention in Colombia, whether it be economic, military or political.

Despite the strength of this popular movement, the justice of their demands, and the democratic and peaceful nature of their protest, the Uribe government carried out its threats of repression. In Bogotá, more than 3,000 youth from all over Colombia marched from the National University to join unionists and campesinos in a march to the Plaza de Bolívar where more than 60,000 people gathered.

They encountered continual state intimidation and police repression. Despite the peaceful nature of the protest, at least 70 protesters were arbitrarily detained and beaten. The police shot canisters of tear gas at the youth march twice and tried to split the joint march, unsuccessfully.

In Bucaramanga 15,000 protesters took to the streets and over 300 campesinos took over INCORA, the Colombian Institute for Agrarian Reform. In the department of Tolima, 5,000 people blocked the roads. In the same department, the military raided a gathering of campesinos preparing to march to the blockade, stole all their food and arrested 12 people.

In Cauca, paramilitaries stopped campesinos from demonstrating in the municipalities of La Vega, Argelia, Balboa, Corinto, Peindemo, and El Tambo with threats of death. In Caldas, 90 families from the Indigenous communities were detained by the army for merely attempting to join the demonstrations there. These measures, of which the above are only examples, show that the Uribe government intends to repress the popular movements, which are a just manifestation of the social and economic conditions that his government perpetuates.

Uribe's policies of war and repression are only possible because of the billions of dollars that the United States has given to the Colombian government, furnishing it with the weapons it uses to repress anyone who speaks out for a more just society. Since the United States increased its military aid to Colombia in 1998, war and repression in Colombia have expanded greatly.

In 1998, the Colombian military was a poorly trained conscript force that was under-equipped and ineffective. After $2 billion in mostly military aid from the United States, the Colombian military now has a trained force of 50,000 paid soldiers, fleets of U.S. made helicopters and advanced intelligence and combat equipment.

The connection between the military and the national police is much stronger in Colombia than in the United States. The aid the United States government had given to Colombia has gone to both forces, which participated directly in the repression of the national mobilization on September 16th. This repression is not limited to that day but is common practice for both the national police and military and their paramilitary allies.

Trade Unions vs. Coca-Cola

"We Are Not Alone"

Rebeca Toledo

A 22-member International Action Center delegation from the U.S. went to Bogotá, Colombia in December 2002 to attend the Tribunal Against the Violence of Coca-Cola which was part of the International Conference on Transnational Corporations and Human Rights.

POWELL IN COLOMBIA

U.S. Secretary of State Colin Powell had just left Bogotá when the international delegates arrived. Powell had arrived Dec. 3, 2002 at a military airport amid heavy security. Two military helicopters circled over the city while more than 50 motorcycle police officers and hundreds of soldiers were deployed to guard the route to his hotel.

Through Plan Colombia and the Andean Initiative, the U.S. government has provided well over $1 billion in aid to Colombia since 2000—mostly in military goods to stop the strong movement for social justice in Colombia, which includes insurgency groups, labor unionists, students, campesinos and human-rights and community leaders.

During Powell's visit he promised to pour another $200 million into the military and police forces. There are now reportedly more U.S. troops in Colombia than there were in Central America in the 1980s.

Powell was also motivated by Washington's search for broader support in the United Nations Security Council for its planned war on Iraq. Colombia currently chairs the Security Council.

So the IAC delegation was an important show of defiance against U.S. war plans in Colombia. More than two-thirds of the U.S. delegates were unionists who serve on executive boards, negotiating committees or as shop stewards. Others were students, lawyers and anti-war activists. They were young and older, women and men, Latino, African American and white.

The tribunal was the third in a series of hearings that began July 22, 2002 in Atlanta. The second hearing was held in Brussels on Oct. 10, 2002. The tribunals were called to bring international attention to the plight of the Coca-Cola workers and all Colombians targeted for repression by the Colombian government, the paramilitaries and the transnational corporations.

Along with holding the tribunals, the National Union of Food Industry Workers (Sinaltrainal), the United Steel Workers of America and the International Labor Fund have filed a lawsuit in U.S. courts accusing Coca-Cola of using paramilitaries to intimidate and assassinate union organizers.

The conveners of the tribunal included the United Center of Colombian Workers (CUT), the General Democratic Workers Confederation (CGTD), the Campaign Against Impunity-Colombia Clamors for Justice, Sinaltrainal, the Corporation for Education and the Development and Popular Studies-National Union Institute (Ced-Ins).

The opening remarks indicted not only Coca-Cola but the Colombian state for terrorism against workers. The speaker outlined how in the past 12 years, eight Coca-Cola workers have been killed, 48 have been displaced and several exiled.

In closing he said, "We don't ask for silence, instead we know that like our beloved Ché, these heroes live more than ever here in this tribunal."

The president of the CGTD, remarked that "capitalist globalization and neoliberalism grows like a stench in the world." He declared that the rulers in Colombia today are assassins. In 2001, 240 unionists were assassinated worldwide. Two hundred of them were in Colombia.

In 2002, more than 150, especially members of the CUT, were assassinated in Colombia.

"It is a massacre of union activists," he said. "This is a national crisis." He added that not only unionists but also campesinos and other social forces are being killed.

The standing-room-only crowd of about 500 people responded to each speaker with chants such as "Organization, unity and struggle" and "The road of justice is the road to victory."

An Indigenous leader said, "We are also struggling against the transnationals for our survival, against genocide." He thanked the unionists for their support.

A Colombian senator spoke as a representative for the seven Colombian members of Congress who have signed a letter calling for the cessation of violence against unionists. He spoke strongly against the labor "reform" law that Colombian President Álvaro Uribe Vélez is trying to impose. This law would dismiss 45,000 federal workers, strip away freedoms and rights such as collective bargaining and striking, impose more taxes on workers and freeze wages, social spending and benefits.

"We will vote against this law," the senator vowed. "And we invite all Colombians to boycott the ensuing referendum to be held in March 2003."

International delegates who addressed the tribunal said what impressed them most was that although repression is severe in Colombia, the people continue to find new space and ways to struggle. The heroism is palpable.

There were eight international delegations. A Mexican delegate announced that 2003 had been declared the year in solidarity with Colombian labor unionists. A representative from the Basque region in Spain called for more international solidarity actions. Delegates from Germany, Italy and England and the U.S. also addressed the tribunal, as did a representative from the IAC delegation.

Sinaltrainal President Javier Correa explained that December 5 had been chosen for the event because six years ago on that date Isidro Segundo Gil Gil was assassinated at his work post inside the Coca-Cola plant in Carepa del Urabá, Antioquiá. Gil was a union leader in the northwestern banana region.

BLOODY REPRESSION OF COCA-COLA WORKERS

Correa went over Coca-Cola's bloody history in Guatemala and India, and more recently in Venezuela. He also cited the company's discriminatory practices in Atlanta, Georgia.

He recounted how the Sinaltrainal union, as a result of systematic repression, has been reduced from 5,400 to 2,300 members. Unionists' family members have been killed. Attempts have been made to kidnap the children. Paramilitary forces have left graffiti in the plants threatening unionists.

"Coca-Cola has done nothing to curb this repression. This is the situation for all trade unionists in Colombia," he said.

He explained that Coca-Cola, like other transnationals, has done much damage and contributed to the pauperization of the Colombian people by taking money out of the country over the last 100 years.

The case against Coca-Cola was then presented. Survivors of its repression spoke.

One union leader was arrested along with two others in a Coca-Cola plant and accused of terrorism. The three were held for six months; no charges were ever filed against them. The wife of one of the three testified that after her husband's arrest, her family was stripped of all benefits, such as health care. Her daughter was harassed at school. She was allowed to see her husband only once a week; her children could see their father once a month.

"The overriding fear was that they would kill or disappear him," she said. Another survivor told of being tortured eight years ago by paramilitaries. He said he is still unable to sleep through the night.

One of the final speakers said, "The goal of the Uribe Vélez government is to open up the country to the imperialists, wipe away trade unions so that it will be easy for them to enact the Free Trade Areas of the Americas."

The tribunal closed with the adoption of a plan of action and a political declaration.

Among the demands on Coca-Cola were that July 22 be declared a day against transnationals and violence, that the corporation publicize its crimes on its soft drink bottles, pay reparations for family victims, clean up the environment and demilitarize the work place.

The International Conference on Transnational Corporations and Human Rights was held over the next two days. There were panels on globalization, neoliberalism, public services, health and education, Indigenous rights, finance, mineral and energy, human-rights violations and, finally resistance and plans of action.

One of the key speakers was José Fernando Ramírez from the Commission for Peace and Human Rights of the Trade Union of Workers (USO).

IAC Co-Director Teresa Gutierrez told the conference, "It is exactly for the benefit of corporations such as Coca-Cola that the U.S. aggressively intervenes in Colombia's internal affairs with Plan Colombia, the military wing of the FTAA."

She commended the labor unionists for their courage, for being on the front lines of the struggle. She said that they gave the delegates strength and inspiration to go back to the United States to fight against Pentagon intervention in Colombia.

Sinaltrainal hosted an important meeting for the IAC delegation at its union headquarters. The hours-long meeting inspired all those attending.

It began with a presentation from a student group called Focus, based at the National University in Bogotá. The three representatives, full of energy and optimism, warmly greeted the delegates.

One of the students recounted how after the murder of Jaime Alfor Acosta Campos, a student at the University of Santander, students stepped up their protests. The students at the National University set up an encampment there to protect themselves against riot police and university officials. The officials responded by closing down the university on Nov. 28, 2002. After heavy protests from the students, the university reopened on Dec. 5, 2002. The students remain steadfast against privatization plans and will be carrying out more actions on Dec. 10, 2002.

Another student impressed upon the delegation that all the money used to repress the movement in Colombia came from the United States. He said that Colombians do not want U.S. intervention and that it is a crime that arms are being bought while people are dying of hunger.

The three pledged never to stop fighting for justice, no matter what it takes.

'WE ARE NOT ALONE'

Javier Correa summarized the meaning of the tribunals: "At first these tribunals were just a dream. What they have proved is the resistance of the national unions, the unconditional support from social groups in Colombia and international solidarity. Coca-Cola and the government had us down for dead. But we have shown that we are not alone."

This is what really worries them, Correa continued. International support especially worries them because the crimes they get away with now will become international scandals in the future.

Correa said that the tribunal helped increase consciousness because it challenged the Colombian state, demonstrating that the movement does not accept the level of terror waged with impunity against the people.

He said the most difficult struggles against the government and Coca-Cola lie ahead. "That is why we are so grateful for compañeros like you. Your solidarity makes our struggle possible." He added that next they would like to confront Nestlé—like Coca-Cola, a big enemy of the workers.

Edgar Paez, another Sinaltrainal leader, told the delegates, "We must find a different road for Colombia, because capitalism and neoliberalism are no good for Colombia or the world. Our struggle against capitalism is for the development of communities where the people decide their own futures, where the power is with the people."

He made it explicit: "For every can of Coca-Cola that you buy, you are buying a bullet to assassinate a Colombian. We do not believe in consultation with the transnational corporations. Imperialism doesn't just want a little piece of Colombia, it wants the whole country. And it doesn't just want Colombia, it wants all of Latin America. It wants us all to kneel and continue to be exploited."

He said he is grateful to Coca-Cola in one way: It brought the delegation to Colombia. He concluded, "You have strengthened our work and helped us to continue our struggle."

V.
THE PEOPLE
OF THE
U.S. SAY
NO

THE POOR OF COLOMBIA ARE NOT GETTING RICH FROM COCA

BISHOP THOMAS GUMBLETON

Bishop Thomas Gumbleton of Detroit has participated in several delegations to Colombia. The following article is based on a speech given on April 6, 2001, after his January 2001 trip to Colombia.

In November 2000, the Bishops' Conference of England and Wales issued a statement on Colombia. I would like to share some of my own experiences within the framework of the statement.

The Bishops' Conference

- expresses its distress at the plight of the people of Colombia who have endured a long-running civil war...
- recognizes that this concern is widely shared by governments and other international bodies...
- affirms that a peace process in Colombia, which implies a concerted response to the linked problems of violence, poverty, extreme economic inequalities, drug cultivation and trafficking, deserves the urgent and committed support of the international community, and that this support will need to include a close control of the arms trade with Colombia.
- expresses grave concern that the implementation of Plan Colombia will damage any peace process, since the plan appears to centre on a massive military intervention directed towards the selective eradication of drug cultivation (almost exclusively, that controlled by the most prominent Colombian guerrilla groups, not by paramilitary groups), and will therefore
  - further exacerbate the widespread abuse of human rights;
  - destroy the livelihood of rural communities by the indiscriminate fumigation of crops with little attempts to promote alternative forms of agricultural production;
  - fail to tackle the gross inequalities and the political disabilities that underlie and transcend the patterns of violence and drug production;
  - further marginalize from the peace process those groups within Colombian civil society that have suffered most from the violence of both paramilitary and guerrilla groups;
  - distract attention from the equally urgent need to reform the judicial structures of Colombia so as to enable access to justice for all citizens;

• declares its support for all those, whether within or outside Colombia, who are working for the reforms necessary to make possible for the people of Colombia an integral human development.

I think the bishops have summarized the situation in Colombia, so I will just try to elaborate. Colombia is a country of about 42 million people. It has a large Afro-Colombian population: 11 million people of Colombia are of African descent, 26 percent of the population. Of the 42 million, already 200,000 people have been killed in the struggles that have been going on for the last 10 years. Nearly 2 million people have been displaced. Every year, 300,000 more people are displaced; almost all are Indigenous or Afro-Colombian people.

In Colombia, the majority of the people are desperately poor. There are a small number of people, mostly landowners, who are very wealthy. But the peasants, who are the majority, have to work the land without being able to earn a livelihood. There has been an attempt to change that situation: there are currently two revolutionary movements that have developed within Colombia. Both of them are committed to violent revolution, and they definitely are a part of the reason for so much of the violence and the killing that goes on in Colombia. However, the violence occurs because of the repression that goes on.

Human-rights reports by Amnesty International, Human Rights Watch, and even our own State Department indicate that the military has historically been the greatest perpetrator of the violence. However, in the last several years the paramilitaries have been at the fore of this violence. "Paramilitary" means that they act like military people, they arm themselves and become like a private police force. The large landowners, originally in official cooperation with the military, developed their own private armies. These forces carry out violence against anyone who dares to speak out against them or works to bring about change to redistribute land. This violence has become extreme. That's the major reason why 300,000 people annually are displaced—a total of 2 million people—because of the paramilitary violence and the military violence. This is the situation in Colombia.

In January 2001, when I was in Colombia, we met with about five priests from the area who came to a meeting to talk with us and to share their difficulties. It's difficult to give a sense of how isolated they feel and how they are up against an almost impossible situation. If they try to preach against the structures of violence, they are preaching against the landowners and they will be killed. If they don't try to reach out to the guerrillas, who are part of the revolutionary violence, and try to support them, they feel they are failing the poor. They get very little support from the bishops of the town. They are in areas where the military is present in huge numbers. Paramilitary forces are there. They have to somehow try to preach the gospel of justice.

It is a similar situation for the peasants who are caught among these forces (the military, the paramilitary, and sometimes guerrillas) if they are accused of cooperating with the paramilitary or the military. The guerrillas will tax them and if they do not pay the taxes, the guerrillas will destroy their villages. However, if they do cooperate in any way with the guerrillas (which they are inclined to do because the guerrillas are the poor), then the paramilitary or military will burn their crops and destroy their villages.

Both times I have been to Colombia, I have met with the military high command. It is very discouraging, because the generals will claim that they are trying to discipline their troops and trying to keep them from carrying out these atrocities. Yet they have almost no success. Also, while military forces are unable to legally commit these atrocities, they simply allow the paramilitaries to do it. They work closely together.[1]

Eleven captains and five majors dismissed in October 2000 from the Colombian Army for human-rights violations have since joined a right-wing paramilitary group that massacres villages suspected of sympathizing with the rebels.[2] Citing documents and interviews, El Espectador reported the 16 officers joined the illegal United Self Defenses of Colombia (AUC). They went from the military right into the paramilitary forces, and the military does nothing to stop them.

We met with the equivalent of the attorney general of Colombia and asked him why the government doesn't do anything about the AUC, which is the largest paramilitary group. He said that they have issued indictments. Later, when we talked to the head of the Army he said they wouldn't dare send troops in; the paramilitary forces are too heavily armed and there would be, in effect, another civil war.

Drug trafficking and drug cultivation are the main pretext for our so-called Plan Colombia. I say pretext because I am totally convinced that Plan Colombia really has nothing to do with ending drug cultivation and drug trafficking. I am also convinced that our political leaders know that as well. It is true that the peasants cultivate coca and they sell that to the paramilitaries or to the guerrillas. Both the paramilitaries and the guerrillas are making huge money off of the drug trade—the paramilitaries much more than the guerrillas, but both are involved. The peasants get more than they would get from other crops, although they are still not getting enough to have any kind of a decent living.

One group of peasants that we met said that they grow coca and that is part of their tradition. They do not make it into cocaine; they use it for medicinal purposes. There may be some drug aspects to it but they never sold it before. They grow coca for themselves. They were much more interested in selling other crops.

However, as the struggle developed, it became necessary for them to grow coca because of pressure from the armed actors (the paramilitaries are involved in the drug trade and the guerrillas tax it). Peasants were offered money for coca. This is how they got involved in the drug trade. The coca travels from there to North America, the main market for the drug trade. Of everyone who makes money from the drug trade, the farmers get hardly anything.

The United States has said that, together with President Pastrana and Colombia, we want to stop this cultivation of coca and stop the drug trade. We are providing $1.3 billion to do this. When the bill was passed in Congress in 2000, it was passed with the Leahy Amendment, the stipulation of Sen. Leahy who had insisted that if Colombia could not pass human-rights criteria then the aid would not be delivered. Our own State Department report said Colombia was not abiding by human-rights criteria, but President Clinton gave a waiver so the $1.3 million could be sent in spite of serious human-rights violations.

The central part of Plan Colombia is to get rid of the drug cultivation by fumigating crops using chemicals like glyphosate produced by Monsanto here in the United States. We are asking for a halt to these aerial eradication programs in Colombia. On July 25, 2000, the governor and 13 mayors of Putumayo state declared their opposition to aerial eradication. When I met with various peasant groups there, they told us that they are willing to get rid of the coca. But they want to get rid of it through manual eradication: by pulling out the plants one by one. It takes longer, of course, but it will not have any of the evil side effects that go along with fumigation.

The U.S. Drug Enforcement Agency places the chemicals that are being used for aerial fumigation in categories 1 (the most toxic chemicals) or 2 (for primary eye or skin irritation). The same chemicals were responsible for many illnesses among California agricultural workers in the 1980s and have led to many health problems in England. In fact, in 1996, Monsanto agreed to stop claiming their product was safe, non-toxic or harmless.

When Colombians reported health problems due to spraying—complaints including respiratory, digestive, skin, and other ailments—the U.S. State Department claimed that since their "illegal livelihood" has been affected by the spraying, these people were not offering objective information about the program. Our U.S. government claims you cannot believe what the peasants are saying.

The peasants told us that animals died, other crops were destroyed, people have skin rashes or eye infections and are becoming seriously ill from the side effects of the chemicals. The planes spray chemicals over whole areas so that even the food crops that they are growing for basic sustenance are destroyed.

Pastrana's government offered a program to try manual eradication. But the government only gave peasant communities $1000 and 12 months to get rid of all the coca and to plant substitute crops—an impossible task. The peasants said they needed four or five years for the transition. Both the Colombian and the U.S. governments refused, in spite of the fact that the people in the area say this is the only way they could eradicate the coca. The people most affected were totally disregarded and the government proceeded with the aerial fumigation.

One of the disturbing things for me on the trip was when we flew in a military helicopter over the whole area. You could see all the crops that had been destroyed by the chemicals; it looked as if they had been burned away. This was a very quick way to get rid of the coca but it has terrible effects for the people, and it does not end the cultivation of coca. Cultivation only moves to other areas.

A recent article in the *Chicago Tribune* was headlined "Colombia Drug War Spills Into Ecuador."[3] Ecuador is just south of the state of Putumayo in Colombia. After eradicating coca from Peru, it began to move into Colombia. Now, coca will be eliminated from Colombia but will move into Ecuador. Brazil is very concerned because it is also crossing the border there as well.

The production of coca cannot be stopped. There is too much money involved in drug trafficking, made by people all the way in the United States. The peasants themselves said to us, "Look, the problem is not our growing the coca, the problem is the demand in the United States for the cocaine that is made from coca."

If we do not do something to stop the consumption of cocaine in this country, we will never stop the growing of coca. Too many people are involved in making huge amounts of money. Eradication does nothing but cause a lot of suffering, and if you are successful in eradicating it in one area, it just goes someplace else. Our government knows that truth and that's why I'm sure they don't really expect to stop the drug trade through Plan Colombia.

Colombia's traditional rural economy is in crisis. Since Colombia opened its agricultural markets in the early 1990s, the coffee harvest has been reduced almost by half. Ten years ago, agricultural imports into Colombia were 700,000 tons. Today they are 7 million tons. The same thing that is happening to Colombia has already happened to Mexico and the other countries of Latin America. They are forced to open up to so-called free trade, but they are unable to compete. The peasants in Colombia who were able to make a living growing coffee are now all displaced from their land. Some of them turned to growing coca instead of growing coffee. One million rural jobs have been lost in the past decade, and a quarter of a million peasants have turned to coca production. That's a part of the dilemma they are up against. They cannot compete in "free trade," so the peasants are forced to leave their land and give up the coffee growing or turn to coca. Then the United States fumigates and tries to destroy the coca and leaves them without anything.

While I was down there, I met with various groups of people. They pleaded with us to do what we could to bring about changes. One of the first meetings that I had was with 14 Indigenous people, men and women from a number of small communities, from the Inca nation. They are the people who are originally from that area. They had to walk three or four hours to get to the meeting. They are leaders in their own communities and expressed gratitude for our visit, especially at this time of crisis. They wanted first of all to know what we could do to help them. They believe that they are being exterminated. Every year the government is destroying their land, their crops and their livelihood. This group never grows coca for dollars; they only use it within the community. They explained how they are being displaced. They are assaulted, murdered, kidnapped, tortured by the military and paramilitary. They had five proposals discussing what they would like to see happen, including the appointment of an international commission of investigation regarding human rights, the recuperation of their territory, legal recognition of their land and their right to it, protection of Indigenous people and their land giving them opportunity to protect the fragile environment. They also suggested addressing the problem of consumption of drugs in the developed countries. The poor of Colombia are not getting rich from coca.

---

[1] See, for example, "The 'Sixth Division': Military-paramilitary Ties and U.S. Policity in Colombia," *Human Rights Watch Report*, October 4, 2001 and "The Ties That Bind: Colombia and Military-Paramilitary Links," *Human Rights Watch Report*, February 1, 2000 and "Colombia's Killer Networks: The Military-Paramilitary Partnership and the United States," *Human Rights Watch Report*, November 1, 1996.

[2] *El Espectador* (Colombia), April 3, 2001.

[3] *Chicago Tribune*, February 13, 2001.

Drugs, CIA and Plan Colombia

Representative Cynthia McKinney

Statement on Colombia to the Western Hemisphere Subcommittee of the House International Relations Committee delivered on September 21, 2001.

Thank you for this opportunity to speak. And I would like to thank the Chairman and the Ranking Member for calling this very important hearing.

Our relationship with the people of Colombia is about to fundamentally change and I hope we know that going into this massive projection of U.S. force into that country.

I am especially appreciative of the opportunity to put my thoughts on the record because more than anything else, I care about the most fundamental aspects of human rights and how Plan Colombia will affect the human-rights climate in Colombia today and the notions about the United States that Colombians affected most will have about us after implementation of Plan Colombia.

As citizens of the most powerful nation in the world, it's our duty to ensure that this power is used responsibly and that we are not confused when we use it. Bobby Kennedy once said that we used to be a force for good in the world. I would like to hope that peoples around the world still see us as a force for good. However, I fear that this is far from the thoughts of the Colombian people from whom I have heard.

Some 80% of the aid in Plan Colombia comes in the form of military weapons. This, more properly, should be called a military aid package, and this meeting must include the military component if we are to truly grasp the full meaning of the U.S. role in implementing Plan Colombia.

Congress actually voted to fund a counter-attack against an army of 20,000 guerrillas in the Amazon jungle. We did this act alone, without the support of our European allies. The European Union does not support our involvement of this nature in Colombia. And because we've voted to give approximately $1 billion to the Colombian military, not very many other donors want to be associated with this kind of contribution.

So, although Plan Colombia was originally intended by President Pastrana to be a multinational aid package, it has now morphed into a U.S. military operation.

About two weeks ago, the presidents of the 12 Latin American countries met for the first time in a historic summit in Brasilia. Although it was not the intended theme of the meeting, the leaders resolved their opposition to the U.S. aid package. Brazil's Fernando Cardoso spoke against it, Venezuela's Hugo Chávez spoke against it. In Ecuador they believe that tens of thousands of refugees are going to spill across the border from the violence this plan is going to generate. This is what Colombia's neighbors think of the plan.

Thirty-seven Colombian NGOs, including the Center for Investigations and Popular Education and the Consortium for Human Rights and the Displaced, have signed a letter saying they would reject any aid offered to them as part of Plan Colombia. They are completely unwilling to be associated with this program in any way no matter how much money they are offered.

Amnesty International, Human Rights Watch, and the Washington Office on Latin America all denounced President Clinton's decision to waive the human-rights conditions that had been placed on the aid by Congress. The human-rights groups had hoped that by placing such conditions on the aid, Colombia would be forced to choose between the modern weaponry and the dirty war of assassination they are currently engaged in. I am extremely disappointed that the Clinton Administration once again has taken human rights completely off the table for discussion. Now there is no incentive whatsoever for Colombia to reform its military and abandon its paramilitary strategy.

I will also note for the record that the push into southern Colombia, which has been described today, violates the Geneva Conventions, which prohibit the forced displacement of civilian populations as a tactic of war.

In the whole world, only the Congo has more displaced people than Colombia. At a forum recently sponsored by my office, I have quite sadly learned that the vast majority of those displaced persons are Afro-Latinos. Two-thirds are minors. Only one in eight has access to education. One in three has access to health care. These poor children suffer from the neglect of the Colombian State and the ignorance of Washington policy makers.

My third and final point is that not only is this plan immoral, it's impractical. Spraying chemicals on Third World farmers is not an effective way to discourage people in the United States from using cocaine.

We are not immune to the lure of quick cocaine cash ourselves, as has been made embarrassingly clear recently.

How can Col. James Hiett, smuggling cocaine and laundering money with his wife while overseeing anti-drug operations for the U.S. Southern Command in Bogotá, how could this narco get off with five months in jail while today there are more African Americans in prison than in college?

So now, the U.S. is about to implement a plan to spray chemicals on Third World subsistence farmers and attack them with helicopter gunships while the Colombian government allows paramilitary groups to massacre them.

One thing is for sure in this plan, it isn't about drug abuse control and won't help my friends who are strung out on dope.

I would rather have from the CIA a truthful accounting of how crack cocaine came to flood every Black neighborhood in America and affect every Black family. Telling the truth about the relationships between federal agencies, U.S. multinational banks and elites in this country and abroad will do more to eradicate the scourge of drugs in America than this proposed Plan Colombia.

An Empire in Search of War

Mumia Abu-Jamal

Colombia has been the leading recipient of U.S. military support and training in the hemisphere in the 1990s, now increasing still further. The pretext is the drug war. The aid, in fact, goes to military forces that have compiled the worst human-rights record in the hemisphere and are closely linked to paramilitary terrorists and drug lords. Information about the matter is voluminous, and shocking, but little of it reaches the general public, who would be appalled if they knew.[1]

The national corporate media are beating the drums for the heightened intervention of the U.S. military into the internal affairs of the Latin American nation of Colombia. According to the establishment media, forces aligned with the Revolutionary Armed Forces of Colombia-People's Army (FARC-EP) are "narco-terrorists," a clever term that unites the demonized figures of drug dealers and "terrorists." It is what the media don't tell Americans that tells the real story.

Colombia is far more than simply a country situated in Latin America; it is a nation with over 45 percent of its population that is African-Colombian. Most African-Colombians live along the coastal regions of the country, in the Pacific Coast region called Chocó and in the Atlantic region called Urabá. It is in these regions that armed paramilitaries are active, and where they have staged a number of massacres of Afro-Colombians. The names of villages like Urrao, La Jagua de Ibirico, Dabeiba, Antioquiá and Pavarando are more than places in the nation; they are shorthand for massacres of people by U.S.-backed paramilitaries. One of the U.S.-backed paramilitaries is known as ACCU (Peasant Self Defenses of Córdoba and Urabá).

Guess which group is supported by the CIA? The FARC-EP or ACCU? And when people consider the history of drug trafficking by the CIA in other parts of the world, what do you think is happening in Colombia? Freelance journalist Frank Smyth, writing in the quarterly *Colombia Bulletin*, reports:

"Indeed most of Colombia's leftist guerrillas, especially among the formerly pro-Moscow FARC-EP, are also involved with drugs. But a U.S. interagency study recently ordered by the Clinton administration's former ambassador in Bogotá, Myles Frechette, found the guerrillas' role to be limited to mostly protecting drug crops, and, to a lesser degree, processing operations. Meanwhile, rightist paramilitaries allied with the military protect far more drug laboratories and internal transit routes, according to both U.S. intelligence and Colombian law enforcement reports. Drug trafficking today is again the paramilitaries' 'central axis' of funding."[2]

You won't read this in the regular newspaper, and you won't see it on the regular network TV newscast, but one wonders: Why not? These facts should be reported regularly on the U.S. news, to inform a people who are being asked to "stop narco-terrorism"!

The media manufacture new enemies for the empire to destroy, more rebellions to crush, in the name of capital. Meanwhile, no one dares even question that the drug industry is driven by the largest appetite in world history—that of Americans hungry for more and more cocaine! By the same token, American military intervention in Colombia has nothing to do with "narco-terror" and everything to do with quelling an insurgency that threatens imperial control of a hemispheric neighbor. Scholar Rensselaer W. Lee III wrote years ago that U.S. and Latin American attempts to curb the flowing river of cocaine northward were almost destined to fall. Writing in the September 1988 issue of Orbis, Lee wrote: "The solution, if there is one, lies not in the Andean jungles but in the United States. The 6 million people who now consume cocaine must be persuaded to change their habits."

Let us say no to this false "narco-war"!

---

[1] Noam Chomsky, *Colombia Bulletin*

[2] Smyth, F., "Colombia's Blowback: Formerly CIA-backed Paramilitaries are Major Drug Traffickers Now," Colombia Bulletin, Spring 1998.

UNIONS UNDER SIEGE IN COLOMBIA

SENATOR PAUL WELLSTONE

Speech delivered on the floor of the United States Senate on September 6, 2001.

Mr. President, I rise today to address the disturbing level of violence perpetrated against Colombia's union leaders.

As another Labor Day passes, I could not in good conscience neglect to mention the plight of our brothers and sisters in the Colombian labor movement. There has been a dramatic escalation in violations against them and the response by the Colombian authorities in the face of this crisis has been negligible.

For the past 15 years, Colombia has been in the midst of an undeclared war on union leaders. Colombia has long been the most dangerous country in the world for union members, with nearly 4,000 murdered in that period. Today, three out of every five trade unionists killed in the world are Colombian.

Union members and activists are among the main targets of human-rights violations, including murders, disappearances and threats, in the escalating conflict in Colombia. Paramilitary groups, who are linked with Colombian security forces, are responsible for most of these attacks, although guerrilla groups have also targeted activists.

The right-wing AUC has been especially brutal, killing hundreds simply because they view union organizers as subversives. One of the most recent killings occurred on June 21 2001, when the leader of Sinaltrainal, the union that represents Colombian Coca-Cola workers, Oscar Darío Soto was gunned down. His murder brings to seven the number of unionists who worked for Coca-Cola and were targeted and killed by paramilitaries. Earlier this summer, the International Labor Rights Fund and the United Steelworkers of America brought a suit against the Coca-Cola company alleging that the Colombian managers had colluded with paramilitary security forces to murder, torture and silence trade union leaders.

According to a recent *New York Times* report by Juan Forero, the number of union workers at Coca-Cola plants in Colombia has dropped to 450 from 1,300 in 1993. The total membership of the National Union of Food Industry Workers (Sinaltrainal) has dropped to 2,400 from 5,800 five years ago.

Regardless of the outcome of this particular legal case, US companies with subsidiaries in Colombia have an obligation to address the upsetting trend of violence against workers, particularly union representatives. It is clear that some companies regularly hire out paramilitary gunmen to intimidate and kill in order to break labor unions. In 2000 alone, at least 130 Colombian labor leaders were assassinated. Four times as many union workers have been killed this year as during the same time last year. That's more than 80 unionists killed since the beginning of this year.

Colombia, like the United States, guarantees workers a legal right to organize. However, when they do, they face grave threats. This is a serious violation of human rights under Article 22 of the International Covenant on Civil and Political Rights. The Colombian government must take an active role in protecting and ensuring that these rights are enjoyed by all its citizens.

Likewise, the Senate should bear in mind the deteriorating plight of union membership in Colombia before sending additional military aid to a government that can't—or won't—crack down on paramilitary forces.

SOLIDARITY WITH COLOMBIAN TRADE UNIONISTS

AFL-CIO EXECUTIVE COUNCIL

February 17, 2000

Colombia's trade unions have been the leading advocates for peace, human rights, and economic justice in a nation afflicted by internal violence and external economic pressures.

According to the International Confederation of Free Trade Unions (ICFTU), more than 90 Colombian trade unionists were murdered in 1998, mostly at the hands of paramilitary organizations supported by government security forces. Among the victims was Jorge Ortega, Vice President of the Confederacion Unitaria de Trabajadores (CUT) and one of many union leaders who have denounced both guerrilla and government violence and played key roles in efforts by civil society to achieve an effective and lasting peace. The violence continued in 1999, culminating in the assassination on December 13 of César Herrera, president of the banana workers' union Sitrainagro. In the past five years, not a single assassin responsible for the murder of unionists has been arrested or tried. Yet unionists who strike or otherwise defend their rights have been prosecuted in regional courts, where judges' and witnesses' identities are hidden and secret evidence can be admitted.

While physical terror against unionists has drawn international condemnation, the government's program of privatization and economic deregulation to create "flexible" labor markets, as required by the IMF, has also undermined freedom of association and taken a severe toll on working families. The official unemployment rate now exceeds 20 percent, and mass dismissals and firings are widespread. Because of high unemployment and poverty, child labor is common in the cut flower and coal mining industries: there are 784,000 working children between the ages of 6 and 11. Yet the IMF has opposed indexing of the minimum wage to protect working families from inflation.

Despite these threats to human and worker rights, the U.S. administration is proposing a $1.6 billion aid package for Colombia, mostly to assist the military.

In solidarity with our Colombian trade union sisters and brothers, we condemn violence and drug trafficking, whether carried out by the military, paramilitary forces, or the guerrillas. Nevertheless, we think the United States should not deepen its entanglement with a military which has been responsible for the violence perpetuated against trade unionists.

Our government should do more to promote peace negotiations that include unions, religious bodies, and other civil society groups. More aid should be provided for human rights, including assistance to promote worker rights and protect the physical security of union members; strengthen the Colombian government's ability to investigate human-rights violations and assist non-governmental organizations engaged in peace, human rights, economic development, and humanitarian relief efforts. At a minimum, existing pre-conditions on disbursement of aid to the military should be retained and broadened to cover all military units, and any such aid should be pre-conditioned on clear progress in investigating the murders of union members and human-rights activists, including the adjudication of those responsible and the dismantling of the regional courts.

We look forward to the report of the ILO Direct Contacts Mission which is visiting Colombia this week, and reaffirm our support for a Commission of Inquiry as recommended by the Workers' Party at the ILO. And we renew our commitment to defend our Colombian union sisters and brothers whose lives are endangered because of their attempts to exercise their fundamental human rights.

Coca-Cola Leaves a Bad Taste in the U.S. and Colombia

Dianne Mathiowetz

Coca-Cola is accused by Colombian trade unionists of working hand in hand with paramilitary groups there to murder, intimidate and harass union members. The National Union of Food Industry Workers (Sinaltrainal) has filed a suit against Coca-Cola in Florida to stop the murders and has been holding international tribunals against the company.

Coca-Cola, the dominant soft drink brand throughout the world, has carefully crafted its public image as being associated with harmony, good times and family. Its billion-dollar ad campaigns saturate people's consciousness using catchy jingles and upbeat music to encourage sales of a non-essential item. The people pictured in the commercials are from varied ethnic backgrounds, always smiling, happy together.

Here in the U.S., according to Motisola Abdallah: "None of that is true inside the corporation. There is no harmony, no peace and no justice within Coca-Cola."

Abdallah, an African American woman who worked at the corporation's headquarters in Atlanta, is one of the original four plaintiffs who brought a lawsuit against Coca-Cola in April 1999. Based on the voluminous evidence of unequal pay, biased promotions, a racially hostile work environment and retaliation against anyone who challenged the status quo, the case was expanded to a class-action lawsuit. This judicial decision brought an additional 1,500 employees into the legal battle.

In June 2000, Coca-Cola brokered a settlement in an attempt to do some damage control. It was also dealing with a sexual discrimination lawsuit based on similar practices toward female employees. Besides monetary compensation to the African American workers who had been underpaid and denied promotions based on their race, Coca-Cola had to establish a "diversity task force" to oversee changes in internal policy.

"Window dressing" is what Abdallah calls the measure. Seventeen workers, including Abdallah, are pressing the lawsuit.

In the midst of the publicity over the lawsuit, Coca-Cola laid off hundreds of workers, many of whom were in the lower-paid classifications where women and people of color predominate.

Abdallah had already been fired. Many of those who actively backed the lawsuit were among those laid off. Abdallah, who gathered much of the early evidence of Coca-Cola's discriminatory policies, is frank in her opinion of the grossly overpaid upper management.

"In court documents, they claimed to know nothing about the racist practices of their subordinates. But just like in the human body, the brain is the source of the messages that determine what the rest of the body does."

She continued, "For many years, this corporation robbed African Americans of their dignity, their pride, their right to be paid on the basis of merit. And then those who profited mightily from this theft claimed to have no responsibility."

Abdallah sees the legal case as a way to expose this global corporation's dirty laundry. She said, "Coca-Cola counts on its name and billions of dollars in assets to intimidate the average person to back down and submit to injustice." She explained however, that the struggle always breaks out no matter what the bosses do.

Referring to the many other campaigns that have targeted Coca-Cola in recent years, she applauded the efforts of Florida farm workers in the 1970s, the anti-apartheid divestment movement in the 1980s, the Teamsters union in the 1990s and the Colombian trade unionists today.

"I'm happy that the struggle against Coca-Cola is long-term and global. It proves that workers wherever they live are all in this together. A corporation like Coca-Cola isn't just unfair to its workers in one place. Injustice runs throughout a business where profit is the driving motivation."

She concluded by saying: "Anyone fighting for justice can't give up. Together we can bring change, real harmony, real justice."

Building ties between U.S. workers and workers around the world, especially in Colombia, will be key in winning justice.

PLAN COLOMBIA AND THE SCHOOL OF THE ASSASSINS

FR. ROY BOURGEOIS AND LINDA PANETTA

Over the past decade we have been part of the growing movement to close the infamous School of the Americas (SOA), renamed the Western Hemisphere Institute for Security Cooperation (WHISC). The School of the Americas/WHISC is a military training facility established in Panama in 1946, ostensibly "to bring stability to Latin America." In 1984 the SOA was kicked out of Panama and was quietly resettled at Fort Benning, Georgia. Over the years, the SOA has trained more than 60,000 Latin American soldiers in courses such as counterinsurgency techniques, interrogation tactics, sniper training, commando and psychological warfare and military intelligence.

In 1996, the State Department was forced to release to the public, training manuals used at the SOA that advocated the use of torture, assassination and false imprisonment.

Many SOA graduates have been responsible for orchestrating coups and promoting civil instability. They have terrorized, tortured, raped, "disappeared" and massacred tens of thousands of Latin Americans. Their primary targets have been educators, union organizers, religious workers, student leaders, Indigenous populations and those who advocate for the rights of the poor.

The United Nations Truth Commission Report on El Salvador identified two-thirds of those who committed the worst atrocities during El Salvador's brutal civil war as SOA alumni. More recently, the UN's report on Guatemala stated that training such as that at the SOA "had a significant bearing on human-rights violations during the armed conflict."

Ironically, former Secretary of the U.S. Army Louis Caldera, responding to opposition to the SOA, said, "Sovereign nations have the right, and even the duty, to keep military forces to protect their people and territories from all manner of scoundrels." The thousands of human-rights abuses in Latin America attributed to SOA graduates show that the SOA has trained, currently trains, and will continue to train its own "scoundrels."

Henry Kissinger said, "Those who lend support, financing and encouragement to them [terrorists] are as guilty as the terrorists." Echoing Kissinger's remarks, President George W. Bush later said, "If any government sponsors outlaws and killers of innocents, they have become outlaws and murderers themselves."

In regard to supporting, training, and propping up dictators and assassins, the school's own documents state: "...we cannot wait until a so-called 'good' government comes along to create an instrument for national good." Perhaps this is why throughout Latin America more than a dozen SOA alumni have been responsible for orchestrating coups. In fact, hundreds of SOA graduates should immediately be placed on President George W. Bush's list of terrorists.

One cannot disregard the body count: tens of thousands of civilians who the Pentagon seems to have looked upon as mere "collateral damage."

A 1997 Pentagon document states that the purpose of the U.S. military is "to protect US interests and investments." But there is a hidden agenda to U.S. involvement in Latin America, including the current "drug war": The goal is to acquire and maintain control of the plethora of resources throughout the Latin American region, including gold, silver and copper as well as the great expanses of oil. It is to secure the interests and investments of U.S. and multinational corporations. For this Washington has forged ties with, supported and let loose bloodletters. The SOA, specifically, has been a major player in training corrupt and oppressive militaries and promoting ties with fanatical regimes.

As word about the SOA spread, people began to respond. Tens of thousands of individuals from across the Americas have participated in protests, lobbying initiatives, civil disobedience, fasts and other solidarity actions in protest of the School of the Americas.

Over the past several years, thousands have risked arrest by "crossing the line" in an attempt to close the SOA. Since 1990, over 70 people have been selected for prosecution. They have collectively served over 40 years in U.S. prisons for nonviolent actions against the SOA.

On Sept. 10, 2002, an additional 23 human-rights activists joined five others already in prison, to serve out sentences ranging from three to six months.

In November 2001, shortly after President George W. Bush declared that "every known terrorist camp must be shut down," nearly 10,000 people gathered to protest at the Fort Benning base to demand that the "School of Assassins" be closed immediately. The weekend gathering was filled with an incredible spirit as a puppet pageant, musicians and speakers invoked feelings of unity, hope and joy—as well as outrage at injustice. Labor groups and veterans gathered en masse. There was a diverse collective of religious groups and students who turned out by the busload.

On the second day of the protest, thousands participated in a solemn procession to the base. The diversity of those gathered was as apparent as the barbed wire that lined the newly erected security fence. At the gates, some left behind their former military fatigues and flags, others left crosses and photos of victims.

Children placed flowers. Others simply wept. The symbols and the witness of those who gathered transformed the high-security gate into a living memorial for all victims of U.S.-sponsored terrorism perpetrated by graduates of the School of the Americas. The common theme was: "Not in my name!"

The SOA has not only graduated some of the most notorious dictators, death-squad leaders, and human-rights violators in our hemisphere. SOA-trained militaries have also been used in promoting initiatives such as NAFTA and the FTAA, to oppress the poor and working classes of Latin America. Today most of the soldiers trained at this combat school are from Colombia.

Consistently, SOA alumni top the lists of perpetrators of atrocities in human-rights reports from and about Colombia. They include those responsible for both the Trujillo "chainsaw" massacre of over 100 villagers and the brutal murder of 20 striking banana workers—eight of the 11 Colombian military officers cited for these slayings were SOA graduates. SOA-trained Capt. Tomas Monroy Roncanico was convicted of detaining six workers and slitting their throats. SOA-trained members of the Colombian Air Force under the command of SOA graduate Juan Raffael Bustillof targeted, tortured and murdered union leaders María Gómez and Miguel Quintanilla. SOA alumnus Capt. Cenen Darío Jiménez León was cited for the assassination of Manuel Gustavo Chacón Sarmiento, whose murder incited five days of strikes and confrontations between the military and civilians.

The 2000 *Human Rights Watch Report* "The Ties That Bind," additionally cites several high-ranking Colombian officers who are SOA graduates and have direct links to paramilitary death squads responsible for the death and dismemberment of many civilians from 1997 to 1999.

In 2001, we traveled to Colombia to bear witness to the violence perpetrated not only by the Colombian military—more than 10,000 of whose soldiers have been trained at the School of the Americas—but also by the paramilitary forces, who are responsible for 80 percent of the massacres in Colombia. We also wanted to see first-hand and to better understand the effects of fumigations in the Putumayo region.

The fumigations are part of the "anti-drug" campaign called Plan Colombia, which is a multi-billion-dollar program purportedly developed by the government of Colombia to deal with the many conflicts in its country. To date, the United States has pledged over $2 billion in Plan Colombia aid—primarily paid to U.S. weapons and chemical corporations—in the form of military training, helicopters, and fumigation-related expenses.

Throughout our meetings and visits in Putumayo we saw vivid evidence that the indiscriminate fumigation campaign was targeting not only coca, the raw material of cocaine, but food crops and medicinal plants as well. All were being eradicated. And water supplies were being contaminated.

The herbicide glyphosate, the primary ingredient in Roundup, is produced and manufactured by the U.S. chemical corporation Monsanto. Monsanto also produced Agent Orange for the U.S. Air Force during the Vietnam War. That deadly weed killer was dropped on jungles and farms throughout Vietnam to kill trees and crops with no regard for the health effects on people or the long-term environmental devastation that would ensue.

The herbicide in Colombia is being used in a highly concentrated form along with a surfactant that increases the chemical's adherence. It does not discriminate among coca plant, birds, children, farmers and subsistence crops. The chemical can obliterate a food crop with a single aerial application. Worse yet, new research is aimed at developing other substances, biological agents such as a mutating fungus that would have greater adherence to the vegetation. The effects of this new agent could have a catastrophic impact on the overall rainforest ecology—aquatic life, animals and people already bombarded with chemical toxins on a continuous basis.

The fumigation campaign has not only had disastrous ecological and health consequences for the region. It has also significantly increased the expansion of coca crops throughout Colombia. While the State Department and authorities in Colombia cite the fumigation's overall effectiveness as low as 15 percent, a 2002 CIA report stated that coca production in Colombia had increased by 25 percent.

Coca is big business. In addition to the paramilitary forces, which receive most of their funding from the coca industry, the various guerrilla groups have also greatly profited from coca. And coca provides U.S. and multinational corporations the opportunity to make millions of dollars by exploiting the "war on drugs." Responding to an article posted on the SOA Watch/NE website, a former employee of the State Department's International Narcotics Unit sent an email to SOA Watch. He wrote: "I cannot agree more with you ... [I] can unequivocally say that the main reason we are there [in Colombia] with our spray planes is economic advantages for U.S. contractors."

Corporations such as United Tech, Sikorsky, Dyncorp, MPRI and Rockwell have received millions of dollars from the sale of weapons and helicopters as well as from outsourcing to mercenaries. These corporations, in collaboration with the U.S. military, are vying to wage biological and civilian-targeted warfare that would bring Colombia to its knees. Already, as the pillage and rape of the land continues, Colombia, which has some of the greatest diversity of animal life in the world, is now losing both plant and animal species to the point of extinction at a calamitous rate.

As soon as we arrived in the Putumayo—the focal point of Plan Colombia—we were taken aback by an eerie presence around us. It was not the many bunkers we saw, nor the stares we received from the countless armed soldiers. The most haunting sound in this majestic Amazon region was the silence.

As our attention was turned to a beautiful bird perched on a cable overhead we saw four planes flying in formation. As they shot through a set of clouds someone yelled, "Those are the fumigation planes!" Glancing back for the bird, which was now gone, we could only ponder how many birds would take flight that day only to be doused in toxic chemicals. How many children would be sprayed while playing in fields?

How many mothers bathe their infants with noxious water? How many campesinos try to harvest their food crops only to find them in ruins?

The State Department would like you to believe that glyphosate "is as safe as baby shampoo." Yet in the areas that have been sprayed, children are developing skin lesions and respiratory ailments at an alarming rate. Farmers complain of severe visual problems. Health experts attribute these problems to direct exposure to the fumigations.

Dr. Francisco José Ruiz, who works for the Colombian Environmental Ministry overseeing the impact of public spending on the fumigations, said that to date there had not been any research into the relationship of the fumigations and the developing health afflictions. "It is outright negligence," said Ruiz.

During a meeting with Dr. Gonzalo de Francisco, who heads the fumigation campaign in Colombia, we handed him pages of data that were given to us by community leaders in the Putumayo. This data documents thousands of acres of subsistence crops decimated and hundreds of cases of livestock killed by the fumigations. De Francisco attempted to sweep aside our report. He said he had heard of such stories but believed that they were greatly exaggerated.

But we confronted him with actual videotaped footage that we had shot in the Putumayo region. The videotape clearly revealed the extent of the devastation to the food crops. Realizing he had been caught up in his own deception, he became flustered and assured us that he would research the matter more thoroughly.

In La Hormiga, a small city in the Putumayo region, we viewed the effects of glyphosate on food crops. The fumigations had killed subsistence crops such as yucca, corn and banana. Adjacent coca fields not only survived but flourished. Unlike most vegetation in this region, the coca plant is quite resilient. Like a weed, it is able to grow under even the most extreme conditions.

Many people with whom we met had horror stories to tell about abductions, tortures and massacres by the paramilitaries. We were also shown photos of a murderous rampage committed by the paramilitary in which bodies were mutilated, faces were mauled, heads decapitated, torsos cut in two.

The paramilitary acts by using terror against any individuals and communities who have not expressed support for them. They deem everyone—whether an active, passive or presumed supporter of a guerrilla group—as an enemy to be destroyed. The paramilitaries use selective killings as well as indiscriminate massacres to elicit absolute terror in the civilian population.

Over and over again people in the Putumayo confirmed that the military and paramilitary are a unified force. Both act with 100 percent impunity. With military support, the paramilitaries have operated as surrogate death squads and thugs.

Dr. Alfonso Gómez Méndez, the former attorney general of Colombia, expressed to us his complete frustration with Colombia's justice system. He said he had issued more than 40 warrants for the arrest of Carlos Castaño, the head of the paramilitary forces, but neither the military nor the police responded to the warrants. We later confronted Gen. Fernando Tapias, the commander in charge of all military forces in Colombia, and asked him why Castaño had not yet been apprehended. Tapias used the excuse that Castaño is elusive, difficult to track, and is supported by his own militant army. Despite this statement, Tapias acknowledged that he knew exactly where Castaño lives.

While in the Putumayo, we also met with Gen. Mario Montoya, a former instructor and graduate of the SOA. At the time Montoya commanded the 24th Brigade, which was responsible for all military activities in the Putumayo region. The 24th Brigade is infamous for human-rights abuses, and upon our return to the United States we learned that Montoya had been cited (in *Terrorismo De Estado En Colombia*, 1992) as having direct ties with the paramilitary groups.

During a meeting with U.S. Ambassador to Colombia Anne Patterson, she stated that the 24th Brigade was not entitled to receive funding through Plan Colombia because of the human-rights abuses associated with the brigade—yet we clearly witnessed a completely different policy being implemented with this brigade in the Putumayo.

Not surprisingly, Plan Colombia and the fumigations are focused not on areas where the paramilitaries have a stronghold, rather, they are generally aimed at regions where the guerrillas occupy and maintain control. The U.S. government's initiative to give Colombia nearly $2 billion is not to fight a "war on drugs." It is to secure the interests of U.S. and multinational corporations and their investments. For this, Washington has forged ties with, supported and funded bloody killers. With the support of the United States, the paramilitaries act with complete impunity and without any regard for human life.

By overriding the human-rights clause in Plan Colombia and with complete disregard for the well-being of the Colombian people, Presidents Clinton and Bush have been accomplices to not only murder, but to genocide.

No matter how many hectares of coca the fumigations destroy, additional hectares (at minimally a twofold ratio) of rainforests will be cut down to keep the supply moving. In the end, once all the forests have been decimated, the medicinal plants eradicated, and all the Indigenous people have been killed off or forced from their land—what will be left? Only the barren soil, from which the oil companies, supported and protected by the military, will have free range to finalize their annihilation of the Amazon.

One Indigenous leader commented to us: "We are used to being exploited and attacked [by the U.S.], but now they are killing themselves by killing the lungs of the world."

We demonize or give meritorious status to leaders and countries in order to package a particular foreign policy. We cater to the interests of an elite minority at the expense of the vast majority of the population. Monsters become heroes, heroes monsters. We funnel millions of U.S. taxpayer dollars into despotic governments and train the thugs at the SOA/WHISC who impose authoritarian rule and are responsible for genocide.

Colombians are counting on their new president, Harvard-educated Álvaro Uribe Vélez, to end the fighting between the Revolutionary Armed Forces of Colombia-People's Army (FARC-EP) and the paramilitary groups closely allied with the Colombian military. But human-rights groups are very concerned by Uribe's tough talk—and by his plan to double the security forces to 400,000 and increase the military budget, which was $2.1 billion in 2001, by another $1 billion.

Once again we find a country's leader advocating the use of force rather than diplomacy. And once again, the U.S. government and corporations are there to provide the arms, deadly chemicals and military training in Colombia and at the School of the Americas. The SOA has a long and tainted history, especially with regard to Colombia. Shutting down this breeding ground for terrorists and assassins is long overdue. Investigating the trail of crimes perpetrated by SOA graduates is crucial. Dramatically shifting policies toward Colombia to include a peace initiative is not only central for democracy to be achieved, but integral for life to be sustained.

Just before we left the Putumayo an Indigenous person submitted this urgent appeal: "We beg you, be our voices. ... We are not only being displaced, we are being exterminated."

How can the U.S. government justify sending millions of dollars of U.S. taxpayer money into one of the most corrupt and violent countries in the world? The "drug war," and now the "war on terrorism," has taken the place of "communism" as the new boogieman. Yet time and time again, from the grassroots level to senior-level government officials in Colombia, it was made clear that the fumigations are being imposed by the United States. The drug problem is not Colombia's problem, it's a U.S. demand-side problem and should be addressed as such. The international community is not fooled, and soon, through ongoing outreach the deception inside the United States will also be revealed.

See the Appendix for an abbreviated list of Colombian officers trained at the School of the Americas who are responsible for many massacres, tortures and disappearances in Colombia.

VI.
APPENDIX

THE AGRARIAN PROGRAM

REVOLUTIONARY ARMED FORCES OF COLOMBIA (FARC)

Proclaimed July 20, 1964, in the heat of the armed struggle of Marquetalia, corrected and broadened by the 8th National Conference of the FARC-EP, April 2, 1993.

Comrade peasants, workers, students, artisans, intellectuals, patriotic soldiers, police and officers, men and women of Colombia:

The Victims of Five Wars:

We are at the heart of a revolutionary movement originating in 1948. Since then, the force of the big landowners and cattle ranchers, grand commerce, the bosses of official politics and the merchants of violence has been thrown against us, peasants of southern Tolima, Huila and Cauca. We have been the victims of the policy of "blood and fire" supported and put into practice by the oligarchy that holds power.

During the last 45 years, five wars have been unleashed against us. One started in 1948, another in 1954, yet another in 1962, and again from May 18, 1964, when the high command officially declared the beginning of "Operation Marquetalia." And we have faced the current one since Dec. 9, 1990, when the dictator Gaviria and the military high command initiated the operation of extermination against the Secretariat of the FARC-EP at Casa Verde and militaristic aggression against the popular movement in the whole country.

We have been victims of the fury of the military and the big land-owners because here, in this part of Colombia, the interests of the big landlords predominate, linked to those of the most obscurantist reaction in the country. This is why we have had to suffer in body and spirit all the bestialities of a rotten regime that sprouts from the domination of the financial monopolies, blood brothers of imperialism.

A PATHWAY BLOCKED

This is why in this war, U.S. planes, specialists and high commands are in action against us. This is why they send against Marquetalia 16,000 men equipped with all manner of arms. This is why they use against us the tactics of economic blockade, extermination encirclement, land and air attacks and, finally, bacteriological warfare. This is why the government, the military high command and U.S. imperialism employ hundreds of millions of dollars in arms, equipment and money for spies and informers. This is why the government and high command bribe and corrupt consciences, kill, pursue and jail Colombians who rise up in struggle in solidarity with us, victims of a cruel and inhuman war of extermination.

We have knocked on all possible doors in the search for help to avoid this anti-communist crusade, this crusade against our people, which would lead us to a prolonged and bloody struggle.

We are revolutionaries who are fighting for a change using the way least painful for our people: the peaceful way, the mass democratic way. That path was violently closed to us with the fascistic official pretext of combating supposed "Independent Republics." But since we are revolutionaries who one way or another shall fulfill our historic role, we had to pursue the other path: the armed revolutionary path of struggle for power.

The present regime has incorporated openly fascist forms into its system of government. The most provocative and adventurist elements are found in command of the forces of repression. The official armed forces are putting into practice the "Theory of National Security." This is the philosophy of terror, dirty war, paramilitarism and death, under the sponsorship and command of the oligarchy and a group of high officials who make their own the policy, tactics and strategy of "preventive war" and the "internal enemy" to maintain the social discipline of the monopolies and the exploitation of our people and natural resources by imperialism and the rapacious and reactionary Colombian ruling class.

Therefore, this war has assumed a genuinely national character that shall necessarily incorporate the broadest masses of our people into the armed struggle against the military underpinnings of the regime.

Thus, the FARC-EP has constituted itself as a political-military organization that takes up the Bolivarian banners and freedom-loving traditions of our people in order to struggle for power, to bring Colombia to the full exercise of its national sovereignty and to make popular sovereignty a reality. We fight for the establishment of a democratic political regime that guarantees peace with social justice, respect for human rights and economic development with well-being for all who live in Colombia.

We fight for an agrarian policy that provides the peasants with land from the large holdings. Therefore, from today, July 20, 1964, we are a guerrilla army that fights for the following agrarian program:

First: Against the oligarchy's agrarian policy of lies, we put forward an effective revolutionary agrarian policy that would change the social structure of the Colombian countryside, providing land completely free to the peasants who work it or want to work it on the basis of confiscation of large landholdings for the benefit of all working people.

The Revolutionary Agrarian Policy shall provide the peasants it benefits the technical assistance, infrastructure, tools and work animals for proper economic exploitation of the land. The Revolutionary Agrarian Policy is the indispensable condition to raise the standard of material and cultural life of the whole peasantry, free it from unemployment, hunger, illiteracy, and the endemic illnesses that limit its ability to work, to eliminate the fetters of the large landholding system and to promote the development of agricultural and industrial production. The Revolutionary Agrarian Policy shall confiscate the lands occupied by U.S. imperialist companies, whatever title they may have and to whatever activity they may be dedicated.

Second: Tenant farmers, occupants, renters, sharecroppers, lessees, and farmhands on the large holdings and lands of the nation shall receive property titles for the lands they exploit. All varieties of backward exploitation of the land, systems of sharecropping and rent in kind or in money shall be eliminated.

The size of economic unit in the countryside shall be established in accord with the fertility and location of the lands, having a minimum of 10-20 hectares where lands are flat and border on villages or cities and, on other lands, according to fertility and the communications network. All the debts of the peasants owed to usurers, speculators and official and semi-official institutions of credit shall be erased.

Third: The Revolutionary Agrarian Government shall respect the property of rich peasants who personally work for their lands. Industrial forms of work in the countryside will be preserved. Large agricultural units, which for social and economic reasons should be conserved, shall be destined for planned development for the whole people.

Fourth: The Revolutionary Agrarian Government shall establish a broad system of credit with facilities for payment, provision of seed, technical assistance, tools, animals, equipment and machinery, etc., for individual peasants and for co-operatives, which arise in the process. A planned system of irrigation and electrification and a network of official agri-technical experimentation stations shall be created.

Adequate health services for complete attention to the problems of public health in the countryside shall be organized. The problem of peasant education shall be dealt with, as shall the total eradication of illiteracy, and a system of scholarships for technical and superior studies for the children of those who work the land shall be created. A vast peasant housing plan shall be carried out, as shall the construction of communications routes from the rural centers of production to the centers of consumption.

Fifth: Sufficient basic support prices for agricultural products shall be guaranteed.

Sixth: Indigenous communities shall be protected, providing them sufficient land for their development, returning to them lands usurped by big landowners and modernizing their systems of cultivation. The Indigenous communities shall enjoy all the benefits of the Revolutionary Agrarian Policy. At the same time, an autonomous organization of these communities shall be established, respecting their councils, way of life, culture, languages, and internal organization.

Seventh: Realization of this Revolutionary Agrarian Program will depend upon the worker-peasant alliance and the United Front of all Colombians in the struggle for the change of regime, which is the only guarantee for the destruction of the old structure of big landowners of Colombia. Realization of this policy will depend upon the broadest masses of peasants who will contribute decisively to the destruction of the big landholding system. For that end, potent organizations of peasant struggle shall be organized, and strong unions, committees of land users and neighborhoods. Therefore, this program puts forward as a vital necessity the struggle for the formation of the broadest united front of all the democratic, progressive, and revolutionary forces of the country to carry out a permanent struggle until the oligarchic regime at the service of U.S. imperialism, which impedes the realization of the desires of the Colombian people, is brought down.

Eighth: At the right time, the FARC-EP shall promulgate the First Law of the Revolutionary Agrarian Policy. Therefore, we invite peasants, workers, employees, students, artisans, small industrialists and merchants, the national bourgeoisie prepared to fight against imperialism, democratic and revolutionary intellectuals, and all parties and currents of the left and center that want a change in the direction of progress, to join the great patriotic revolutionary struggle for a Colombia for Colombians, for the triumph of the revolution and for a democratic government of national liberation.

Manuel Marulanda Vélez	Judith Grisales	Pedro Ipús
Jacobo Arenas	Jesús Ortíz	Evaristo Lozada
Rigoberto Lozada	Rogelio Diaz	Vicente Torres
Isauro Yosa	Miguel Aldana	Desiderio García
Isaías Pardo	Hernando González Acosta	Agustín Cifuentes
Luis Pardo	Gabriel Gualteros	Abraham García
Jesús María Medina	Miguel Pascuas	Ismael Valderrama
Darío Lozano	Jaime Bustos	Miguel Garzón
Tarcisio Guaracas	Alcides González & brothers	Jaime García
Parménides Cuenca	David González	José Domingo Rivera
Roberto López	Andrés López & brothers	Mariano Pérez Montes
Miryam Narváez	Luis Salgado	

GOVERNMENT OF NATIONAL RECONCILIATION AND RECONSTRUCTION

REVOLUTIONARY ARMED FORCES OF COLOMBIA-PEOPLE'S ARMY (FARC-EP)

Proclaimed April 30, 1993 at the Eighth National Conference of the Guerrilla Movement.

We invite all Colombians who desire a peaceful, developing and pleasant country to work for the formation of a PLURALISTIC, PATRIOTIC, and DEMOCRATIC national government that commits itself to the following:

1. Political Solution of the grave conflict through which the country is passing.

2. The National Defense and Military Doctrine of State shall be BOLIVARI-AN. The liberator said: "The purpose of the army is to garrison the frontier. May God save us from it turning its weapons against the citizens." The Armed Forces shall be guarantors of our national sovereignty, respectful of human rights and shall have a size and budget appropriate to a country that is not at war with its neighbors.

3. National, regional and municipal democratic participation in the decisions that involve the future of the society. Strengthening of the instruments of popular accountability.

The Office of the Attorney General shall be an independent branch of public power and the Attorney General shall be popularly elected.

The parliament shall be unicameral.

The opposition and minorities shall have full political and social rights with their access to the mass communications media guaranteed by the state.

There shall be freedom of the press.

The Electoral Branch shall be independent.

The Supreme Court of Justice, the Constitutional Court and the National Judicial Council shall be elected by the direct vote of all the judges and magistrates of the country.

The morality of the public administration and the civil and military institutions of the state shall be raised.

4. Economic modernization and development with social justice.

The state must be the principal owner and administrator of the strategic sectors: in energy, in communications, public services, roads, ports and natural resources, to benefit the harmonious social-economic development of the country and its regions.

The emphasis of economic policy shall be on the broadening of the internal market, self-sufficiency in foodstuff and the permanent stimulation of production, small, medium and large private industry, of self-management, micro-enterprise and the solidarity economy.

The state shall invest in strategic areas of national industry and develop a protectionist policy for them. Official economic management must be characterized by its efficiency, ethics, productivity and high quality. There shall be participation by the economic associations, unions and popular organizations and academic and scientific entities in the elaboration of decisions about economic, social and energy policy and on strategic investments.

5. Fifty percent of the national budget shall be invested in social well-being, paying attention to the Colombian, his/her employment, income, health, housing, education and recreation as the focus of state policies, supported in our democratic cultural traditions and pursuing equilibrium between society and the natural environment. Ten percent of the national budget shall be invested in scientific research.

6. Those who possess more wealth shall make greater tax contributions in order to bring about a redistribution of income. The Value Added Tax shall only affect luxury goods and services.

7. An Agrarian Policy that would democratize credit, technical aid and marketing. Complete stimulation of industry and agricultural production. State protectionism in the face of unfair international competition. Each region shall have its own development plan elaborated together with all organizations of the community, eliminating feudalistic landholding where it survives, redistributing the land, defining agricultural frontier that rationalizes colonization and protects against the destruction of our reserves. Permanent assistance for national and international marketing.

8. Exploitation of natural resources like petroleum, gas, coal, gold, nickel and emeralds, etc., for the benefit of the country and its regions.

Renegotiation with the multinational companies of the contracts that are harmful for Colombia. The National Energy Commission shall have participation by the state, the workers of the sector and the regions, and shall plan the energy policy.

More refineries shall be constructed and the petrochemical industry shall be developed. The government shall openly inform the public as to the terms of the contract existing for the exploitation of CUSIANA. Just the 5 billion barrels of petroleum reserves which it possesses, at today's prices and exchange rate, would produce 80 trillion pesos, that is, more than six times the national budget of 1993.

All Colombia shall know how and at what rate CUSIANA will be exploited and how we shall include its production in the general plans for our development. We must "plan petroleum" for the following generations because crude oil belongs to all Colombians as do its benefits.

9. International relations with all countries of the world on the principle of respect for the free self-determination of the peoples and mutual benefit. Priority to tasks for regional and Latin American integration.

Respect for the political commitments of the state with other states. Total revision of the military pacts and of the interference of the big powers in our internal affairs.

Renegotiation of external debt to achieve a 10-year moratorium on debt servicing.

10. Solution of the phenomenon of production, commercialization and consumption of narcotics and hallucinogenics, it being understood above all as a grave social problem that cannot be dealt with militarily. It requires agreements with the participation of the national and international community and the commitment of the big powers, the principal sources of the world demand for narcotic.

THE MANIFESTO OF SIMACOTA

NATIONAL LIBERATION ARMY (ELN)

Declared in the town of Simacota, province of Santander, January 7, 1965.
The ELN is struggling for the complete realization of the following program in our country:

1. The taking of power for the popular classes and the installation of a democratic and popular government that will free our country from the international monopolies and the local oligarchy and will guarantee the complete equality of our people, will grant complete democratic freedoms to the popular sectors, will grant women their legitimate rights, will free the creative forces of the masses and will guarantee the respect for human dignity and the free development of the Colombians.

2. An authentic agrarian revolution involving the elimination of the big latifundist landholdings, the minifundist land holdings and one-crop cultivation that will realize a technical and fair distribution of the lands to the peasants that work them; grant credits, fertilizer, farming equipment, seeds and tools to the growers; encourage the mechanization and use of technology in agriculture, the creation of adequate entities for distribution, eliminating the need for intermediaries, speculators, and monopolists; assures medical and educational assistance to the peasants, along with developing systems for irrigation, electrification, housing and adequate communications routes.

The properties of the landowners on the big latifundist holdings will be confiscated, and those properties that benefit the national economy will be respected. The creation of production, distribution and consumption cooperatives and state farms will be encouraged, along with the planning of agriculture, with the aim of crop diversity and the development of cattle ranching.

3. Economic and industrial development, by means of scientific planning, through the protection of the national industry, encouraging semi-heavy industry, along with the confiscation of imperialist interests and those of the traitorous oligarchies. Small industrialists and merchants who are not speculating will be protected.

The diversification of industry and an industrial economy based on our own resources will be sought after, guaranteeing the complete utilization of our workforce. The subsoil and its exploitation will be effectively nationalized for the benefit of the national economy. A plan for electrification, irrigation and taking advantage of the hydraulic resources of our country will be drawn up and carried out. Trade will be carried out with all countries of the world for the benefit of our people with no other interests than the collective ones.

4. A plan for housing and urban reform will guarantee a clean and adequate home for the workers in the country and the city and will eliminate the exploitation of renters by long-term amortization, eradication of slums, shacks and shantytowns in the city and countryside.

5. The creation of a popular system of credit, eliminating usurers and stock speculators, encouraging industrial-economic, agricultural and commercial development, and improving the quality of living for the workers.

6. The organization of a national public health plan, making possible medical, pharmacy and hospital attention to every sector of the population without burdening household budgets; development of preventative medicine and fighting against endemic diseases. Health care posts and hospitals will be set up in the city and country.

Children and elderly will be efficiently protected, and social security will be regulated to serve the needs of our people.

A centralized body will be created for developing and carrying out public health programs.

7. The creation of a road and highway plan in order to match the needs of the national economy, to deliver an efficient service to densely populated regions and to make economic development possible. This program will be centralized and planned with the aim of avoiding unnecessary costs. Agricultural and grazing lands will be penetrated; transportation and tolls technically stipulated by state entities will be organized by the state.

8. Education reform, eliminating illiteracy and promoting the creation of urban and rural schools, and training competent teachers. Education will be obligatory and free.

Programs of study will be reformed to align them with the needs of the country and modern science, students will be linked to the national reality, and the technical level of the workers will be raised; high school and university instruction will be nationalized, with the goal that the university will fulfill its social function, putting itself in harmony with scientific advances, that all people have access to it, eliminating obscurantism and academic dogmatism, and that can thus unleash the intellectual and cultural vanguard role for the Colombian workers.

A National Academy of Sciences will be created that will unify the demands and the efforts of the development of scientific research.

In the same way, student cafeterias will be set up, a wide number of children's scholarships will be granted, the network of public libraries will be widened, and necessary academic and educational materials will be provided for educational establishments.

Sports and physical culture will be promoted and encouraged.

The state will take upon itself the defense, stimulation and development of national culture, people's folkloric art and the protection of national writers and artists. Likewise, all artistic and freethinking manifestations that display popular and democratic forms of other peoples will be widely promoted.

9. The incorporation of the Indigenous population into the economy and culture of the nation, respecting its customs, lands, language, traditions and the development of its cultural life. The rights of Colombians will be granted completely to the Indigenous population.

10. Freedom of thought and worship. Separation of church and state. The elimination of every form of discrimination on the basis of race, gender, social origin or religious belief.

11. An independent foreign policy based on mutual respect, self-determination of peoples, and non-intervention of any state in the internal affairs of another, opposition of every form of oppression and imperialist, colonialist or neocolonialist domination, defense of world peace and solidarity with the struggle of peoples against their oppressors for national independence.

All agreements that damage national sovereignty will be annulled. Military missions of U.S. imperialism will be expelled.

Diplomatic, cultural and commercial relations with every country of the world will be established on the basis of mutual respect.

12. The formation of a permanent people's army, disciplined and technically gifted, that will guarantee the conquests of the people, defend national sovereignty and will be the most firm support of the people. This people's army will be formed initially by the ELN detachments and will maintain solid and constant ties to the popular masses, from whose breast their squads and combatants have arisen.

The people's army will defend the most authentic patriotic interests and will never be an instrument of repression against any people of the world.

THE COUNTRY WE WANT

NATIONAL LIBERATION ARMY (ELN)

This minimum program was approved at the National Congress of the ELN held in July 1996 and replaces the previous official text in place since 1993 with the same name.

We want to form a new people's democratic government with the participation of the social and popular organizations, the different political parties and organizations and other active forces in the country, in which the revolutionary forces play an important leadership role. We want a government standing for peace, democracy, national dignity, social justice and development.

We want to create organs of judicial power that guarantee the suppression of impunity, promote civic harmony, punish corruption and crimes against humanity. A legal system based on procedural guarantees and due process, in which the law is applied justly, must be in effect in order to judge crimes against society and to serve as the underpinning for the new constitution.

We want to create a new system in which effective means of community decision-making will ensure the people's participation in their municipality, region, neighborhood, city and work place, as well as mechanisms for direct popular participation in the important political and economic decisions at the different levels.

Everyone's participation is welcomed, with the exception of imperialist interests, the representatives of the monopolies and the large landowners, the drug traffickers, the paramilitary and those who bear primary responsibility for the war and the crimes unleashed against our people.

NATIONAL SOVEREIGNTY

We wish to act in accordance with a patriotic sense of sovereignty, national self-determination and independence vis-a-vis the United States, other imperialists and the transnational corporations, developing our own conception of national sovereignty.

Neocolonial relations—with the multinationals' plunder of our resources and the oligarchy's subordination to the economic and political interests of their masters to the North—have been the main obstacle to our development.

Therefore new relations will be established with foreign capital and new conditions will be placed on foreign investment and the exploitation of our natural resources. Foreign investment will be accepted only if there is a transfer of technology, if we are left with resources and if it corresponds to the priorities set for our economic and social development.

The relations subordinating us to the demands of the IMF will be revised. We will renegotiate and declare a moratorium on our foreign debt and set out a new framework for relations with the World Bank. Treaties deemed harmful to the new nation will be declared null and void. Treaties governing borders will be respected in accordance with international law.

ARMED FORCES

We will organize a new army with the rebel forces as its core, and new police and security forces, and will punish war criminals. The new patriotic army will act in accordance with the postulates of the new government. It will be internationalist, independent from the United States, and act in keeping with the new political realities that will come into effect when power is seized from a tiny handful of oligarchs. This army and the new security forces will be guided by respect for human rights and the people's just right to protest and make demands.

DEVELOPMENT

We will establish an economic policy based on the interests of Colombia, rather than those of the United States and the transnational corporations. There will be an equitable redistribution of wealth and an improved standard of living for the poorest and most marginalized sectors.

We will seek to attain growth without sacrificing workers' jobs or incomes; we will seek to increase wealth and guarantee economic development to benefit not the few but the majority.

We support sustainable development that will permit new advances, while setting out conditions for Colombia itself to attain higher scientific and technological levels that, in time, will enable us to exploit our own resources.

We will also apply a policy for the country's exploitation of its natural resources in accordance with our interests and needs and maintaining reserves, guaranteeing their future use.

We will respect and protect small and medium-sized industrial, craft and mining enterprises, developing an incentive policy in accordance with the interests laid out in the National Development Plan.

We will establish and combine different forms of property: private, state, collective, communal and joint. Self-management processes will be stimulated, with special emphasis by the state on the development of a popular economy as the basis in the future for true economic democracy.

The multinationals and the big monopolies will either have their property seized or will be negotiated with, depending on their behavior with respect to the people's struggle and the people's desire for change, and on the attitude they adopt toward the new government and the economic and political goals of the new Colombia.

In any event, the monopolies and all foreign investment will be limited and controlled. They will be subjected to the parameters of national development, favoring entrepreneurial and industrial competitiveness but without detriment to small and medium enterprises.

RURAL POLICY

An agrarian reform will take place with the property of the large landowners, drug traffickers and latifundists being distributed among the landless peasants. A new credit policy will be devised which will be especially concerned with the poor and medium peasantry, stimulating cooperatives, communal associations and profit sharing. Marketing systems will be organized which will do away with middlemen and will lower costs and prices and provide technical assistance to increase productivity and efficiency.

Momentum will be given to the creation of a national food industry to meet the demand for internal consumption; at the same time attempts will be made to establish commercial relations on the international market.

Support will be provided to small and medium-sized agricultural and agro-industrial enterprises and in general to all non-monopolistic enterprises that contribute to the new government's economic plans. These enterprises must conform to new wage scales, regional development plans, the redistribution of profits and new employee-employer relations.

Families that were forcibly displaced during the war will be guaranteed their return to their land. All possible efforts will be made to improve their situation.

WELFARE

Efforts will be made to significantly increase social spending and to provide a better and more extensive network of basic services: water, light, sewage, housing, health, education and broad access to culture, sports and recreation.

A national health system will be established which will train healthcare workers who will act with a revolutionary morale and provide care of the highest scientific quality possible to the people nationwide.

Educational, art and cultural workers and students will be called on to participate in the construction of a national education system which will eradicate illiteracy, lead to the socialization of knowledge and engender critical thinking in the people, all in benefit of the transformations which society demands.

Special efforts will be made to change and improve the critical situation confronted at present by the poorest people in the cities and the countryside. We will also concern ourselves with the elderly, with children and with the rehabilitation of those crippled and injured by the war.

ENVIRONMENT AND ECOLOGY

We believe that scientific-technical development and progress in different areas should occur as part of a necessary balance with nature and preservation of the environment, which is the patrimony of humanity.

We are for the preservation of animal and plant species, for guaranteeing their rational use and survival.

We will exercise sovereignty over our biodiversity and its rational use.

We will ask the international community to call on the transnational corporations to make payment for and rectify the damage done to the ecosystem through their irrational use of our resources. Efforts will be made in the scientific-technical area to eliminate waste to avoid environmental and ecological damage.

INDIGENOUS AND BLACK COMMUNITIES

The rights of Indigenous peoples to their culture, territory, autonomy and authorities, and their social, economic and cultural development will be made a reality.

Recognition and support will be given to Colombia's Black communities in their struggle to recover their culture and for recognition of their lands as collective property, and in their efforts to gain respect as an ethnic group and for the end of racial discrimination.

NATIONAL IDENTITY

In order to strengthen the formation of the national identity and unity, which the Dominant Bloc was unable to achieve, a new popular, democratic sentiment is needed, which combines both the will and the understanding necessary to undertake change.

A new ideological plan will be implemented, combining actions in the fields of education, culture and popular communication, to recover the Colombian and Latin American people's historic and culturally rooted progressive community-based practices and values.

This plan respects freedom of expression and belief and recognizes cultural diversity.

It proposes, as well, supporting initiatives taken by individuals and different social groups toward the construction of the New Colombia.

DRUG TRAFFICKING

The problem of drug trafficking will be dealt with in an autonomous and sovereign manner in our national territory. We will seek a global agreement, internationally, on effective measures to be taken to control the consumption of drugs, and the mafias that process and deal in drugs in their own territory. We will not permit the extradition of Colombian nationals.

Any imposition or interference by the U.S. government will be rejected and we will demand that the U.S. reciprocate Colombia's efforts.

With the eradication of drug cultivation and trafficking, it will be very necessary to seek economic alternatives for the peasants linked to the raising of drug crops and new sources of income for those people involved in the different activities in drug trafficking.

We will develop educational processes and recovery centers for addicts, aiming at their development and the elimination of their dependence on drugs.

FOREIGN POLICY AND CONTINENTALISM

An autonomous foreign policy, independent of any center of power, will be developed. It will express solidarity with the Third World countries, and respect and support for the self-determination of all peoples, and in particular, for the Cuban people and their revolution.

It will be an explicitly Latin American policy, since it is to the extent that the continent acts as a bloc and strengthens its bonds of brotherhood, cooperation and integration that Latin America will win for itself a place on the international stage, and each of its countries will be able to define, in an autonomous and sovereign manner, its own direction, future and development. As part of our foreign policy we will establish relations with all states in the world.

SCHOOL OF THE AMERICAS GRADUATES

Following is an abbreviated list of Colombian officers who were trained at the School of the Americas by U.S. military personnel in tactics of murder, torture and disappearances. In short, the U.S. trained these officers in terror.

1Lt. Pedro Nei Acosta Gaivis, 1986, Cadet Arms Orientation Course, Murder of 11 peasants, 1990. Ordered the massacre of 11 peasants, had his men dress the corpses like guerrilla forces, and then dismissed the killings as an armed confrontation between the Army and guerrillas. (*Terrorismo de Estado en Colombia*, 1992)

Lt. Carlos Alberto Acosta, 1992, Cadet Infantry Orientation Course (Commandant's List), Massacre, 1994. Fled after receiving notice of a 58-year sentence for his participation in the massacre of three people in Lebrija in June 1994. (*Vanguardia Liberal*, 11/15/97)

Gen. Norberto Adrada Córdoba, 1978, Training Management Course; 1975, Special Maintenance Administration, Disappearance, June 18, 1986. Covered-up of the murder of William Camacho Barajas and Orlando García González, who were last seen alive in the hands of soldiers under Adrada Córdoba's command. (*Terrorismo de Estado en Colombia*, 1992)

Cpt. Juan Carlos Álvarez, 1987, Psychological Operations Course, Death Squad Activity. According to testimony given by Álvarez' fellow officers to the Colombian attorney general, Álvarez was the officer who gave the go-ahead for death squad killings. ("Colombia's Killer Networks" *Human Rights Watch Report* and *Covert Action Quarterly*)

Cpt. Gilberto Alzate Alzate, 1983, Cadet Arms Orientation Course, Segovia Massacre, 1988. Implicated in the massacre at Segovia in which 43 people died, including several children. (*Terrorismo de Estado en Colombia*, 1992)

1Lt. Luis Enrique Andrade Ortiz, 1983, Cadet Arms Orientation Course, Massacre of a judicial commission, 1989. Believed to be the intellectual author of the paramilitary massacre of 12 officials, including 2 judges, who were investigating military/paramilitary cooperation. Assassination, 1988. Ordered the assassination of farmer Jorge Ramírez, carried out by a military/paramilitary patrol under his command. Assassination, 1988. Ordered the assassination of José Sánchez, also carried out by military/paramilitary soldiers under his command. Then he had the corpse put on display for the benefit of the public. Ramírez family massacre, 1986: Andrade Ortiz was one of officers in charge of military/paramilitary soldiers who broke into the home of the Ramírez family, killed two members outright; and captured four others whose bodies were found later with signs of torture. (*Terrorismo de Estado en Colombia*, 1992)

2Lt. Julio Arenas Vera, 1985, Combat Arms Orientation Course, Assassination, 1986. Implicated in the revenge-killing of communist Gustavo Alfonso Macias Borja. (*Terrorismo de Estado en Colombia*, 1992)

Gen. Harold Bedoya Pizarro, 1978-79, SOA Guest Instructor; 1965, Military Intelligence Course, Paramilitary death squad activity, 1965-present. "Throughout Bedoya's entire career, he has been implicated with the sponsorship and organization of a network of paramilitary organizations. Bedoya, who has never undergone any investigation for his involvement in the massacres of non-combatants or other dirty-war crimes, is an articulate proponent of the continued 'legal' involvement of local populations in counterinsurgency operations." (Ana Carrigan, *NACLA Report on the Americas*, March/April 1995) Paramilitary death squad activity ("AAA"), 1978: Believed to be the founder and chief of the paramilitary death squad known as "AAA" (American Anti-communist Alliance). (*Terrorismo de Estado en Colombia*, 1992)

Ltc. Victor Bernal Castaño, 1992, Command and General Staff College, Fusagasugá massacre, 1991. Colombian legislature asserts that Bernal Castaño was enrolled at the SOA to avoid having to answer to investigators about the Fusagasugá massacre of a peasant family. (Charles Call, *Miami Herald*, 9/9/92) The SOA enrolled him in its longest and most prestigious course, the Command and General Staff College, and made him Chief of Course, Disappearance, 1989. Implicated in the disappearance of peasant Sandra Vélez Vélez. Paramilitary death squad activity. Protected and aided the "Hure" death squad in its criminal activities, including assassinations and disappearances. (*Terrorismo de Estado en Colombia*, 1992)

Henry Borda, 1980, Cadet Arms Orientation Course, Segovia Massacre, 1988. Judge Marta Luisa Hurtado issued an arrest warrant against Borda and other officials for their failure to prevent the massacre of 43 people in Segovia. All evidence indicates that the police and military officials knew the attack was coming and did nothing to prevent it, to stop it while it was occurring or to detain the attackers as they escaped, driving right by the police station. ("Informe Sobre Derechos Humanos en Colombia," *Americas Watch Report*, 1989)

Gen. Martín Orlando Carreño Sandoval, 1990, Comando and State, Major threats and intimidation of human rights workers, 1998. On May 24, troops under his command entered a farm located near San José de Apartado. They shot a cow, proceeded to carve it up, and stated to all those present that they would do the same to Eduar, a member of the Missionary Team of Justice and Peace. On June 17, soldiers from the same brigade came back and sought out Eduar, demanding that he give them a statement and identify the witnesses of the earlier incident so they could also provide statements. The military did not hide the fact that among them were the very soldiers who had reportedly threatened Eduar. (Inter-Congregational Justice and Peace Commission)

Col. Luis Arturo Cifuentes Mogollón, 1973, Auto Maintenance Officer Course, Torture, assassination, 1986. Strongly implicated in the torture and extrajudicial execution of M-19 member Yolanda Acevedo Carvajal. (*Terrorismo de Estado en Colombia*, 1992)

1Lt. Edgar Ferrucio Correa Copola, 1986, Cadet Arms Orientation Course, Llana Caliente massacre, 1988. One of the officers responsible for the massacre of 20 or more peasants detained during a march demanding schools and health clinics. (*Terrorismo de Estado en Colombia*, 1992)

Maj. Jorge Enrique Duran Arquelles, 1991, Cadet Calvary Orientation Course, Massacre, 1991. Named in the massacre of 20 Indigenous people in Caloto. ("Colombia: Human Rights Abuses against Indigenous Peoples," Amnesty International)

Ltc. Manuel José Espitia Sotelo, 1991, Command and General Staff College;1982, Tactical Officer, Escape of Pablo Escobar, 1992. Espitia Sotelo was forced into early retirement in August 1992 after drug kingpin Pablo Escobar "escaped" from prison, where he was living in grand style. Espitia Sotelo was commander of the military police battalion guarding the prison. ("State of War: Political Violence and Counterinsurgency in Colombia," *Americas Watch Report*, 1993)

Col. Edgar Hernando Falla Alvira, 1967, Cadet Orientation Course, Assassinations, 1987. "Intellectual author" of the assassinations of Unión Patriótica leaders José Darío Rodríguez and Fabiola Ruiz. (*Terrorismo de Estado en Colombia*, 1992)

Maj Jorge Flóres Suárez, 1972, Military Intelligence Officer Course, Paramilitary death squad ("AAA") activity, 1978. Strongly implicated in the activities of the military/paramilitary death squad "AAA." (*Terrorismo de Estado en Colombia*, 1992)

2Lt. Octavio Fonseca Hoyos, 1985, Combat Arms Orientation Disappearance, 15 September 1987: Strong evidence links Fonseca Hoyos to the disappearance of Ramón Salvador Angarita Solano. (*Terrorismo de Estado en Colombia*, 1992)

Cpt. Héctor Alirio Forero Quintero, 1977, Small Unit Infantry Tactics, Disappearances, torture, 1988. Commanded a patrol that disappeared four people on February 11, 1988. On the same day, he himself detained two more individuals and tortured them with the help of fellow SOA graduate Carlos Morales del Río (below). The last two victims were released to civilian authorities several days later. (*Terrorismo de Estado en Colombia*, 1992)

Gen. Mario Hugo Galán, 1971, Threats to human rights workers, 1998. Recently in the news for calling Human Rights Watch/Americas director José Miguel Vivanco and a *Washington Post* reporter "enemies of the people" for reporting that the 20th Brigade was being investigated in connection with the murders of human rights defenders. Such a label is tantamount to a death threat.

Ltc. Luis Fabio García Correra, 1985, Command and General Staff College, Denouncing human rights workers, 1993. "In May-July 1993, senior army officers of the Nueva Granada Battalion based in Barrancabermeja verbally attacked CREDHOS (Regional Committee for the Defense of Human Rights) workers when they inquired about or tried to visit detainees on the army base. On several occasions, officers, including battalion commander Luis Fabio García, accused CREDHOS members of being spokespersons for the guerrillas." ("State of War: Political Violence and Counterinsurgency in Colombia," *Americas Watch Report*, December 1993)

Gen. Daniel Enrique García Echeverry, 1976, Command and General Staff College; 1961, Military Intelligence, Paramilitary activity, 1983-88, including Urabá massacre. García Echeverry established and ran paramilitary forces wherever he was stationed. Witnesses and ex-members of his units have testified as to his role in planning and running squads in Antioquiá and Santander, including his involvement with the paramilitaries who carried out the Urabá massacre of 20 banana workers in 1988. (*Terrorismo de Estado en Colombia*, 1992)

Oscar Gómez, 1987, Cadet Arms Orientation Course C-3A (Infantry), Murder. Gómez is charged with the "aggravated murder" of grassroots leader Antonio Palacios Urrea as well as six other people. ("Political Murder and Reform in Colombia," *Americas Watch Report* 1992)

Gen Manuel Jaime Guerrero Paz, 1988, SOA "Hall of Fame," Mistreatment of prisoners, 1982. In 1982, soldiers under Guerrero Paz' command tortured four prisoners, one of whom died of his injuries. (*Terrorismo de Estado en Colombia*, 1992) Illegal detention, 1988. In a measure of questionable legality, he personally issued orders for the arrest of 10 union leaders, most of whom were released later without charge. (Amnesty International, 1989) Paramilitary activities. Throughout his tenure as armed forces chief and defense minister, the relationship between the Colombian military and paramilitaries remained close, and impunity was the rule for crimes committed by both. (*Colombia: Inside the Labyrinth*)

Cpt. David Hernández, 1985, Cadet Arms Orientation Course, 1991, Psychological Operations, Firing indiscriminately on civilians. In August 1996, troops under Hernández's command fired on and used tear gas against a group of protesting peasants, which resulted in four wounded. The soldiers also burned the protesters' tents and stole money that was intended for the purchase of food.

("Noche y Neblina: Panorama de Derechos Humanos y Violencia Politica en Colombia," Banco de Datos de Violencia Politica)

Col. Roberto Hernández Hernández, 1970, Automotive Maintenance Officer; 1976, Tactical Officer, Small Unit Infantry Tactics, Paramilitary activity, 1980-90. Consistently implicated in paramilitary activities in association with members of the extreme right. Torture, 1990. Supervised the illegal detention and torture of 42 people, most of whom were union members and human rights workers. Trujillo massacre, 1990. Implicated in the gruesome killings in Trujillo, in which many victims were dismembered with chain saws. (*Terrorismo de Estado en Colombia*, 1992)

Cpt. Gilberto lbarra, 1983, Cadet Arms Orientation Course, Used children to detonate mines, 1992. On February 12, 1992, Ibarra forced three peasant children to walk in front of his patrol to detonate mines and spring ambushes. Two were killed; one was seriously wounded. ("Feeding the Tiger: Colombia's Internally Displaced People," *U.S. Committee for Refugees Report*, 1993)

Cpt. Cenén Darío Jiménez León; 1980, Cadet Arms Orientation Course, Assassination, 1988. Strongly implicated in the assassination of union leader Manuel Gustavo Chacón Sarmiento, whose assassination in broad daylight incited five days of strikes and confrontations between the military and the citizens of Barranca. (*Terrorismo de Estado en Colombia*, Inter-American Commission on Human Rights, 1992; *Colombia: Inside the Labyrinth*) Disappearance, 1988. Strongly implicated in the illegal detention, beating and disappearance of Héctor Suárez. (*Terrorismo de Estado en Colombia*, 1992)

Gen. Fernando Landázabal, 1950, Basic and Heavy Weapons, Refusal to submit to civilian democratic authority, 1983. Landazábal was forced to retire as Colombia's defense minister in 1983, when he refused to honor a government mandated amnesty for certain guerrilla factions. (*Colombia: Inside the Labyrinth*)

Paucelino Latorre Gamboa, 1980, Commando Operations Commander of notorious 20th Brigade, 1998: Latorre was the commander of the 20th Brigade when it was implicated in the murders of three human rights workers in 1998. The Colombian government recently disbanded the 20th Brigade because of its involvement in grave human rights violations.

Maj. Jorge Alberto Lázaro Vergel, 1981, Orient/Armas p' Cadetes C-3 Puerto Patiño, Massacre, 1995. Lázaro was arrested by the attorney general's office in Barranquilla on charges that he had directed the massacre of eight people in Puerto Patiño. A local police commander quoted Lázaro as saying, "no one[can] operate here without my order and I tell them yes or no, they are under my command and we're not going to leave dead people around, we are going to grab people and disappear them because the dead make a lot of noise." ("Colombia's Killer Networks," *Human Rights Watch Report* 1996) Links to Drug-Trafficking:

Cited in a Colombian police report, which was published by Human Rights Watch in 1996, for involvement in the drug trade. (Frank Smyth, freelance journalist)

Cpt. Fernando López Cifuentes, 1992, Combat Arms Officer Advance Course, Torture, murder, 1987. Implicated in the brutal torture and murder of César Aqite Ipia and Miguel Ipia Vargas. (*Terrorismo de Estado en Colombia*, 1992)

Maj. Luis Fernando Madrid Barón, 1978, Small Unit Tactics, Paramilitary activity, 1987. Implicated in the activities of a paramilitary group which killed 149 people from 1987 to 1990. Cited as the intellectual author of many of the assassinations. (*Terrorismo de Estado en Colombia*, 1992)

Maj. Carlos Enrique Martínez Orozco, 1975, Guerrilla Warfare Operations, Massacre, 1988. Implicated in the massacre of 18 miners in Antioquiá, whose body parts washed in pieces down the river Nare. Martínez Orozco was subsequently promoted. Paramilitary activity, 1990. Protected a chief paramilitarist responsible for high-profile assassinations; and in June 1992 was charged in a military court for his connection to paramilitaries. ("Colombia: Political Violence: Myth and Reality;" *Amnesty International Report*; *Terrorismo de Estado en Colombia*, 1992)

Gen. José Nelson Mejía Henao, 1989, SOA "Hall of Fame"; 1961, Counter Resistance Course, Use of U.S. counter-narcotics funds for counterinsurgency campaign. Former Chief of Staff, Colombian Army Generals Nelson Mejía Henao and Luis Eduardo Roca thanked the U.S. Congress in 1991 for $40.3 million in anti-narcotics aid which was used (illegally) in counterinsurgency campaigns in northeastern Colombia, where narcotics are neither grown nor processed. (Ruth Conniff in *The Progressive*, May 1992)

Cpt. Carlos Armando Mejía Lobo, 1989, Psychological Operations Course; 1980, Cadet Arms Orientation Course, Assassination, 1984. Ordered the extrajudicial execution of communist Oscar William Calvo. (*Terrorismo de Estado en Colombia*, 1992)

Cpt. Tomas Monroy Roncancio, 1981, Patrol Operations; 1976, Small Unit Infantry Tactics, Murder (6 counts, convicted), 1986. In June 1992, a military court convicted Monroy and two sergeants for detaining six workers ("suspected subversives"), forcing them into a cave, and slitting their throats. ("State of War: Political Violence and Counterinsurgency in Colombia," *Americas Watch Report* 1993)

Cpt. Rafael Neira, 1980, Cadet Arms Orientation Course, Cover-up, 1991. Neira claimed that Gildardo Antonio Gómez had escaped following his arrest by soldiers from the Nueva Granada Batallion, which was under Neira's command. Gomez' body was subsequently found with signs of severe torture. (*OMCT News*, 1991)

Maj. Hernán Orozco Castro, 1981, Cadet Arms Orientation Course, Mapiripán Massacres, 1997. During 1998, the Colombian Attorney General's office was investigating Orozco Castro for complicity in the Mapiripán massacre in which paramilitary groups cut the throats of 30 peasants, causing the flight of at least 500 of the town's inhabitants. During the five days that the massacres were taking place, a judge from the town made repeated calls for help to the army, but Hernán Orozco refused to provide assistance to prevent the massacres. ("State Department Report on Human Rights in Colombia;" *Colombia Bulletin*, 1998, Vol. 2, No. 3)

2Lt Germán Darío Otalora Amaya, 1988, Cadet Arms Orientation Course, Massacre in El Sande. In 1990, troops under Otalora's command entered the village of El Sande threatening them and accusing them of being guerrillas. Several people were killed, including the religious lay worker from Switzerland, Hildegard María Feldmann. Sande, firing indiscriminately at the inhabitants. They rounded up all of the villagers. (*Aquellas Muertes que Hicieron Resplandecer la Vida*, 1992)

Gen. Gustavo Pardo Ariza, 1971, Irregular Warfare Operations, Escape of Pablo Escobar, 1992. Pardo was one of three Army officers (two of them SOA graduates) forced into retirement upon the "escape" of Pablo Escobar from prison. Pardo was head of the Fourth Brigade in Medellín; soldiers under his command were supposed to be guarding the prison from which Escobar literally walked away. ("State of War Political Violence and Counterinsurgency in Colombia," *Americas Watch Report* 1993)

José Pereira, 1987, Cadet Arms Orientation Course C-3A, Illegal arrest, 1991. Pereira was indicted for the illegal arrest of Gildardo Antonio Gómez and one of his employees. The two were taken to an abandoned house and questioned about their involvement with the guerrillas. The employee managed to escape, but Mr. Gómez' body was later found with signs of torture. ("Political Murder and Reform in Colombia," *Americas Watch Report* 1992)

Gen. Rafael Peña Ríos, 1971, Special Maintenance Orientation Course; 1967, IW Operations. Stated baldly in an interview with El Tiempo that the military should be a force of repression. He bemoaned the fact that the military no longer had complete control of Colombia, equated political opposition (such as the Patriotic Union) with guerrilla warfare, and said that the way to end military abuse of authority was to give back to the military complete authority. (*Colombia: Inside the Labyrinth*)

Maj. William Fernando Pérez Laiseca, 1977, Small Unit Infantry Tactics, Torture, 1988. Participated in the detention and torture of 19 people in Pereira (Risaralda). (*Terrorismo de Estado en Colombia*, 1992)

CPT. Gustavo Adolfo Pizza Giviria, 1982, Cadet Arms Orientation Course, Assassination, 1987. Implicated in the assassination of Unión Patriótica presidential candidate Jaime Pardo Leal. (*Terrorismo de Estado en Colombia*, 1992)

1LT. José Oswaldo Prada Escobar, 1986, Cadet Arms Orientation Course, Disappearance, paramilitary activity, 1988-89: Implicated in paramilitary activities including disappearance, assassination, and the massacre of a judicial commission investigating military/paramilitary cooperation. (*Terrorismo de Estado en Colombia*, 1992)

Gen. Néstor Ramírez Mejía, 1985, Command and General Staff College (Distinguished graduate), Beating of journalist, 1996. In 1996, journalist Richard Vélez was attempting to film a confrontation where army troops under Ramírez' command fired on a group of demonstrating peasants. When the soldiers saw Vélez filming, they began to kick and beat him, demanding that he give up the tape. He managed to hand the tape to another journalist who was able to smuggle it out, but Vélez himself was severely wounded, his liver perforated and testicles destroyed. This incident occurred after Vélez had publicly challenged Ramirez Mejia at a press conference, providing video evidence that contradicted Ramirez' account of an armed confrontation. Vélez was later granted political asylum in the United States. (*Colombia Update*, Fall/Winter 1998) Failure to comply with judicial order, 1996: A judge sentenced Ramírez Mejía to 30 days in prison and a fine for failure to comply with an order to remove barricades constructed by the army at a bridge to block protesting peasants. (*Colombia Bulletin*, Vol. 1, No. 2) Assassination, 1986: Implicated in the revenge-killing of Gustavo Alfonso Macías. (*Terrorismo de Estado en Colombia*, 1992)

Gen. Luis Eduardo Roca Malchel, 1991, SOA "Hall of Fame," Misuse of counter-narcotics funds. In 1991, this former Army chief of staff, with cohort José Nelson Mejía Henao (above), thanked Congress for $40.3 million in anti-narcotics aid, which they said would be used (illegally) in counterinsurgency campaigns in northeastern Colombia, where narcotics are neither grown nor processed. (Ruth Connill, *The Progressive*, May 1992) Torture, 1988: Covered for those who tortured 19 people over three weeks in June 1988, one of whom sustained permanent damage to both arms. (*Terrorismo de Estado en Colombia*, 1992)

Gen. Luis Alberto Rodríguez, 1978, Command and General Staff College; 1970, "O-7." Former head, joint chiefs of staff, dismissed along with five other top military officers: Rodríguez was dismissed on November 22, 1994 by President Ernesto Samper. Samper overhauled the military leadership in the hopes of decreasing corruption and drug trafficking among the armed forces, and improving the human rights record of the military. (*Reuters*, November 22, 1994)

Cpt. Mario Raúl Rodríguez Reynoso, 1978, Small Unit Tactics, Murder, 1989. Implicated in the disappearance of Amparo Tordecilla. (*Terrorismo de Estado en Colombia*, 1992)

2Lt. Alejandro Rojas Pinilla, 1985, Cadet Arms Orientation, Disappearance,

1987. Implicated in the abduction and disappearance of Ramón Salvador Angarita Solano from his home in the Santander department. (*Terrorismo de Estado en Colombia*, 1992)

Ltc. Francisco E. Ruiz Florian, 1976, Tactical Officer, Small Unit Infantry, Assassination, 1986. Obstructed investigations into the revenge-killing of communist Gustavo Alfonso Macías. (*Terrorismo de Estado en Colombia*, 1992)

Gen. Juan Salcedo Lora, 1979, SOA Guest Instructor; 1971, Special Maintenance Orientation, Illegal detention, 1988: Ordered the illegal and clandestine detention of Manuel Reyes Cárdenas. (*Terrorismo de Estado en Colombia*, 1992)

Gen. Rafael Samudio Molina, 1988, SOA "Hall of Fame"; 1970, SOA Guest Instructor, Massacre at the Palace of Justice, November 7, 1985: Oversaw the Army massacre at the Palace of Justice following an attempt by the M-19 to take it over. The Army under his command set the building ablaze, resulting in the needless and horrifying deaths of many of the hostages. Other hostages were killed in Army crossfire, or, as some suspect, direct assassination. Even the hostages who lived through the horrifying ordeal were not safe; some were killed before exiting the palace and others were arrested and disappeared immediately upon leaving the building. Taped conversations between Samudio Molina and his commanders in the building establish that at no time did Samudio Molina act as an agent of the civilian government, but rather used the situation to prove the brutality of the Colombian military and to eliminate individuals, including Supreme Court justices, who were not staunch enough allies of the Colombian Army. (POJ) Samudio Molina has also been implicated in paramilitary activities since 1978. (*Terrorismo de Estado en Colombia*, 1992)

Col. Ramón de Jesús Santander Fuentes, 1986, Command and General Staff College (Distinguished graduate), Massacre, 1989: Implicated in the military/paramilitary massacre of a judicial commission investigating military/paramilitary cooperation. (*Terrorismo de Estado en Colombia*, 1992)

Maj. José Ismael Sierra Sierra, 1976, Small Unit Infantry Tactics, Disappearance, 1982. Covered for those who disappeared Gustavo Albeiro Muñoz Hurtado. (*Terrorismo de Estado en Colombia*, 1992)

Maj. Jairo Solano, 1976, Small Unit Infantry Tactics, Ordered killing, 1992. He ordered the death of Dr. Adalbulo in 1992. (*Colombia's Killer Networks*)

Maj. Carlos Arturo Suárez Bustamante, 1981, Tactical Officer, Cadet Arms Orientation, Assassination, 1986. Commanded the company that conducted the revenge-killing of Gustavo Alfonso Macias Borja. (*Terrorismo de Estado en Colombia*, 1992)

Gen. Hugo Arturo Tovar Sánchez, 1967, Tactical Officer, Cadet Orientation

Course, Clandestine detention, 1989. Ordered the illegal clandestine detention of Argiro Alonso Avendano Palacio and Maricela Cuello Villamil. (*Terrorismo de Estado en Colombia*, 1992)

1Lt. Orlando Ulloa Gaitán, 1980, Cadet Arms Orientation Course, Assassination, 1987. Implicated in the drug-financed assassination of Patriotic Union presidential candidate Jaime Pardo Leal. (*Terrorismo de Estado en Colombia*, 1992)

Cpt. Jairo John Uribe Cárdenas, 1980 Cadet Arms Orientation Course, Paramilitary activity, 1986. Implicated in paramilitary activities, including assassinations and disappearances, in Llanos Orientales. Ramírez massacre, 1986: Implicated in the murder of two members of the Ramírez family, and the torture and murder of four others. (*Terrorismo de Estado en Colombia*, 1992)

Col. Alirio Antonio Urueña Jaramillo, 1976, Small Unit Infantry Tactics, Trujillo chain saw massacres, 1988-1991. From 1988-1991, at least 107 citizens of the village of Trujillo were tortured and murdered. An eyewitness said Major Alirio Antonio Urueña tortured prisoners (including elderly women) with water hoses, stuffed them into coffee sacks, and chopped them to pieces with a chain saw. The eyewitness was soon disappeared; Major Urueña was promoted to Colonel. After intense international outcry, Urueña was dismissed from the Army in February 1995. (*Associated Press*, 2/7/95; *Terrorismo de Estado en Colombia*, 1992)

Cpt. César Augusto Valencia Moreno, 1980, Orientacion para Ramas de Cadete, Linked to death of Sergio Restrepo Jaramillo: Cpt. Valencia repeatedly pressured Jesuit Sergio Restrepo to change a mural painted on a church wall that depicted soldiers torturing a priest. Restrepo refused to do so, and was murdered a short time later by paid assassins who carried Army Intelligence cards. Eyewitnesses state that shortly before the shots were fired, Valencia became nervous and went out onto the balcony as though expecting something to happen. When he heard the shots, he was visibly relieved and came back inside. (*Aquellas Muertes que Hicieron Resplandecer la Vida*, 1992)

Ltc. Bayardo Vásquez Valdes, 1977, Automotive Maintenance Officer, Disappearance, 1989. Implicated in the disappearance of Sandra Vélez Vélez. (*Terrorismo de Estado en Colombia*, 1992)

Lt. Alfonso Vega Garzón, 1985, Combat Arms Orientation Course, Massacre, 1993. Implicated in the massacre of 13 people. (*Colombia's Killer Networks*)

Cpt. Freddy José Velandia Bottia, 1980, Cadet Arms Orientation Course Torture, 1989: Commanded the patrol that detained and tortured a union leader and two banana workers over several days in March 1989. (*Terrorismo de Estado en Colombia*, 1992)

Col. Carlos Velásquez, 1976, Small Unit Infantry Tactics, Coup Plot, 1995. As commander of the 17th Brigade, Velasquez planned to seize Colombian

President Samper during a visit to an army base in the northwest banana-growing region of Uraba and send him into exile in Panama. The attempt was called off after a general, one of Velásquez's superiors, arrived unexpectedly at the base. Interior Minister Alfonso López immediately announced an investigation and said that Velásquez would be punished. Prior to serving as a commander of the 17th Brigade, Velásquez headed an anti-drug unit that lead the search for the kingpins of the Cali cartel, but he was transferred after the leak of a video showing him in a motel room with a known female member of the cartel. (*Reuters*)

Gen. Nacim Yanine Díaz, 1971, 'O-7,' Disappearance, 1982. Implicated in the disappearance of 13 people between March and September of 1982. (*Terrorismo de Estado en Colombia*, 1992)

INTERNATIONAL ACTION CENTER

The IAC was initiated in 1991 by former U.S. Attorney General Ramsey Clark and other anti-war activists who had rallied hundreds of thousands of people in the United States to oppose the U.S./UN war against Iraq. Tribunal hearings were then organized in 20 countries and 30 U.S. cities against U.S. war crimes in Iraq. It incorporates opposition to U.S. militarism and domination around the world with the struggle to end poverty, racism, sexism, and oppression of lesbian, gay, bisexual and transgendered people in the United States.

The IAC has led delegations to Colombia for eyewitness accounts from Colombians on the frontlines of the struggle. In 2000, Ramsey Clark and others visted Colombia and as a result, meetings and video showings were held throughout the U.S. In December 2002, the IAC led a 22-member delegation to Colombia to attend the Tribunal Against the Violence of Coca-Cola—part of the International Conference on Transnational Corporations and Human Rights. The IAC has also hosted meetings of Colombian trade unionists, human rights activists and others across the U.S.

The IAC has fought the blockade against Cuba, led the movement to end the U.S./UN sanctions that caused the death of 1.5 million Iraqis, including a half million children, battled the use of radioactive "depleted-uranium" weapons that have endangered both the Middle East and the Balkans and fought against U.S. military intervention in Latin America.

After September 11, 2001, the IAC distinguished itself by immediately calling for anti-war protests. It helped form the new coalition called International ANSWER, or Act Now to Stop War and End Racism. This new group drew tens of thousands of people to Washington and San Francisco on September 29, 2001, to say no to the U.S. war drive. In 2002, two historic demonstrations were held on April 20 and October 26.

The IAC has played a leading role in the struggle to end the death penalty and, especially, the mobilizations to win freedom for Black liberation fighter and death-row political prisoner Mumia Abu-Jamal. IAC organizers coordinated a mass demonstration in Philadelphia in April 1999 and a rally in New York's Madison Square Garden in May 2000.

A major part of the IAC's work is to expose the intricate web of lies woven before, during and after each U.S. military intervention. It shows instead that U.S. intervention is dictated by the drive for profits and that as military funding expands, the money available for education, healthcare and needed social programs contracts. Much IAC material is published first on its increasingly popular web site, www.iacenter.org, which has made the "top one percent of web sites" list for the thousands of sites that link to it.

The IAC is a volunteer activist organization. In its campaigns opposing U.S. intervention, the center relies totally on the donations and assistance of supporters around the country. To be a part of a growing network or to make a donation, request a speaker or volunteer your support, contact the IAC.

International Action Center
39 West 14th Street, Room 206, New York, N.Y. 10011 USA
Tel: 212-633-6646; fax 212-633-2889
Email: iacenter@action-mail.org
Web page: http://www.action-mail.org

War in Colombia: Made in the U.S.A.

This book powerfully counters the Pentagon and media propaganda with facts about what's really happening in Colombia.

In these pages you will find the truth about the almost 40,000 Colombians who have died in the last several years, the more than 2.5 million who have been displaced, the broad sectors who are heroically fighting inhumane policies mandated by the multinational corporations like Coca-Cola.

This book is a compilation of voices that oppose Plan Colombia and express solidarity with the Colombian people. Authors include: Ramsey Clark, Fidel Castro, Teresa Gutierrez, James Petras, Rep. Cynthia McKinney, Javier Correa Suárez and Manuel Marulanda Vélez.

INTERNATIONAL ACTION CENTER, New 2003. 300 pages, indexed, chronology, maps, softcover. $19.95

Hidden Agenda *U.S./NATO Takeover of Yugoslavia*

The International Action Center's second full-length book on the Balkans conflict exposes the illegal roots and procedures of the International Criminal Tribunal for the former Yugoslavia and its effort to stage a show trial of former Yugoslav President Slobodan Milosevic as an attempt to find the Serb and Yugoslav people guilty of resistance to NATO. Using evidence presented to dozens of popular international tribunal hearings in 1999 and 2000, it turns the tables on NATO by exposing and demonstrating the war crimes of Milosevic's accusers, including their decade-long conspiracy to wage war on Yugoslavia. With articles by Mumia Abu-Jamal, former Yugoslav President Slobodon Milosevic, Ramsey Clark, Michel Chossudovsky, Sara Flounders, Gloria La Riva, Michael Parenti, Michel Collon and other leading anti-war activists and analysts from many countries.

INTERNATIONAL ACTION CENTER, New 2002.
400 pages, pictures, indexed, chronology, maps, softcover. $19.95

NATO in the Balkans *Voices of Dissent*

Confused about the REAL reasons the United States bombed Yugoslavia? This book, released in 1998, will give you the secret background and hidden role of the U.S. and Germany in the dismemberment of Yugoslavia. *NATO in the Balkans* shows how sophisticated, "Big Lie" war propaganda nearly silenced popular debate and opposition. Authors Ramsey Clark, Sean Gervasi, Sara Flounders, Thomas Deichmann, Gary Wilson, Richard Becker and Nadja Tesich will take you through the ins and outs, the framework and media lies that led to the series of bloody conflicts that have characterized central Europe in the last years of this century.

INTERNATIONAL ACTION CENTER, 1998. 230 pages, indexed, softcover. $15.95

Plan Colombia: We Say No!

This video documents the growing movement to stop U.S. war in Colombia. See footage from interviews with Raúl Reyes, other FARC-EP members, Wilson Borja, labor leaders, human rights activists and youth in Colombia. Also see excerpts from speeches by Ramsey Clark, Teresa Gutierrez and others.

Video

VHS, 2000, 29 min. $20 *individual* $50 *institutions*

The Fire This Time *U.S. War Crimes in the Gulf*

BY RAMSEY CLARK A book that tells the truth about the Gulf War tragedy—a sharp indictment of U.S. foreign policy that led to the Gulf War and its devastating human and environmental consequences. *The Fire This Time* stands out amid the deluge of self-congratulatory accounts which do injustice to history. Updated introduction since 9/11/01 by Sara Flounders and Brian Becker. *"A strong indictment of conduct of the war and especially of the needless deaths of civilians caused by bombing."*—New York Times *"Not academic. ... Clark risked his life by traveling through Iraqi cities at a time when the U.S. was staging 3,000 bombings a day."*—Los Angeles Times

INTERNATIONAL ACTION CENTER, 2002. 352 pages, indexed, pictures, softcover. $19.95

War, Lies & Videotape
How media monopoly stifles truth

What passes as news today has been predigested by a handful of megamedia corporations. In this book, hard-hitting media critics, journalists, and activists examine:

- The ever-increasing media monopoly that stifles dissent and information
- Links between the government, the media and the military
- War propaganda & NATO's expanding role in Yugoslavia
- Role of Big Oil, the Pentagon & the media in the Gulf
- How new technologies can help break through the media monopoly

Edited by Lenora Foerstel. Chapters by: Jean-Bertrand Aristide, Scott Armstrong, Ben Bagdikian, Brian Becker, Ramsey Clark, Thomas Deichmann, Nawal El Saadawi, Sara Flounders, Diana Johnstone, Michael Parenti and others.

INTERNATIONAL ACTION CENTER, 2000. 288 pages, indexed, softcover. $15.95

Metal of Dishonor–Depleted Uranium
How the Pentagon Radiates Soldiers & Civilians with DU Weapons

A devastating exposé of the Pentagon's new weapons comprised of depleted uranium. This is the book you've heard about, but won't see in most bookstores. Now in its second printing, Gulf War veterans, leaders of environmental, anti-nuclear, anti-military and community movements discuss: The connection of depleted uranium to Gulf War syndrome and a new generation of radioactive conventional weapons. Understand how the bizarre Pentagon recycling plans of nuclear waste creates a new global threat. Authors include former U.S. Attorney General Ramsey Clark, Dr. Michio Kaku, Dr. Helen Caldicott, Dr. Rosalie Bertell, Dr. Jay M. Gould, Dan Fahey, Sara Flounders, Manuel Pino and many others.

INTERNATIONAL ACTION CENTER, 1997, 2nd edition 1999, 272 pages, indexed, photos, tables, softcover. $12.95

Metal of Dishonor

Interviews with noted scientists, doctors, and community activists explaining dangers of radioactive DU weapons. Explores consequences of DU from mining to production, testing, and combat use. Footage from Bikini and atomic war veterans.

PEOPLES VIDEO NETWORK, VHS, 1998, 50 min. $20 *individual* $50 *institutions*
PAL version for Europe $35

Challenge To Genocide Let Iraq Live

Contains essays and detailed reports on the devastating effect of the economic sanctions on Iraq since the beginning of the Gulf War. It features "Fire and Ice," a chapter by former U.S. Attorney General Ramsey Clark. Also included are personal memoirs from many who defied the sanctions and U.S. law by taking medicines to Baghdad as part of the May 1998 "Iraq Sanctions Challenge." Contributers include Ramsey Clark, Bishop Thomas Gumbleton, Rania Masri, Sara Flounders, Ahmed El-Sherif, Brian Becker, Barbara Nimri Aziz, Kathy Kelly, Monica Moorehead and Manzoor Ghori.

INTERNATIONAL ACTION CENTER, 1998. 264 pages, photos, indexed, resource lists, softcover. $12.95

Genocide By Sanctions

Excellent for libraries, schools, and community groups and for cable-access television programs. This powerful video documents on a day-to-day, human level how sanctions kill. It contains an important historical perspective that explains why the United States is so determined to maintain the sanctions. An important tool in the educational and humanitarian "Medicine for Iraq" campaign to collect medicine while educating people so U.S. policy will be changed. This excellent video by Gloria La Riva took second prize at the San Luis Obispo International Film Festival.

Video

VHS, 1998, 28 min. $20 *individuals* $50 *institutions*

The Children Are Dying The Impact of Sanctions on Iraq

Report of the UN Food and Agriculture Organization, supporting documents, and articles by Ramsey Clark, Ahmed Ben Bella, Tony Benn, Margarita Papandreou, and other prominent international human rights figures. Shows the human face of those targeted by the weapon of sanctions. The UN FAO report showed with facts and statistics that over 500,000 Iraqi children under the age of five had died as a result of U.S./UN imposed sanctions. Photos and chapters define the social implications.

INTERNATIONAL ACTION CENTER, 1998. 170 pages, resource lists, photos, softcover. $10

Nowhere to Hide

Video

Traveling with Ramsey Clark in Iraq in 1991, award-winning video journalist Jon Alpert captured what it was like to be on the ground during the allied bombing. In dramatic, graphic scenes, *Nowhere to Hide* shows a different reality from what was on the nightly news. Tom Harpur wrote in the *Toronto Star*: "Only by knowing the true nature of 'Operation Desert Storm' can similar wars be prevented...send for the video."

VHS, 28 min. $20 *individuals* $50 *institutions*

Eyewitness Sudan

An exposé of the 1998 U.S. bombing of El Shifa, the small factory that produced more than half the medicine for Sudan. The smoking ruins are skillfully juxtaposed to footage of Bill Clinton, Madeline Albright and Berger's charges. This documentary by Ellen Andors connects the years of sanctions to the cruise missiles sent against an African country.

PEOPLES VIDEO NETWORK VHS, 1998, 28 min.,
$20 *individual* $50 *institutions*

The Prison Industrial Complex
An interview with Mumia Abu-Jamal on death row   Video

Censored journalist, political activist and death-row inmate Mumia Abu-Jamal, framed for his ideas, speaks about the current political scene in the United States. In an excellent interview Mumia discusses racism, prison labor in the United States, youth, elections, economics and the state of the world. See and hear the "Voice of the Voiceless" in this unique uncensored interview. Interview by Monica Moorehead and Larry Holmes.

PEOPLES VIDEO NETWORK VHS, 1996, 28 min. $20 *individual* $50 *institutions*

Mumia Speaks *An interview with Mumia Abu-Jamal*
by **Mumia Abu-Jamal** with forewards by Monica Moorehead, Larry Holmes and Teresa Gutierrez.

Political prisoner and award-winning journalist Mumia Abu-Jamal speaks from his cell on Pennsylvania's Death Row. In this far ranging interview, Mumia talks about prisons, capitalism, politics, revolution and solidarity. The pamphlet also includes two articles— "The Oppressed Nations, the Poor and Prisons," by Monica Moorehead. and "The Death Penalty and the Texas Killing Machine," by Teresa Gutierrez.

WORLD VIEW FORUM, 2000, 33 pages, softcover. $3

ON A MOVE *The Story of Mumia Abu-Jamal*
BY TERRY BISSON

Covering Mumia Abu-Jamal's childhood in the North Philly projects, a turbulent youth in Oakland and New York, a promising career in radio journalism, and a fateful sidewalk altercation that changed everything, Bisson's colorful sketches tell the story of one of the stormiest periods in American history, and of a young rebel who came of age in its crucible. *"The next time you see Mumia demonized in the mainstream media, pick up this book. It chronicles the evolution of an eloquent advocate for the damned."*—Martin Espada, author, *Zapata's Disciple*

PLOUGH PUBLISHING, 2000, 240 pages, 36 photos, softcover. $12

TO ORDER: All mail orders must be pre-paid. Bulk orders of 10 or more items available at 40% off cover price. Include $5 U.S. shipping and handling for first item, $1.50 each additional item. International shipping $12 for first item, $4 each additional item.

Send check or money order to:
INTERNATIONAL ACTION CENTER
39 W. 14th St., Rm. 206, New York, NY 10011 (212) 633-6646 iacenter@action-mail.org

To place individual CREDIT CARD orders (VISA & MC only), order on-line at:
www.leftbooks.com
For bookstore and university invoice orders and discounts, call the IAC in advance for specific information.

DATE DUE
